s/c 3.6   ORD 96.

JESUS

A Prophet
of Islam

Muhammad Àta ur-Rahim

MWH London Publishers

First Published in 1977 by Diwan Press

Second Edition © 1979 by MWH London Publishers

ISBN 0 906194 08 3

 MWH London Publishers

233 Seven Sisters Road
LONDON
N4 2DA
England

Printed and bound in Great Britain by
Redwood Burn Limited
Trowbridge & Esher

CONTENTS

PREFACE

An eminent scholar of Christian history admits that the present-day Christianity is a "mask" on the face of Jesus, but goes on to say that a mask worn for a long time acquires a life of its own and it has to be accepted as such. The Muslim believes in the Jesus of history and refuses to accept the "mask". This, in a nutshell, has been the point of difference between Islam and the Church for the last fourteen hundred years. Even before the advent of Islam, the Arians, the Paulicians, and the Goths, to mention only a few, accepted Jesus, but rejected the "mask". The Holy Roman Emperors forced Christians to think alike. To achieve this impossible goal, millions of Christians were killed. Castillo, an admirer of Servitus, said that "to kill a man is not to prove a doctrine." Conviction cannot be forced with a dagger.

It is suggested in some quarters that, to achieve integration in England, the Muslims should change their two festivals to synchronise with Christmas and Easter. Those who say this forget that these are pre-Christian pagan festivals. One is the ancient birthday of the sun-god and the other is a sacred festival for the old Anglo-Saxon goddess of fertility. In this situation, one begins to wonder who in reality is "Anti-Christ".

In this book an attempt is made, perhaps for the first time, to study the sacred life of Jesus, using all available sources, including the Dead Sea Scrolls, Christian Scripture, modern research, Qur'an and Hadith. Christian scholars who attempt to write the history of Jesus never completely free themselves of the idea of his divinity. When they fail to prove his divinity, they sometimes conclude that he did not exist at all, or that he is "everything to everybody". An

1

objective study is impossible to anyone with this frame of mind. This book starts with the conviction that Jesus did exist. He was a man and a prophet of Allah.

This work is the result of thirty years of study. My thanks are due to Amatur Raquib who went to the trouble of searching for out-of-print books sold on the streets of many cities in the U.S.A. These books were unavailable in the libraries of Karachi, so the help she gave me was of vital importance.

His Excellency Mr. Ahmad Jamjoom of Jeddah visited me in Karachi, and his encouragement and support were always available to me whenever I was facing any difficulty.

Thanks are also due to His Eminence Shaykh Mahmoud Subhi of Jamiat Dawa Islamia in Tripoli for making it possible for me to come to London in order to undertake the study of this subject in depth.

In London, I met His Eminence Shaykh 'Abd al-Qadir as-Sufi. At every step, he extended his helping hand to me. This resulted in the collaboration of Mr. Ahmad Thomson with me. He helped me to collect the material and without him work would have been painfully slow. Hajj 'Abd al-Haqq Bewley was always ready with useful suggestions and advice.

The affection and heart-warming friendship I received from Dr. Ali Aneizi cannot be described, only deeply felt.

Lastly, in the words of Qur'an,

Nothing from me except with the help of Allah

و ما توفيقي إلا بالله

Muhammad 'Ata ur-Rahim

London
7 Jumada al'Awal, 1397 A.H.

INTRODUCTION

The author of this book, Muhammad 'Ata ur-Rahim, felt passionately that if only the peoples of the Christian countries had some knowledge of the Islamic faith, together with a realistic understanding of Jesus, the prophet, may he rest in peace, a great deal of unnecessary distress could be avoided in the future. A brilliant, cosmopolitan scholar, the author knew no national boundaries so far as the happiness and well-being of people are concerned. Inter-cultural ignorance, he maintained, is the greatest single cause of today's suffering and hardship.

So this book is written, primarily, for the western world, but also for all who seek enlightenment amidst the tangle of conflicting ideas surrounding the birth of Jesus, his mission and his death. Muhammad 'Ata ur-Rahim attacked the muddle with the logic of a pure historian; he found most of the confusion is caused by those two dogmas which defy rational explanation — the supposed Divinity of Jesus and the Trinity.

This work demolishes a great deal of the myth upon which the Christian Church leans and shows Jesus as the highly orthodox Jew he actually was; as a teacher of the unitarian faith sent as a messenger by Allah to destroy those base elements which had grown to such enormous proportions within the Jewish priesthood.

But I do not wish this introduction to be a synopsis of a book which stands entirely on its own. The author wrote this as but a single part of his overall desire to help non-Muslims towards the truth and to lessen the superstitious fear of Islam held by most Christians.

We, as Muslims, know how baseless are these fears. We are secure in our knowledge of Allah as One all merciful, all beneficent to man; untouchable by human qualifications: "There is nothing like unto Him, and He is the All-Hearing, the All-Seeing." (The Qur'an; XLII:11).

We are secure in our knowledge of His prophets, may peace be upon them; secure in the knowledge they have given us of Allah and His covenant for us to follow on earth. Muslims following the unchanging completeness of the Holy Qur'an know all this but, perhaps, fail at times to make it obvious to others. The author, from the depths of his great sympathy for all people — especially those less fortunate than himself — was aware of this failure in communication. He was also aware of a great deal of regional tradition which has grown up within Islam; tradition which is capable of confusing those looking at us across the fence of fear; even of causing confusion and misunderstanding between Muslims of different nations.

Only great determination, great sympathy, can bring true brotherhood and understanding between nations and fear of the unknown is the greatest obstacle. Many Muslims looking westward at the lost moral values feel it should be a simple matter to introduce Islam into the spiritual vacuum, but such hopes are a matter of building castles in the sky. Mass education of the people necessary for the growth of western technology and industry has shown those people all too clearly that religion, as they know it, is based on dogmas unsupported by fact. Consequently, it is small wonder that the intellectual elite of this industrial society were the first to withdraw their support, finding a great sense of freedom in their new-found independence from the monopolistic priesthood of the Christian Church; a priesthood which had contained the spread of education over the centuries. For such people, religion, whatever its name, is seen not only as outdated superstition but as a restrictive force and a hindrance to the quest for further scientific knowledge. Born Muslims, unused to interference between themselves and Allah, appear not to appreciate that, for the lapsed Christian, the loss of faith is only the dropping of a man-made philosophy which, in the past, had some expediency as a method of maintaining law and order.

Before Islam can fill the west's spiritual vacuum, these

now purely materialistic people have to be convinced of the actuality of Allah and that knowledge of Him does not depend upon acceptance of the priestly hierarchy they have deposed. They also have to be given a new image — by example — of Muslim peoples.

If the Islamic countries had not, almost overnight, gained great riches, the western world would have retained its ignorance of Islam for a great deal longer. As it is, all of Europe — including Russia — and America are suddenly faced with not only a faith they know nothing of, but a faith backed by the one commodity they recognise — money, in enormous quantities. And that means power; the power to overcome.

It is not surprising that there is very real fear of this power. It is a long time since the Muslim world held a monopoly of scientific knowledge, and it is long forgotten that western technology is based upon that eastern science. The Arab nations have, only recently, found true nationhood: Pakistan has, as a part of the sub-continent, been kept in subjugation by the strength of western industrial power until a few short years ago. And yet, now, these same people of Islam are showing the west the possibility of overwhelming its society despite that society's ability to walk upon the moon; despite the ability to produce test-tube babies and a near-capability of, maybe, doubling the present expected lifespan.

Having fought so hard to free themselves and their countries from the domination and jurisdiction of the Roman clergy, and to replace these by civil government and civil law, those born in Christian lands now see the possibility of this freedom being swept away.

Unless Islamic scholarship, directed with loving care for people, such as this work by Muhammad 'Ata ur-Rahim, creates a climate of close communication with the west, only conflict can emerge from this atmosphere of fear. Upon Muslim countries, especially those with so much financial power, lies an enormous responsibility of example to be set. Hopefully, the proliferation and growth of universities and cultural centres in the west, and in the Muslim world itself, will make greater opportunities available for serious and constructive Islamic research and scholarship, and thereby allowing these fears, Allah willing, to recede gradually.

We, as Muslims, know that all will follow the pattern of Allah, but that does not mean that we may sit back in complacency. We have the great gift of the example of the Prophet Mohammad, peace and blessings of Allah be upon him, and the unchanging instruction and inspiration of the Holy Qur'an to guide us. But the instruction is clear; we must work to the Will of Allah if we are to attain peace in this life and His most favourable reward in the next.

ANDREW DOUGLAS-HAMILTON

Jumada al-Thani, 1399 A.H.
April, 1979 A.D.

TEXT

Chapter 1

THE UNITARIAN VIEW AND CHRISTIANITY

Historical research has shown that the animism and idol worship of primitive peoples in the world is in all cases a regression from an original unitive belief, and the One-god of Judaism, Christianity and Islam grew up in opposition to many-gods rather than evolving out of them. Thus in any tradition, the pure teaching is to be found at its beginning and what follows is necessarily a decline, and it is from this perspective that the history of Christianity should be viewed. It began with the belief in One God and was then corrupted, and the doctrine of the Trinity came to be accepted. The result was a confusion which led men more and more away from sanity.

In the first century after the disappearance of Jesus, those who followed him continued to affirm the Divine Unity. This is illustrated by the fact that the *Shepherd of Hermas,* written in about 90 A.D. was regarded as a book of Revelation by the Church. The first of the twelve commandments which it contains begins:

> First of all, believe that God is One and that He created all things and organised them and out of what did not exist made all things to be, and He contains all things but alone is Himself uncontained. . .[1]

According to Theodore Zahn, the article of faith up until about 250 A.D. was, "I believe in God, the Almighty."[2] Between 180 and 210 A.D. the word "Father" was added before the "Almighty." This was bitterly contested by a number of the leaders of the Church. Bishop Victor and Bishop Zephysius are on record as condemning this movement, since they regarded it an unthinkable sacrilege to add or subtract any word to the Scriptures. They opposed the tendency to regard Jesus as divine. They laid great stress on the Unity of God as expressed in the original teachings of Jesus and asserted that although he was a prophet, he was essentially a man like other men, even if highly favoured by his Lord. The same faith was held by the Churches which had sprung up in North Africa and West Asia.

As the teaching of Jesus was spread, it came into contact with other cultures and into conflict with those in authority. It began to be assimilated and adapted by these cultures and was also altered to diminish persecution by the rulers. In Greece, especially, it became metamorphosed, both by its being expressed in a new language for the first time, and by its realignment with the ideas and philosophy of that culture. It was the many-gods viewpoint of the Greeks which largely contributed to the formulation of this doctrine of the Trinity, together with the gradual elevation of Jesus by some, notably Paul of Tarsus, from a prophet to God.

It was only in 325 A.D. that the doctrine of the Trinity was declared to be the orthodox Christian belief. Even then some of those who signed the creed did not believe in it, as they could find no authority for it in the Scriptures. Athanasius, who is considered to be the father of this creed, was himself not very sure of its truth. He admits that, "Whenever he forced his understanding to meditate on the divinity of Jesus, his toilsome and unavailing efforts recoiled on themselves — that the more he wrote the less capable was he of expressing his thoughts." At one point he even wrote, "There are not three but ONE GOD." His belief in the doctrine of the Trinity was not based on conviction but on policy and apparent necessity.

That this historic decision was based just as much on political expediency as on the faulty reasoning of philosophy is shown by the part played by Constantine, the pagan emperor of Rome, who presided over the council of Nicea. The growing communities of Christians were a force whose opposition he had no wish for, who weakened his Empire and whose support would be invaluable in strengthening it. By remodelling Christianity, he hoped to gain the Church's support and at the same time end the confusion which had arisen within it and which was the source of yet more conflict within his Empire.

The process by which he partially achieved this aim may be illustrated by an incident which occured in the Second World War. Once, as the time for the Muslim festival of the 'Id drew near, propaganda from Tokyo began to concentrate on an 'Id prayer that was going to be held in Singapore, then under Japanese occupation. It would be an historic occasion, it was announced, and its effect would be felt throughout the Muslim world. This sudden emphasis on the prayer abruptly stopped after a few days. The mystery was solved when a Japanese prisoner was taken in a skirmish and interrogated. He said that Tojo, the head of the Japanese government, was planning to take on the role of the greatest Muslim reformer of modern times. He had a scheme to adjust the teachings of Islam to the requirements of the modern age. It had therefore become necessary, according to him, that the Muslims, instead of facing Mecca in prayer, should start facing Tokyo, which would become the future centre of Islam under Tojo. The Muslims refused this reorientation of Islam, and so the whole project was dropped. As a result, there was no 'Id prayer allowed in Singapore that year. Tojo had realised the importance of Islam and he wanted to use it as a means to further his imperialistic designs, but he was unsuccessful. Constantine succeeded where Tojo failed. Rome replaced Jerusalem as the center of Pauline Christianity.

This degeneration of the pure teachings of Jesus, which resulted inevitably in the acceptance of a many-god Christianity, never went unchallenged. When, in 325 A.D., the doctrine of Trinity was officially proposed as the orthodox Christian doctrine, Arius, one of the leaders of the Christians in North Africa, stood up against the combined might of Constantine and the Catholic Church and reminded them that Jesus had always affirmed the Divine Unity. Constantine tried to crush the troublesome One-God people with all the force and brutality at his command, but he failed. Although, ironically, Constantine himself died a unitarian, the doctrine of Trinity eventually became officially accepted as the basis of Christianity in Europe. This doctrine caused much confusion among men, many of whom were told to believe it without trying to understand it. Yet it was not possible to stop people from trying to prove and explain it intellectually. Broadly speaking, three schools of thought developed. The first is associated with St. Augustine, who lived in the 4th century and was of the view that the doctrine could not be proved but could be illustrated. St. Victor, who lived in the 12th century, is associated with the second school, who believed that the doctrine could both be demonstrated and illustrated. And the 14th century saw the growth of the third school, which believed that the doctrine of Trinity could be neither illustrated nor proved, but should be blindly accepted and believed.

Although the books into which Jesus's teaching had gone were either completely destroyed, suppressed, or changed in order to avoid any blatant contradictions of the doctrine, a good deal of truth remained in the ones which survived, and therefore to sustain belief in the doctrine of Trinity, there was a shift in emphasis from what the Scriptures said, to what the leaders of the Church said. The doctrine, it was asserted, was based on the special revelation made to the Church, the "Bride of Jesus." Thus, for instance, Fra Fulgentio was reprimanded by the Pope in a letter saying: "Preaching of the Scriptures is a suspicious thing. He who keeps close to the Scriptures will ruin the Catholic faith." In his next letter he was more explicit, warning against too much insistence on the Scriptures: "...which is a book if anyone keeps close to, he will quite destroy the Catholic Church."[3]

The effective abandoning of the teaching of Jesus was largely due to complete obscuring of his historical reality. The Church made religion not only independent of the Scriptures but also independent of Jesus, so that the man Jesus became confused with a mythological Christ. Belief in Jesus, however, does not necessarily mean belief in a resurrected Christ. Whereas the immediate followers of Jesus had based their lives on his example, Pauline Christianity was based on a belief in Christ after his supposed crucifixion, and the life and teaching of Jesus while he was alive was no longer important.

As the established Church distanced itself further and further from the teaching of Jesus, so its leaders became more and more involved in the affairs of those in authority over the land. As the distinctions between what Jesus had taught and what those in authority desired became blurred and began to merge into each other, the Church, while asserting its separateness from the State, became more and more identified with it, and grew in power. Whereas in the early days the Church was subject to imperial power, once it had compromised itself completely, the position was reversed.

There was always opposition to these deviations from what Jesus had taught. As the Church became more powerful, it became very dangerous to deny the Trinity, and led to almost certain death. Although Luther left the Roman Church, his revolt was only against the authority of the Pope, rather than against the fundamental doctrines of the Roman Catholic Church. The result was that he founded a new Church and became its head. All the basic Christian doctrines were accepted, and remained. This led to the establishment of a number of Reformed Churches and sects, but pre-Reformation Christianity remained undisturbed. These two main bodies of the Pauline Church have continued to exist up to the present day.

In North Africa and West Asia the teachings of Arius were accepted by the majority of the people who readily embraced Islam when it later came to them. Because they had held to the doctrine of One-God and the pure teaching of Jesus, they recognised Islam as the truth.

In Europe the thread of unitarianism within Christianity has never been broken, and the movement has in fact grown in strength, surviving the continual and brutal persecution of the established Churches in the past and their indifference today.

More and more people are now aware that the Christianity they know has little to do with the original teaching of Jesus. During the last two centuries the research of the historians has left little room for faith in the Christian "mysteries", but the proven fact that the Christ of the established Church has almost nothing to do with the Jesus of history does not in itself help Christians towards the Truth. The present dilemma of the Christians is illustrated by what the Church historians of this present century write. The fundamental difficulty is, as pointed out by Adolf Harnack, that "By the fourth century the living Gospel had been masked in Greek philosophy. It was the historians' mission to pluck off the mask and thus reveal how different had been the original contours of the faith beneath." But then Harnack points out the difficulty of fulfilling this task by saying that the doctrinal mask worn long enough can reshape the face of religion:

> The mask acquires a life of its own — the Trinity, the two natures of Christ, infallibility, and all propositions seconding these dogmas, were the product of historic decisions and of situations that might have turned out quite differently. . . nevertheless. . . early or late, product or reshaping force, this dogma remains what it has been from the beginning, a bad habit of intellectualization which the Christian picked up from the Greek when he fled from the Jews.[4]

Harnack enlarges on his theme in another book, where he admits that:

> . . .the fourth Gospel does not emanate or profess to emanate from the apostle John, who cannot be taken as an historical authority. . . the author of the fourth Gospel acted with sovereign freedom, transposed events and put them in a strange light. He drew up the discussions himself and illustrated great thoughts with imaginary situations.

He further refers to the work of the famous Christian historian, David Strauss, whom he describes as having "almost destroyed the historic credibility not only of the fourth but also of the first three Gospels as well."[5]

According to Johannes Lehmann, another historian, the writers of the four accepted Gospels describe a different Jesus from the one who can be identified by historic reality. Lehmann quotes Heinz Zahrnt who points out the consequences of this:

> If historical research could prove that an irreconcilable antithesis exists between the historical Jesus and Christ as preached, and therefore that belief in Jesus has no support

in Jesus himself, that would not only be absolutely fatal theologically, as N.A. Dahl says, but would also mean the end of all Christology. Yet I am convinced that even then we theologians would be able to find a way out — was there ever a time when we couldn't? — but we are either lying now or would be lying then.[6]

While these few short quotations illustrate the dilemma Christianity is in today, the words of Zahrnt also demonstrate something far more serious which underlies this: that it is possible to get so involved with the details of what became of Jesus's teaching and the Chruches and sects which followed after him, that the original purpose of his teaching is overlooked or forgotten. Thus Theodore Zahn, for instance, illustrates the bitter conflicts within the established Churches. He points out that the Roman Catholics accuse the Greek Orthodox Church of remodelling the text of the holy Scriptures by additions and subtractions with good and bad intentions, the Greeks in turn point out that the Catholics themselves in places depart very far from the original text, and, in spite of their differences, they combine to accuse the non-conformist Christians of deviating from "the true way" and condemn them as heretics, and the heretics in their turn accuse the Catholics of "having recoined the Truth like forgers." He concludes, "Do not facts support these accusations?"[7]

Jesus himself is completely forgotten. Those who are aware of the degeneration that has taken place and who wish in all sincerity to return to and live by the original teaching of Jesus are prevented from doing so because the original teaching in its totality has disappeared and is irrecoverable.

Erasmus had this to say:

> The ancients philosophised very little about divine things. . . Formerly faith was in life rather than in profession of creeds. . . When faith came to be in writings rather than in hearts, then there were almost as many faiths as men. Articles increased and sincerity decreased. Contentions grew hot and love grew cold. The doctrine of Christ which at first knew no hair-splitting came to depend on the aid of philosophy. This was the first stage in the decline of the Church.

Thus the Church was forced to explain what could not be expressed in words, and recourse was taken by both sides to win the support of the Emperor. Erasmus, commenting on this, continued:

> The injection of the authority of the Emperor into this affair did not greatly aid the sincerity of faith. . . When faith is in the mouth rather than in the heart, when the solid knowledge of sacred Scriptures fails us, nevertheless by terrorization we drive men to believe what they do not believe, to love what they do not love, to know what they do not know. That which is forced cannot be sincere.[8]

Erasmus understood that the first Christians, the immediate followers of Jesus, had a recognition of the Unity which they never had to express, and that when his teaching spread and conflict between the Churches grew up, the men of understanding were forced to try and explain their knowledge of Reality. They had by then lost the teaching of Jesus in its totality and the language of Unity that went with it. They only had recourse to the vocabulary and terminology of Greek philosophy which looked not to Unity but to a tripartite view of existence. And so simple and pure trust in Reality became inevitably couched in a language foreign to Jesus, and led to the formulation of the doctrine of the Trinity, with the deification of Jesus and the Holy Spirit. Confusion and schism were the inevitable results which followed when men lost sight of the Unity of Existence.

This understanding is essential to anyone who wants to know who Jesus was and what he really taught, together with the knowledge that once people no longer have recourse to all the everyday actions of a prophet, which are no less than the embodiment of his teaching, they are in loss, whether they believe in the doctrine of the Trinity or vocally affirm the Divine Unity.

Chapter 2

AN HISTORICAL ACCOUNT OF JESUS

The more people have tried to discover who Jesus really was, the more it has been found how little is known about him. There are limited records of his teachings and some of his actions, but very little is known about how he actually lived his life from moment to moment, and how he conducted his everyday transactions with other people.

Certainly, the pictures many people have given of Jesus — of who he was, and what he did — are distorted ones. Although there is some truth in them, it has been established that the four accepted Gospels have not only been altered and censored through the ages, but also are not eyewitness accounts. The earliest Gospel is that of Mark, written about 60-75 A.D. He was the son of St. Barnabas's sister. Matthew was a tax collector, a minor official who did not travel around with Jesus. Luke's Gospel was written much later, and is, in fact, drawn from the same source as Mark's and Matthew's. Luke was Paul's physician, and like Paul, never met Jesus. John's Gospel is from a different source, and was written later still, in about 100 A.D. He should not be confused with John, the disciple, who was another man. For two centuries it was hotly debated whether this Gospel should be accepted as a reliable account of the life of Jesus, and should be included in the Scriptures.

The discovery of the famous Dead Sea Scrolls has thrown new light on the nature of the society into which Jesus was born. The Gospel of Barnabas covers Jesus's life more extensively than the other Gospels, and the Qur'an and the Hadith further clarify the picture of who Jesus really was.

We find that he was not the "son of God", in the literal sense of the word, but, like Abraham and Moses before him and Muhammad after him, a Messenger, who, like all human beings ate food and went to the market place.

We find that he inevitably found himself doing battle with those people whose interests were in conflict with what he taught. They either did not accept the guidance he received, or knowing it to be true, nevertheless chose to ignore it in favour of pursuing power, riches and reputation in the eyes of men.

Further, we find that Jesus's life on earth is an integral part of Jewish history, and to understand his story it is necessary to look at theirs. Throughout his life he was an orthodox practising Jew, and he came to re-affirm and revive the original teaching of Moses that had been altered through the years.

Finally, we find that it was not Jesus who was crucified, but someone who resembled him.

Lentulus, a Roman official, describes Jesus:

> He had nut brown hair that is smoothed down to the ears, forming soft curls and flowing onto his shoulders in luxuriant locks, with a parting in the centre of his head after the fashion of the Nazarenes. A smooth clear brow and a reddish face without spots and wrinkles. Nose and mouth are flawless. He bears a full luxurious beard which is the same colour as his hair and is parted in the middle. He has blue-grey eyes with an unusually varied capacity for expression. He was of medium height, fifteen and a half fists tall. He is cheerful in seriousness. Sometimes he weeps, but no one has ever seen him laugh.

A Muslim Tradition, however, paints a slightly different picture. According to this source:

> He was a ruddy man inclined to white. He did not have long hair. He never annointed his head. Jesus used to walk barefoot, and he took no house, nor adornment, nor goods, nor clothes, nor provisions, except his day's food. His head was dishevelled and his face was small. He was an ascetic in this world, longing for the next world and eager for the worship of Allah.

The exact date of Jesus's birth is not known. According to Luke, it is associated with a census which was held in 6 A.D. It is also stated that he was born in the reign of Herod, who died in 4 B.C. Vincent Taylor, however, concludes that his date of birth could be as early as 8 B.C.[1]; since Herod's decree, set in motion by the news of Jesus's actual or imminent birth, that all newly born infans in Bethlehem should be slaughtered, obviously must have preceded Herod's death. Even if we follow Luke, the discrepancy between the two verses in the same Gospel is of ten years. Most of the commentators believe the second verse, which infers that he was born in 4 B.C., i.e. four years "Before Christ."

The miraculous conception and birth of Jesus have been the subject of much discussion. Some people believe that he was no more than the flesh and blood son of Joseph. While others, believing in the immaculate conception, therefore conclude that he was the "son of God," but remain divided as to whether this term should be taken literally or figuratively.

Luke says:

> The angel Gabriel was sent from God to a virgin. . . the virgin's name was Mary. And the angel came in unto her and said: "Hail, thou art a highly favoured woman." And when she saw him, she was troubled at his saying and cast in her mind what manner of salutation this should be. And the angel said unto her: "Fear not, Mary, for thou hast found favour with God. And behold, thou shalt conceive in thy womb and bring forth a son and shalt call his name Jesus. . ." Then said Mary unto the angel: "How shall this be, seeing I know not a man?" . . .And the angel answered . . ."With God, nothing shall be impossible." And Mary said: "Behold the handmaid of the Lord, be it unto me according to thy word." And the angel departed from her.
>
> (Luke 1:26-39)

The same incident is described in the Qur'an as follows:

> When the angel said: "O Mary! Allah has chosen you and made you pure and has preferred you above the women of Creation. . . O Mary! Allah gives you good news of a Word from Him whose name is the Messiah, Jesus, son of Mary, illustrious in the world and the hereafter and one of those brought near (to Allah). . ." She said: "My Lord! How can I have a child when no mortal has touched me?" He said: "So (it will be). Allah creates what He will. If He decrees a

19

thing, He says to it: 'Be!' It is."

(Qur'an 3:42-45)

Out of the four Gospels, Mark and John are silent about Jesus's birth, and Matthew just casually mentions it. Then, again, Luke contradicts himself by giving a human geneology to Jesus, while Mark and John don't mention it. As between Matthew and Luke, the former gives twenty-six persons between Adam and Jesus, while Luke has forty-two names in his list. Thus, there is a discrepancy between the two of sixteen people. If we accept forty years as the average age of a person, then there is a gap of six hundred and forty years between the two records of Jesus's supposed lineal descent!

There are no such contradictions in the Qur'anic doctrine of the immaculate conception and the miraculous birth of Jesus. Yet Qur'an firmly rejects the divinity of Jesus, as is shown in this description of what happened shortly after Jesus's birth:

> Then she brought the child to her people, carrying him; and they said: "Mary, you have surely committed a monstrous thing! Sister of Aaron, your father was not a wicked man, nor was your mother an unchaste woman." Mary pointed to the child then; but they said: "How shall we speak to one who is still in the cradle, a little child?" He said: "I am the servant of Allah; Allah has given me the Book, and made me a prophet. Blessed He has made me, wherever I may be, and He has enjoined me to pray, and to give the alms, so long as I live, and likewise to cherish my mother. He has not made me arrogant, unprosperous. Peace be upon me, the day I was born, and the day I die, and the day I am raised up alive!" That is Jesus, son of Mary, in word of truth, concerning which they are doubting. It is not for Allah to take a son to Him. Glory be to Him! When He decrees a thing, He only says to it: "Be!" It is.

(Qur'an 19:27-35)

The birth of Adam was the greatest miracle, as he was born without a father or mother. The birth of Eve too was a greater miracle than the birth of Jesus, inasmuch as she was born without a mother. Qur'an says:

The likeness of Jesus with Allah is as the likeness of Adam.
He created him of dust, then He said to him: "Be!" and he
is.

(Qur'an 3:59)

It is very important to examine Jesus's life in the context of
what was happening politically and socially in the society
into which he was born. It was a time of great unrest in the
Jewish world.

The Jews in their history have been trampled under the
feet of invaders one after another in a series of invasions,
which will be examined in greater detail further on in this account. Because of the defeats which resulted in their helpless-
ness, the fire of hatred always remained burning in their
hearts. But even in the days of their blackest despair, a large
proportion of the Jews retained their mental balance, and
continued in the expectation of a new Moses who, with his
staff, would succeed in driving away the invader, and the rule
of Jehovah would be ushered in. He would be the Messiah, or
the Annointed.

There was always a section of the Jewish nation who worshipped every rising sun, trimming their sails to whatever
wind prevailed at the time, in order to make the best of a bad
bargain. They acquired wealth and position, both temporal
and religious, but were hated by the rest of the Jews as
traitors.

Apart from these two groups, there was a third group of
Jews who differed widely from them. They took refuge in the
wilderness where they could practice religion according to the
Torah, and prepare themselves to fight the invaders whenever
the opportunity arose. During this period, the Romans made
many unsuccessful attempts to discover their hideouts. The
numbers of these patriots continued to grow. We first knew
about them from Josephus.

He calls these three parties of the Jews — Pharisees, Sad-
ducees, and Essenes, respectively.

The existence of the Essenes was known of, but not in any
great detail. This group of people is not once mentioned in
the Gospels. Then, with dramatic suddenness, the documents
known as the Dead Sea Scrolls came to light in the mountains

of Jordan near the Dead Sea. This discovery took the whole intellectual and ecclesiastical world by storm. The story of of how these documents were found needs some telling.

In 1947, an Arab boy, tending his flock near Qumran, found one of the sheep was missing, so he decided to climb the nearby mountain in search of the missing animal. During his search, he came upon the mouth of a cave into which he thought the sheep had gone. He threw a stone into it and expected to hear stone hitting stone. Instead the stone made a clinking noise as if it had hit an earthen pot. His imagination was fired. He thought that perhaps he had stumbled upon a treasure trove. Next morning, he returned to the cave and, with a friend to help him, entered it. Instead they found several clay jars amongst the fragments of broken pottery. They took one of them to the camp where they were living and were bitterly disappointed when all that they found was a foul smelling leather scroll. They unrolled it until it reached from one side of the tent to the other. It was one of the scrolls which were later sold for a quarter of a million dollars. They sold it to a Syrian Christian named Kando for a few shillings. Kando was a cobbler, and he was only interested in the leather as it might come in handy for resoling old shoes. Kando, however, noticed that the leather sheet was over-written in letters unknown to him. After a closer look, he decided to show it to the Syrian Metropolitan of St. Mark's Monastery in Jerusalem. These two shadowy figures carted the scrolls from one country to another, hoping to make money.

In the American Oriental Institute of Jordan, the scrolls were found to be the oldest known copy of the Book of Isaiah in the Old Testament. Seven years later, the scrolls were placed in the Shrine of the Book in Jerusalem by the government of Israel.

At a rough guess, there are about six hundred caves dotting the hillside above the bank of the river Jordan. In these caves lived the Essenes, a community of people who had renounced the world, because a true Jew could only live under the sovereignty of Jehovah and was not permitted to obey any authority except His. So, according to their beliefs, a Jew living under and recognizing the Roman Emperor as overlord committed a sin.

Tired of the pomp and show of the world and over-whelmed by its uncontrollable forces which lead inevitably to conflict and self-destruction, they sought refuge in the silence of the cliffs rising above the shores of the Dead Sea. They withdrew into the solitude of the mountain caves so that they could concentrate on living a life of purity and so gain salvation. Unlike many of the Jews of the Temple, they did not use the Old Testament to make money, but tried to live according to its teaching. By leading this life, they hoped to achieve perfection and holiness. Their aim was to set an example to the rest of the Jews of how they could escape from the road leading to destruction, which they knew was fast approaching unless the Jews followed the Word of God.

They wrote gnostic songs that must have stirred the hearts of the people too deeply for words to express. A gnostic's life is like a ship in a storm, says one song. In another, a gnostic is described as a traveller in a forest full of lions, each having a tongue like a sword. At the beginning of the path, a gnostic experiences distress like a woman in labour giving birth to her first child. If he succeeds in enduring this distress, he becomes illuminated by God's perfect Light. Then he realizes that man is a vain and empty creature moulded of clay and kneaded with water. Since he has passed through the crucible of suffering and endured the limits of doubt and despair, he attains peace in turmoil, joy in sorrow, and a new life of happiness in pain. Then he finds himself wrapped in God's love. At this stage, with humble thanks, he realizes how he has been snatched from the pit, and placed on a high plain. Walking here in the Light of God, he stands erect, unbending before the brute force of the world.

Before the discovery of the Dead Sea Scrolls, only a little was known about the Essenes. Pliny and Josephus mention them, but they were virtually ignored by later historians. Pliny describes them as a race by themselves more remarkable then any other in the world:

> They have no women, they abjure sexual love, they have
> no money. . . Their membership is steadily increasing
> through the large number of people who are attracted to
> their way of life. . . in this way, their race has lasted for

thousands of years, though no one is born within it.

Josephus, who started life as an Essene writes that the Essenes "believe that the soul (ruach) is immortal. It is a gift from God. God purifies some for Himself, removing all blemishes of the flesh. The person so perfected attains a holiness free of all impurities."

These cave-dwellers continued to lead their life unaffected by the waves of conquerors who destroyed the temple and conquered the Jews so many times. Their life in the wilderness was not an escape from the responsibility of every Jew to struggle for the purity of his religion, and to free Judea from foreign aggression. Side by side with the daily prayers and study of the Scriptures, some of them were formed into an efficient force which not only preached the guidance of Moses, but was also ready to fight for the freedom to live in the way that the teaching indicated. Thus, their fighting could only be in the service of God and not to gain power or for any personal consideration. The members of this fighting force were called "Zealots" by the enemy. They were organised under one flag, and each tribe had its own banner. The Zealots were divided into four divisions, and at the head of each stood a chief. Each division was composed of people from three of the tribes of Israel. In this way, all the twelve Jewish tribes were organised under one flag. The chief had to be a Levite. He was not only a military commander, but was also a teacher of the Law. Each division had its own *Midrash* (school), and the Levite, apart from performing the duties of a military commander, had to give regular *darsh* (lessons) in the school.

Thus, living in the wilderness in these caves, the Essenes shunned pleasure-seeking, scorned wedlock and were contempuous of wealth. They formed a secret society and their secrets were never divulged to a non-member. The Romans knew about their existence, but could not penetrate the mask of secrecy surrounding them. The dream of every adventurous Jew was to become a member of this society, for that was the only practical method available to him of fighting the foreign invaders.

The Essenes, as we already know from Pliny's record,

disdained marriage, but they adopted other men's children while yet pliable and docile, accepting them as their kin and moulding them according to their way of life. Thus, through centuries, incredible though it seems, the Essene society had perpetuated itself, although no one was ever born into it. Thus, Zachariah, the High Priest in the Temple of Solomon, when he had a son in his old age, sent him to the Essenes in the wilderness where the child was brought up. He is known to history as John the Baptist.

Now that we know that the Essene community did exist in the wilderness, Zachariah's action is made understandable. He was not sending his cherished son alone into the desert, but was entrusting him to the most reliable of communities, a community which sought to live in a manner pleasing to Jehovah. Mary, the cousin of Zachariah's wife, Elizabeth, was brought up by Zachariah because she was handed over to the temple in accordance with a vow taken by her mother. It was in this environment that the birth of Jesus took place.

There was among the Jews an expectation of the Messiah, a new leader who would be baptised and annointed their king. The rumour circulating among the Jews of his imminent birth led to Herod's decision to kill all the babies born in Bethlehem where, according to tradition, the Messiah was to appear. The powerful secret society of the Essenes was set in motion by Zachariah, and Mary succeeded in escaping the clutches of the Roman soldiers. She went with Jesus to Egypt where the Essenes had another colony.

The sudden disappearance of Jesus and Mary and their safe escape from the Roman authorities had, until the discovery of the Dead Sea Scrolls, been a mystery and source of speculation. None of the Gospels cover this episode. The existence of the Essene community shows how it was possible for them to evade their pursuers with such success despite the publicity which must have surrounded the birth. Under other circumstances, a child who spoke coherently and with authority from the cradle, and who was visited by shepherds and Magi might not have been able to disappear so easily.

In 4 B.C., when Jesus was three or four years old, Herod

died. And so the immediate danger to the life of Jesus was removed and he could move freely. It appears that he was educated under the hard discipline of the Essene teachers and, being an intelligent pupil, he learned Torah very quickly. When he was twelve years old, he was sent to the temple and it was found that the student, instead of repeating his lessons, was speaking with a certain confidence and authority. There are several Muslim traditions which tell of the singular gifts which Jesus was given so early in his life. The following is from Thalabi's *Stories of the Prophets*:

> Wahb said: The first sign which the people saw from Jesus was that his mother was living in the house of a village headman in the land of Egypt, to which Joseph, the carpenter, had brought her when he went with her to Egypt; and the poor used to repair to that headman's house. Some money belonging to that headman was stolen from his treasury, but he did not suspect the poor, and Mary was grieved over the affliction of that headman. When Jesus saw his mother's grief over her host's affliction, he said to her, "Mother, do you want me to guide him to his money?" She replied, "Yes, my son." He said, "Tell him to gather the poor for me in his house." So Mary said that to the headman and he gathered the poor for him. When they had collected, he went to two of them, one of whom was blind and the other lame, and lifted the lame man onto the blind man's shoulders, and said to him, "Rise up with him." The blind man replied, "I am too weak for that." Jesus said to him, "How were you strong enough for it yesterday?" When they heard him saying that, they beat the blind man till he arose, and when he stood up, the lame man reached to the window of the treasury. Then Jesus said to the headman, "Thus they schemed against your property yesterday, because the blind man sought the help of his strength and the lame man of his eyes." Then the blind man and the lame man said, "He has spoken the truth, by God!" and restored all his money to the headman. He took it and put it in his treasury and said, "O Mary, take half of it." She replied, "I was not created for that." The headman said, "Then give it to your son." She replied, "He is greater in rank than I." . . .And at that time he was twelve years old.

Another sign:

As Sadi said: When Jesus, peace be upon him, was in the school, he used to tell the boys what their fathers were doing, and he would say to a boy, "Go home, for your people have been eating such and such and have prepared such and such for you and they are eating such and such." So the boy would go home to his people and would cry until they gave him that thing. Then they would say to him, "Who told you about this?" and he would say, "Jesus." So they gathered them in a house and Jesus came looking for them. Then they said, "They are not here." He said to them, "Then what is in this house?" They replied, "Swine." He said, "Let them be swine." So when they opened the door for them, lo! they were swine. The Children of Israel were troubled about Jesus, so when his mother was afraid concerning him, she put him on an ass of hers and went in flight to Egypt. . .

Ata' said: When Mary had taken Jesus from the school, she handed him over to various trades, and the last to which she entrusted him was to the dyers; so she handed him over to their chief that he might learn from him. Now the man had various clothes with him, and he had to go on a journey, so he said to Jesus, "You have learned this trade, and I am going on a journey from which I shall not return for ten days. These clothes are of different colours, and I have marked every one of them with the colour with which it is to be dyed, so I want you to be finished with them when I return." Then he went out. Jesus, peace be upon him, prepared one receptacle with one colour and put all the clothes in it and said to them, "Be, by God's permission, according to what is expected of you." Then the dyer came, and all the clothes were in one receptacle, so he said, "O Jesus, what have you done?" He replied, "I have finished them." He said, "Where are they?" He replied, "In the receptacle." He said, "All of them?" He replied, "Yes." He said, "How are they all in one receptacle? You have spoiled those clothes." He replied, "Rise and look." So he arose, and Jesus took out a yellow garment and a green garment and a red garment until he had taken them out according to the colours which he desired. Then the dyer began to wonder, and he knew that that was from God, Great and

Glorious is He. Then the dyer said to the people, "Come and look at what Jesus, peace be upon him, has done." So he and his companions, and they were the disciples, believed in him; and God, Great and Glorious is He, knows best.

During the early manhood of Jesus, a rumour began to spread that John had drifted away from the Essene society and was living alone in the wilderness. "He dressed himself in the simple garment of camel's hair with a leather girdle round his waist. He ate only locusts and wild honey." (Matthew 3:4) He began to preach to the masses directly and did not insist on the long period of apprenticeship which was necessary for a person who desired full membership in the Essene brotherhood. His was thus a public movement. He called on everyone to turn to Jehovah, and assured them that the Kingdom of God would soon be established.

In connection with this, it is of interest to read in the history written by Josephus of another hermit whose disciple this historian was. Josephus had spent three years in the desert as an ascetic. During this time he was under the guidance of a hermit called Bannus who clothed himself with what grew on trees, ate only such food as grew wild and disciplined himself to chastity by constant cold baths. Thus, it is obvious that John was following the tradition common to hermits.

The wilderness had been the place of refuge for David and other Prophets before him. It was a place where the Jews could be free from the domination of their foreign rulers and the influence of false gods. In the wilderness, there was no aspiration to the favours of the pagan rulers. In this atmosphere, there could only be dependance on the Creator and worship of Him alone. It was the cradle of monotheism. The desert wilderness removed any false sense of security, and a man learned to rely on Reality alone: "In the barrenness of the wilderness, all other support falls and one is laid bare to the One God, the Power, the Constant Source of all life, and the Root of all security."[2] Thus, the struggle in the wilderness had two aspects. Primarily, it took place within the hearts of men who had to do battle with themselves if they were to live in a manner pleasing to their Lord. Secondly, as we have already seen, the choice of this course of action inevitably resulted in conflict with those who wished to live otherwise. The first struggle was a question of faith in Jehovah, and of spiritual gain, irrespective of whether the second battle was won or lost.

The clarion call of John began to attract a large crowd. He had ceased to observe one important stipulation in the Essene code of conduct: "to disclose none of the secrets of the sect to others even though tortured to death."[3] The failure to follow this rule made it all the easier for the Romans to infiltrate the movement with spies. John, with his prophetic vision, saw through their guise, and called them "vipers". (Matthew 3:7) Jesus, his younger cousin, joined the movement and was probably one of the first to be baptised. It is likely that Barnabas, who was his constant companion, was baptised with Jesus, and also his other companion, Mathias.

John knew that the "vipers" were going to succeed before he could start the fight and, therefore, the baptism of Jesus gave him great satisfaction inasmuch as he was sure that his movement would not end with his life. As was foreseen by John, King Herod beheaded him and his mantle fell upon the shoulders of Jesus.

Jesus was now thirty years old. His mission lasted for not more than three years. He realised that his period of preparation was over. The significant part of his life had begun. In order to appreciate the full significance of this time, we will have to see Jesus against the background of history, and in particular, the history of the Jews. This will further clarify the picture which has already begun to emerge, that the existence of the Essene community, the activities of John, and finally, the conflict between Jesus and the Romans, were all a part of one pattern which repeats itself again and again throughout the history of the Jews. In every case, what finally moved the Jews to revolt against their foreign invaders was the attempt of these rulers to make them associate partners with their Lord. Their belief in the Divine Unity, and that there is no object of worship other than Him, was categoric.

As rulers, the Jews displayed an utter lack of statesmanship, though they flourished in political slavery. At the dawn of history, we find the Jews intriguing against their own king because he did everything which "was evil in the sight of the Lord." (II Kings 13:11) Nebuchadnezzar of Babylon took Jerusalem. The temple was left intact, but the treasure, both from the temple and the royal palace, was left under the new ruler and the Jews lost no time in rebelling against the Babylonian overlord. This prompted another attack in which the temple and the city were destroyed.

The wheel of fortune took another turn, and the Persians, under Cyrus, conquered Babylon. The Jews once again intrigued for the benefit of the invaders. Cyrus immediately realised the danger of having such a large population of aliens in Babylon, and asked them to leave and go back to Jerusalem. They were also permitted to rebuild the temple.

The cavalcade moving towards Jerusalem was composed of 42,360 Jews. In addition, they carried with them 7,337 servants and women. This included 200 singing men and singing girls. This caravan was carried on 736 horses, 245 mules, 435 camels, and 6,720 asses. (Ezra 2:64-69) This was in addition to the animals which carried the treasure they had amassed.

On reaching Jerusalem, they began to plan the reconstruction of the temple, and for this purpose, they collected 61,000 drams of gold and 5,000 pounds of silver. This was in addition to the treasure they had brought with them from Babylon which was thirty horses laden with gold, and one thousand carrying silver. In addition, there were 5,400 gold and silver vessels to be placed in the temple. (Ezra 1:9-11) The captives who returned to Jerusalem had grown both in number and wealth.

As rulers of Jerusalem, the Jews did not enjoy peace for a long time. The conquest of Alexander the Great, before he died in 323 B.C., had reached India. His generals divided up his empire between them after his death. Ptolemy began to rule Egypt with his capitol in Alexandria. The kingdom of Seleucus was divided into two parts — Antioch became the capitol of the Northern kingdom and Babylon was the centre of the remainder of Alexander's empire. The Ptolemaic and Seleucian rulers were locked in constant feud and, in one of their earlier encounters Jerusalem fell into the hands of the Egyptian Greeks. The new rulers were not happy with the large concentration of Jews in Israel; so a large number were forcibly transported to Egypt. This resulted in what was to become the largest Jewish colony out of Israel. Here they came into close contact with Greek civilization, and the Hebrew scriptures were translated into Greek. To the Ptolemaic rulers, Israel was a far-off colony and the Jews, after they had paid the annual tribute, were very much left to themselves.

In 198 B.C., the Seleucian rulers took over Jerusalem from the Ptolemaic rulers. For them, Jerusalem was very much nearer at hand. So they took a much greater interest in the affairs of the people of Jerusalem than did the earlier rulers. The process of Hellenisation, which had occurred gradually and at a natural pace under the Ptolemaic rule, was accelerated by the new rulers in a deliberate attempt to assimilate the Jews into their way of life. This forced cultural conformity reached its extreme expression during the reign of Antiochus Epeplianus. He made the mistake of installing a statue of Zeus in the Temple of Solomon. This outraged the Jews and they revolted under Judah Maccabees. The hammer was their emblem of revolt. The Greeks were pushed out of Jerusalem. The victorious Jews found the temple in ruins, the sanctuary desolate, the altar profaned and the temple gate burnt. They rebuilt the temple according to the Torah. The new rulers were so popular that they became both the high priests of the temple and the kings of Israel. With the concentration of power in the same hands, the rulers became very strict in the observation of the law, and the people began to pine for the benevolent administration of foreign rulers. Finding dissatisfaction against their rule, the Maccabees became more haughty and arrogant. The Jews once again began to intrigue against their rulers, and this played no small part in ushering in the Roman rule over Jerusalem.

About the time Jesus was born, the Romans repeated the mistake of the earlier rulers. They erected a large golden eagle over the main gate of the temple. This infuriated the Jews and resulted in a series of revolts against the Romans. Two descendants of the Maccabees were the first to unfurl the banner of revolt. Their aim was to destroy the eagle. To the Romans, it was not only an act of sedition, but also an insult to their religion. So, after much bloodshed, the revolt was crushed. The two leaders were caught and burnt alive. Shortly afterwards, the Romans had to face another rebellion. The fight went against the Jews and two thousand rebels were crucified.

Though defeated, tempers were still running very high when in 6 A.D. the Emperor Augustus ordered a census of the Jews in order to facilitate the levying of the taxes. To pay taxes to the deified emperor was against the teaching of the Torah. The Jews recognised only one king: Jehovah. A disturbance followed. The more moderate elements realised that the conflict would result in the complete massacre of the Jews and they counselled compromise and agreed to pay the taxes, to save the people from committing senseless suicide. The leaders who purchased peace at this price were not popular, and were regarded as traitors to the Jewish nation.

The practical and social situation at the time of Jesus's birth, together with the events leading up to the death of John have already been mentioned, and we have now reached a point where the entire resistance movement was concentrated around the divinely inspired figure of Jesus.

Before doing anything else, Jesus had to undergo forty days living and praying in the wilderness. He was now thirty years old. Under Jewish law, this was the age when a man was freed from the domination of his father. Unlike John, he did not openly teach, when he preached to the multitudes, that they should take a stand against the Roman rulers. Discreet preparations needed to be made. The previous attempts had ended in disaster and the recent death of John was fresh in the mind of Jesus. With foresight and prudence, he began to prepare and organise the Jews. He baptised no one. This would have unnecessarily attracted too much attention from the Romans, and would have been a dangerous practise, as he could not have prevented the "vipers" from infiltrating the resistance movement. He appointed twelve disciples, a traditional number representing the twelve tribes of Israel. They further enlisted seventy patriots to serve under their command. The Pharisees had always kept the *Am Al Arez*, the able-bodied Jews who lived in the villages, at arm's length. Jesus took them under his wing. These peasants, many of whom were of the Essene community, became the zealous followers of Jesus, and were ready to lay down their lives for his cause. They were known as Zealots. According to the Bible, at least six of the twelve disciples are known to have been Zealots. Jesus, who had come to reaffirm and not to reject the teaching of Moses, issued the Old Testament appeal: "Whosoever is zealous for the Law and maintains the Covenant, let him come forth after me." (Maccabees 2:27-31) A large number began to enlist, but they were kept underground, and their training was carried out in the wilderness. They were also called *Bar Yonim*, which means "sons of the wilderness." From among these, those who had learned to use the dagger were known as *Sicarii* (dagger-men). A further hand-picked group of men formed a kind of bodyguard, and they were known as *Bar Jesus*, or "sons of Jesus". A number of persons known as *Bar Jesus* are mentioned in historical sources, but a curtain of mystery surrounds these men, and not much is known about them. This is understandable. They belonged to the closest circle of Jesus's followers, and their identities had to be hidden from the eyes of the Roman spies.

Jesus gave the command to his followers: "But now he that hath a purse, let him take it and likewise his scrip; and he that hath no sword, let him sell his garments and buy one." (Luke 22:36) And the number of his followers, inspired also by his teaching and miracles, grew. The net result of all these preparations was that Pilate's successor, Sossianus Hierocles, (quoted by the Church father, Lactanius), says, off-handedly, that Jesus was the leader of a band of highway robbers numbering nine-hundred men. A medieval Hebrew copy of a lost version of a work by Josephus also reports that Jesus had between 2,000 to 4,000 armed followers with him.[4]

Jesus took great care not to deviate from the teaching of the Essenes, which is known by the fact that "the rites and precepts of the Gospels and the Epistles are to be found on every page of the literature of the sect."[5] During his mission, however, Jesus did not disclose the totality of his teaching to most of his followers. The whole truth was known to very few:

> I have yet many things to say unto you, but you cannot bear them now. Howbeit, when he, the Spirit of truth, is come, he will guide you into all truth, but he shall not speak of himself, but whatsoever he shall hear, that shall he speak.

> (John 16:12-14)

He was not seeking worldly power, either as ruler of the country, or within the closed hierarchy of the Scribes and Pharisees. However, his popularity with the common people and the large number of his following caused the Romans and those priests who supported them to fear that this was his intention. It was this apparent threat to their position of power which prompted them to try to dispose of him.

Jesus's mission was solely to establish worship of the Creator in the manner in which the Creator had ordained. He and his followers were prepared to fight anyone who tried to prevent them from living as their Lord wished them to.

The first fighting took place with the Jews loyal to the Romans. It was led by Bar Jesus Barabbas, and it completely demoralised this group of Jews, as their leader was killed in the encounter. Bar Jesus Barabbas was arrested.

The next objective was the temple itself. The Romans had a strong force near at hand, since it was the time of the annual festival and the feast of the Passover was approaching. The Romans who at that time of year were always ready for minor disturbances, were even more alert than usual. In addition, there were the temple police who guarded the sacred place. The entrance made by Jesus was so well-planned that the Roman soldiers were taken completely by surprise, and Jesus took over the control of the temple. This encounter is known as the "cleansing of the temple". John's Gospel describes the event in these words:

> In the temple (Jesus) found those who were selling oxen and sheep and pigeons, and the money-changers at their business. And making a whip of cord, he drove them all, with the sheep and oxen, out of the temple, and he poured

out the coins of the money-changers and over-turned their tables.

(John 2:14-15)

Commenting on the words, "the whip of cord", Carmichael says that

> they unmistakably imply violence and equally unmistakably represent a sort of minimal toning-down of what actually must have been a massive undertaking. If we simply imagine the size of the temple, the tens of thousands of pilgrims thronging into and through it, the numerous attendants, the police force, the Roman soldiers, as well as the normal reaction of the ox-drivers themselves, to say nothing of the money-changers, we see that it must have taken much more than mere surprise to have accomplished it at all. The scene behind this fragmentary recollection in the fourth Gospel must have been vastly different. The chronicler has softened it by "spiritualising" it out of all reality.[6]

One of the lessons of every freedom fighter has been that the local police have their sympathies with the patriots and not with the army of occupation. This could have been a contributing factor in the complete collapse of the defence of the Temple.

The Romans had suffered a local setback, but their power was not crushed. They called for reinforcements, and fresh troops began to move towards Jerusalem. The defence of the gate of Jerusalem lasted for a few days; but, ultimately, the Roman army proved too strong for the patriots, and all the followers of Jesus melted away. Even the disciples ran away, leaving Jesus with very few men around him. Jesus went underground, and the Romans began an intensive search to find him.

The "arrest", the "trial", and the "crucifixion" are hedged around with so many contradictions and mis-statements, that it is extremely difficult to untangle and penetrate through them in order to arrive at what actually happened. We find that the Roman government succeeded in utilising the services of the small minority of Jews who had a vested interest in the continuation of Roman rule over Jerusalem.

Judas Iscariot, a disciple of Jesus, was won over on the

promise of receiving thirty pieces of silver, if, through his help, Jesus was arrested. In order to avoid any further trouble, it was decided to make the attempt at night. On reaching the place where Jesus had gone with a few of his followers, Judas was told to kiss Jesus, so that the foreign Roman soldiers could identify him. The plan miscarried. When the soldiers materialised from the darkness, a tumult ensued. The two Jews were mixed up in the dark, and the soldiers mistakenly arrested Judas instead of Jesus. Thus, the latter made good his escape. Qur'an says:

> . . .yet they did not slay him, nor crucified him, only a likeness of that was shown to them.
>
> (Qur'an 4:155)

When the prisoner was brought before Pilate, the Roman Magistrate, the dramatic turn of events satisfied everyone. The majority of the Jews were happy for, due to a miracle, the traitor was standing in the dock instead of Jesus. The pro-Roman Jews were happy, for, with the death of Judas, the proof of their guilt would be destroyed. Furthermore, because Jesus would be legally dead, he would not be able to come out into the open to give them trouble.

The part played by Pontius Pilate, the Roman Magistrate, is hard to determine. His indecisiveness, as described in the Bible, his partiality towards the Jewish leaders, together with his good will towards Jesus, make a story hard to believe. This could be the result of an attempt by the writers of the Gospels to twist the facts in order to throw the responsibility of the "crucifixion" onto the whole Jewish nation and so to exonerate the Romans completely from their part in Jesus's supposed death.[7] The only way an official account of Jesus's life could survive would be by describing it in a manner which was not offensive to the foreign rulers, and by either omitting, disguising, or even changing those details which would be displeasing to those in authority.

Another explanation is provided by a strong tradition that Pilate was "got at" with a sizable bribe amounting to the equivalent of £30,000. If what is described in the Gospels is true, then it is obvious that Pilate did have a vested interest in the drama enacted that day in Jerusalem.

Finally, there is another significant fact. In the calendars of the Saints of the Coptic Church, both in Egypt and in Ethiopia, Pilate and his wife appear as "saints". This could be possible only if we accept that Pilate, knowing full well that his soldiers had made a wrong arrest, knowingly condemned Judas in place of Jesus, and allowed the latter to escape.

In the account given by Barnabas, we are told that at the time of the arrest, Judas was transformed by the Creator so that even his mother and his closest followers believed him to be Jesus. It was not until Jesus appeared to them, after his supposed death, that they were informed of what had really happened. This would explain why there is such confusion surrounding the events which took place at this time, and why some accounts, written by people who were not present at those events, support the mistaken belief that it was Jesus who was crucified.

Not everyone is in complete agreement as to whether it was Jesus's would-be betrayer who was the one crucified. The Cerinthians and later the Basilidians, who were among the first Christians, denied that Jesus was crucified, but believed that it was Simon of Cyrene who was crucified instead. Cerinthus, a contemporary of Peter, Paul and John, also denied the resurrection of Jesus. The Carpocratians, another early Christian sect, believed that it was not Jesus who was crucified, but one of his followers who very closely resembled him. Plotinus, who lived in the fourth century, tells us that he had read a book called *The Journies of the Apostles* which related the acts of Peter, John, Andrew, Thomas and Paul. Among other things, it stated that Jesus was not crucified, but another in his place, and therefore, he laughed at those who believed that they had crucified him.[8] Thus, although it is known that Jesus was not crucified, sources either differ or are not specific as to who was crucified in his place. Some find it hard to believe anything:

> When one reflects that the catalogue of outrage ascribed to the Roman soldiery, repeats almost verbatim certain passages of the Old Testament. . . one begins to suspect that the entire episode is a sheer invention.[9]

37

There is no other known historical record of what happened to Jesus after the "crucifixion" other than in the Gospel of Barnabas and the Qur'an. These both describe the event which is generally known as the "ascension" in the four accepted Gospels, in which Jesus was taken away from this world.

Chapter 3

THE GOSPEL OF BARNABAS

The Gospel of Barnabas is the only known surviving Gospel
written by a disciple of Jesus, that is, by a man who spent
most of his time in the actual company of Jesus during the
three years in which he was delivering his message. He therefore had direct experience and knowledge of Jesus's teaching,
unlike all the authors of the four accepted Gospels. It is
not known when he wrote down what he remembered of
Jesus and his guidance, whether events and discourses were
recorded as they happened, or whether he wrote it soon after
Jesus had left the earth, fearing that otherwise some of his
teaching might be changed or lost. It is possible that he did
not write down anything until he had returned to Cyprus
with John Mark. The two made this journey some time after
Jesus had left the earth, after parting company with Paul of
Tarsus, who had refused to make any further journeys with
Barnabas on which Mark was also present. But no matter
when it was written, and although it, too, like the four accepted Gospels, has inevitably suffered from being translated
and filtered through several languages, it is, at least, an eye-
witness account of Jesus's life.

The Gospel of Barnabas was accepted as a Canonical Gospel in the churches of Alexandria up until 325 A.D. It is
known that it was being circulated in the first and second
centuries after the birth of Jesus from the writings of Iraneus
(130-200 A.D.), who wrote in support of the Divine Unity.
He opposed Paul whom he accused of being responsible for
the assimilation of the pagan Roman religion and Platonic
philosophy into the original teaching of Jesus. He quoted
extensively from the Gospel of Barnabas in support of his
views.

In 325 A.D., the famous Council of Nicea was held. The doctrine of the Trinity was declared to be the official doctrine of the Pauline Church, and one of the consequences of this decision was that out of the three hundred or so Gospels extant at that time, four were chosen as the official Gospels of the Church. The remaining Gospels, including the Gospel of Barnabas, were ordered to be destroyed completely. It was also decided that all Gospels written in Hebrew should be destroyed. An edict was issued stating that anyone found in possession of an unauthorised Gospel would be put to death. This was the first well-organised attempt to remove all the records of Jesus's original teaching, whether in human beings or books, which contradicted the doctrine of Trinity. In the case of the Gospel of Barnabas, these orders were not entirely successful, and mention of its continued existence has been made up to the present day.

Pope Damasus (304-384 A.D.), who became Pope in 366 A.D., is recorded as having issued a decree that the Gospel of Barnabas should not be read. This decree was supported by Gelasus, Bishop of Caesaria, who died in 395 A.D. The Gospel was included in his list of Apocryphal books. *Apocrypha* simply means *"hidden from the people"*. Thus, at this stage, the Gospel was no longer available to everyone, but was still being referred to by the leaders of the Church. In fact, it is known that the Pope secured a copy of the Gospel of Barnabas in 383 A.D., and kept it in his private library.

There were a number of other decrees which referred to the Gospel. It was forbidden by the Decree of the Western Churches in 382 A.D., and by Pope Innocent in 465 A.D. In the Glasian Decree of 496 A.D., the *Evangelium Barnabe* is included in the list of forbidden books. This decree was re-affirmed by Hormisdas, who was Pope from 514 A.D. to 523 A.D. All these decrees are mentioned in the catalogue of the Greek manuscripts in the Library of Chancellor Seguier (1558-1672), prepared by B. de Montfaucon (1655-1741).

Barnabas is also mentioned in the *Stichometry* of Nicephorus as follows:

Serial No.3, Epistle of Barnabas . . . Lines 1,300

and again in the list of *Sixty Books* as follows:

Serial No. 17. Travels and teaching of the Apostles.
Serial No. 18. Epistle of Barnabas.
Serial No. 24. Gospel According to Barnabas.

This famous list was also known as the *Index*, and Christians were not supposed to read any of the books on it on pain of eternal punishment.

Cotelerius, who catalogued the manuscripts in the Library of the French king, listed the Gospel of Barnabas in the *Index of Scriptures* which he prepared in 1789. The Gospel is also recorded in the 206th manuscript of the Baroccian Collection in the Bodleian Library in Oxford.[1] There is also a solitary fragment of a Greek version of the Gospel of Barnabas to be found in a museum in Athens, which is all that remains of a copy which was burnt:

Βαρνάβας ὁ ἀπόστολος ἔφη· ἐν ἀμίλλαις πονηραῖς ἀθλιώτερος ὁ νικήσας, διότι ἀπέρχεται πλέον ἔχων τῆς ἀμαρτίας[2].

In the fourth year of the Emperor Zeno's rule in 478 A.D., the remains of Barnabas were discovered, and a copy of the Gospel of Barnabas, written in his own hand, was found on his breast. This is recorded in the *Acta Sanctorum*, Boland Junii, Tome II, pages 422-450, published in Antwerp in 1698. It has been claimed by the Roman Catholic Church that the Gospel found in the grave of Barnabas was that of Matthew, but no steps have been taken to display this copy. The contents of the twenty-five mile long library of the Vatican remain in the dark.

The manuscript from which the English translation of the Gospel of Barnabas was made, was originally in the possession of Pope Sextus (1589-1590). He had a friend, a monk called Fra Marino, who became very interested in the Gospel of Barnabas after reading the writings of Iraneus, who quoted from it extensively. One day he went to see the Pope. They lunched together and, after the meal, the Pope fell asleep. Father Marino began to browse through the books in the Pope's private library and discovered an Italian manuscript of the Gospel of Barnabas. Concealing it in the sleeve of his robe, he left and came out of the Vatican with it. This manuscript then passed through different hands until it reached "a person of great name and authority" in Amsterdam, "who, during his lifetime, was often heard to put a high value to this piece." After his death, it came into the possession of J.E. Cramer, a Councillor of the King of Prussia. In 1713, Cramer presented this manuscript to the famous connoisseur of books, Prince Eugene of Savoy. In 1738, along with the library of the Prince, it found its way into the Hofbibliothek in Vienna, where it now rests.

Toland, a notable historian of the early Church, had access to this manuscript, and he refers to it in his *Miscellaneous Works*, which was published posthumously in 1747. He says of the Gospel: "This is in scripture style to a hair," and continues:

> The story of Jesus is very differently told in many things from the received Gospels, but much more fully. . . and particularly this Gospel. . . being near as long again as many of ours. Someone would make a prejudice in favour of it; because, as all things are best known just after they happen, so everything diminishes the further it proceeds from its original.[3]

The publicity which Toland gave to this manuscript made it impossible for it to share the same fate as another manuscript of the Gospel in Spanish which also once existed. This manuscript was presented to a college library in England at about the same time that the Italian manuscript was given to the Hofbibliothek. It had not been in England long before it mysteriously disappeared.

The Italian manuscript was translated into English by Canon and Mrs. Ragg, and was printed and published by the Oxford University Press in 1907. Nearly the whole edition of this English translation abruptly and mysteriously disappeared from the market. Only two copies of this translation are known to exist, one in the British Museum, and the other in the Library of Congress in Washington. A micro-film copy of the book in the Library of Congress was obtained, and a fresh edition of the English translation was printed in Pakistan. A copy of this edition was used for the purposes of reprinting a revised version of the Gospel of Barnabas.

It is now generally accepted that the three earliest accepted Gospels, known as the Synoptic Gospels, were copied from an earlier unknown Gospel which today's researchers refer to as "Q", for want of a better name. The question arises as to whether the Apocryphal Gospel of Barnabas is, in fact, this missing Gospel. It must be remembered that John Mark, whose Gospel is the earliest of the four accepted Gospels, was the son of the sister of Barnabas. He never met Jesus. Thus, what he related of Jesus's life and teaching in his Gospel must have been related to him by others. It is known from the books of the New Testament that he accompanied Paul and Barnabas on many of their missionary journeys up to the point when there was a sharp conflict between them, resulting in Barnabas and Mark going to Cyprus together. It is unlikely that Mark relied on Paul as a source of information since Paul had never met Jesus either. The only reasonable conclusion appears to be that he must have repeated what his uncle Barnabas told him about Jesus. It is said by some that he acted as Peter's interpreter and wrote down what he had learned from Peter. This may be correct, for Mark must have had some contact with the other apostles when he was not journeying with Barnabas or Paul. However, Goodspeed shows us from his research that anything he did learn from Peter was by no means comprehensive:

> He had been an interpreter of Peter and wrote down accurately, though not in order, everything that he remembered that had been said or done by the Lord. For he neither heard the Lord, nor followed him, but afterwards, as I said, attended Peter who adapted his instructions to the needs of the hearers, but had no design of giving a connected account of the Lord's oracles.[4]

Luke, who also wrote the Acts of the Apostles, never met Jesus. He was Paul's personal physician. Matthew, who also never encountered Jesus, was a tax collector.

It has been argued that Mark's Gospel might be the "Q" Gospel and that Matthew and Luke used his Gospel when writing theirs. However, they record details which Mark does not, which implies that Mark's Gospel could not have been their only source. Some have said that this is not important, since it is known that Mark's Gospel was written in Hebrew, was then translated into Greek, and re-translated again into Latin. All the Hebrew and early Greek versions of Mark's Gospel have been destroyed, and people can only speculate as to how much of the Gospel was changed or altered during these transitions from one language to another.

It is interesting to note, in passing, that there have even been attempts to return to the source by synthesising the Gospels, since the contradictions that arise between them have, at times, proved a little awkward for the established Church. Titian attempted to synthesise the four accepted Gospels, which had already been earmarked by the Pauline Church as their official Scriptures in the second century A.D. In this Gospel, Titian used 96% of John's Gospel, 75% of Matthew's Gospel, 66% of Luke's Gospel, and 50% of Mark's Gospel. The rest he rejected. It is significant that he placed little trust in the earliest Gospel and relied most heavily on the last Gospel to be written. His synthetic Gospel was not a success.

Thus it is debatable whether Mark's Gospel can be regarded as the common source of the three Synoptic Gospels, whereas all the events recorded in these three Gospels are contained within the Gospel of Barnabas.

Whether these three men, with such differing backgrounds, derived their knowledge from the same source or not, about Barnabas the commandment is:

If he comes unto you, receive him.
(Epistle to the Colossians 4:10)

Chapter 4

THE SHEPHERD OF HERMAS

Th-

The Shepherd was a book written by Hermas between 88 and 97 A.D. at Patmos, near Ephesus. Like the Gospel of Barnabas, it affirmed the Divine Unity, and it was for this reason that concerted efforts were made to destroy it, once the doctrine of Trinity had become firmly rooted in the established Pauline Church. It was one of the books which was banned as a result of the decisions made by the Council of Nicea in 325 A.D.

It appears that Hermas wrote *The Shepherd* at about the same time that John was writing his Gospel, although some people think that *The Shepherd* was written before this. However, there is no difference of opinion as regards the fact that Hermas had not read or seen any of the four Gospels included in the New Testament. Some believe that *The Shepherd* was inspired by the Gospel According to Hebrews, an earlier Gospel which no longer exists, but this is not supported by the account given by Hermas of how the book came to be written.

Up until the Council of Nicea, the book was accepted and widely used by the early followers of Jesus, who regarded Hermas as a prophet. Towards the end of the second century A.D., it was accepted as part of the New Testament by Clement of Alexandria. Origen (185-254 A.D.) also accepted it as a revealed book, and it was placed at the end of the *Codex Sinaiticus* which was in use in the middle of the fourth century A.D. Tertullian (160-220 A.D.) at first accepted it, but later repudiated it when he became a Montanist. Iranius (130-200 A.D.) accepted it as Scripture. Eusebius of Caesaria rejected it, but Athanasius accepted it in 367 A.D. as being suitable for the private reading of new converts. Manichaeaus, a Christian from Persia, took it far into the East. Dante was also definitely influenced by the book.

Thus, *The Shepherd* was a book which obviously could not be ignored and which was accepted as a revealed book by the majority of early Christian thinkers and lovers of God. It was written when the movement to "Hellenise" the teachings of Jesus was in its infancy, and at a time when many of those who followed Jesus were still aware that Jesus had come to restore and expand the teaching which Moses had brought to the Jews. Like Jesus, they were practising Jews whose understanding of what they were doing was illuminated by the knowledge Jesus had brought. They still believed in and followed the writings of the Old Testament, and since *The Shepherd* affirmed what they already knew, they accepted Hermas's book into their body of Scriptures.

With the teaching by some, notably Paul, that the laws of the Jews need not be followed by a Christian, contradictions began to arise between the body of newly-written Scriptures, which later became known as the "New Testament", and the Old Testament. However, the Old Testament was retained by the established Church in spite of these contradictions, since an outright rejection of the Old Testament would have been regarded by many of the people as a rejection of Jesus himself. Confusion was the inevitable result. In the attempt to accept and reject the Old Testament simultaneously, contradictions arose within the New Testament itself, since it had to be "new" without openly rejecting the old. But, in the early days of the Church, there was no real attempt to formally arrange the books and ensure that all the accounts and doctrines tallied with each other. The leaders of the first Christian communities were free to use their discretion and to refer to those Scriptures which they thought best contained the teachings of Jesus.

With the development, formulation and official acceptance in 325 A.D. of the doctrine of Trinity, such latitude was no longer acceptable to the established Pauline Church. The four accepted Gospels were selected and all the other Scriptures written after Jesus's birth were banned. However, the leaders of the Pauline Church, who were not entirely satisfied with their doctrine of "mysteries", which was now beginning to develop, and who recognised the validity of some of the banned books, wished to retain some of these books even though they directly contradicted the new doctrine of the Church. They were gathered together and their availability was limited to the people in power in the Church. They became known as the *Apocrypha*, which means *"hidden from the people."* They were then removed from the Bible, and only very few people had copies of these books which were being destroyed publicly along with those who were found in possession of them. This, as with the Gospel of Barnabas, was the fate of *The Shepherd* of Hermas. It was removed from the New Testament, and, since it created confusion in the minds of the people who were asked to believe in the doctrine of the Trinity, attempts were made to destroy it completely.

These attempts proved unsuccessful. There are records of references being made about it, but no one in the West had had the opportunity of reading it for a long time. Then, suddenly, in 1922, a third century papyrus manuscript of the text came to light.

It was found that the Greek used by Hermas was a simple vernacular. The language could be understood by the common people and it is clear that the book was written for everyone and not for an intellectual elite. His style was frank and informal and he possessed an originality of expression which made the book easy to read.

Hermas begins by telling of four visions he experienced, the last of which he calls a revelation since on this occasion an angel visited him dressed as a shepherd. The angel informed Hermas that he had been sent by the "most reverend angel" (that is, the angel Gabriel), to live with Hermas for the rest of the days of his life.

The angel then ordered Hermas to write down all "the Commands and the Parables." Since these were dictated to him by the angel, who only related what he was told to say by the "most reverend angel", it was accepted as a revealed book by the earlier Christians.

The commands he was told to write down were these:

47

I.

First of all believe that God is One and that He created all things and organised them, and out of what did not exist made all things to be, and He contains all things but Alone is Himself uncontained. Trust Him therefore and fear Him, and, fearing Him, be self-controlled. Keep this command and you will cast away from yourself all wickedness, put on every virtue of uprightness, and you will live to God if you keep this commandment.

II.

Be sincere and simple-minded.
Speak evil of nobody and do not enjoy hearing anyone do so.
Do right, and give generously.

III.

Love truth.

IV.

Observe purity. Be pure not only in action but in thinking.

V.

Be patient and understanding. The Lord dwells in patience, but the devil in ill-temper.

VI.

Trust what is right, and do not trust what is wrong. Uprightness has a straight and level way, but wrong-doing a crooked one. There are two of angels with men, one of uprightness and one of wickedness.

VII.

Fear the Lord and keep God's commands.

VIII.

Be self-controlled about what is wrong and do no wrong.

But do not be self-controlled about what is right, but do what is right. Restrain yourself from all evil and follow the right path.

IX.

Cast off doubt from yourself. Ask the Lord without doubting, and you will receive everything. God is not like men who hold grudges, but He is forgiving and feels pity for what He had made. So cleanse your heart of all vanities of this world.

X.

Put sadness away from you, for it is the sister of doubt and bad temper.

XI.

A man who consults a false prophet is an idolater and void of the truth.

Hermas asked the angel how to distinguish a true prophet from a false. The angel replied that in the first place the man who has the spirit that is from above is gentle, quiet, and humble. He abstains from all wickedness and the futile desires of the world. . . (He) does not speak by himself. . . but speaks when God wishes him to speak. . . but all power belongs to the Lord.

A false prophet exalts himself and wants to have a front seat. He is bold, shameless, and talkative, lives in great luxury and accepts pay for his prophesying. Can a divine spirit accept pay for prophesying? The false prophet avoids the upright men and attaches himself to those who are doubtful and vain; and he says everything to them falsely in line with their desires. An empty vessel put among empty ones does not break, but they harmonise with one another. Take a stone and throw it up to heaven; see if you can reach it. The earthly things are impotent and weak. On the other hand, take the power that comes from above. Hail is a very small grain, yet when it falls on a man's head what pain it causes! Or again, take a drop of water which falls on the ground from the roof and makes a hole in the stone. So the Divine Power that comes from above is mighty.

XII.

Cast off from yourself every evil desire and clothe yourself in good and holy desires. God created the world for man's sake and made his whole creation subject to man, and gave him complete authority to have dominion over all things under heaven. A man who has the Lord in his heart is able to master all things.

Behave as a slave of God. The devil cannot get control of the slaves of God. The devil can wrestle, but cannot throw them.[1]

Chapter 5

BARNABAS AND THE EARLY CHRISTIANS

Barnabas, or Bar-nabe, which means "son of consolation" or "son of exhortation", was a Jew and was born in Cyprus. He was known as Joses, or Joseph, but was given this new name by the disciples of Jesus. Although little mention is made of him in the four accepted Gospels, it is evident from some of the other books in the New Testament that he became one of the leaders of the disciples after Jesus had disappeared. It was he above all who endeavored to hold to the pure teaching of Jesus and opposed any innovators, notably Paul of Tarsus. Luke, who also wrote the Acts of the Apostles, was Paul's personal physician and therefore gave Paul's point of view. This explains why Barnabas is only mentioned by him when it serves to illustrate Paul's story. Unfortunately, books like *The Travels and Teachings of the Apostles* were destroyed by the Pauline Church, once it had adopted the doctrine of Trinity, in its attempts to eliminate any record which contradicted this dogma. Therefore, much that was known about Barnabas and the early Christians has been lost. It is this policy of the Trinitarians which probably indicates why any reference to Barnabas during Jesus's mission is strangely missing from the four accepted Gospels; and why Barnabas, who, according to Luke, acquires an importance second to none soon after the disappearance of Jesus, himself disappears from the pages of history as soon as he and Paul have a disagreement and part company.

Barnabas was with Jesus from the very start of his mission. His Gospel clearly demonstrates his great loyalty to Jesus and the love he had for him. Barnabas was not only his constant companion, but also absorbed and retained his teaching, so that very soon he must have acquired the reputation, which is attested to so clearly in the Acts, as a man who had the ability to transmit what he had learned from his Master. The name the disciples gave him indicates his power as a speaker who was a source of solace and encouragement. He was sincere, as well as generous. After meeting Jesus, he sold all that he possessed and gave the money for the use of the followers of Jesus. The affection Jesus and the disciples had for him is shown in the number of different names by which he was known. When the apostles decided to elect an apostle in the place of Judas from among those who had constantly been with Jesus "beginning from the baptism of John," they selected two people to choose from: "Joseph, called Barsabas, who was surnamed Justus: and Mathias." (Acts I:22-23) There is no other Joseph who accompanied Jesus during his life referred to in the New Testament except the one who was popularly known as Barnabas. Thus in all probability Barsabas — who, Goodspeed tells us, once drank a deadly poison but experienced nothing unpleasant — was none other than Barnabas. If this is so, then it also shows that if Barnabas was not one of the first twelve apostles, he was certainly one of the first seventy disciples. The fact that he was regarded highly enough to be proposed as someone suitable to make up the number of the first apostles to the original twelve is supported by the tradition that as Mary, the mother of Jesus, lay on her deathbed, she called for the apostles, and Barnabas was one of those who came. Clement of Alexandria always refers to him as an apostle in his writings.

It is likely that Jesus was brought up by the Essene community, and there is a tradition that Barnabas was a student of Gamaliel, the greatest teacher of orthodox Judaism at that time. And so the meeting of Jesus and Barnabas meant the fusing together of all that was best in the gnostic teaching of the Essenes and the orthodox Judaism of the Temple. Doubtless this contributed to the harmonious understanding between them. Since Barnabas was a Levite, he could well have been the commander of a division of the Zealots.

Although so little is known about Barnabas, the latest historical research is slowly uncovering the importance that was his while Jesus was on earth. It is now generally agreed that the Last Supper was held in the house of Barnabas's sister.

Albert Schweitzer in *The Kingdom of God and Primitive Christian Belief* writes:

> It may be inferred from the Acts that the disciples and the believers from Galilee met in the house of the mother of John Mark, who later accompanied Barnabas and Paul on the First Missionary Journey (Acts 12:25) . . .The meeting place of the believers was the "upper room", which means the room situated immediately under the flat roof (Acts I:12-14). It must have been a large one to hold the entire company. It was in this room that the believers were "all together in one place" on the day of Pentecost (Acts 2:1). How did it come to be identified with the one in which Jesus celebrated the Last Supper with the disciples?
>
> When Jesus sent two disciples from Bethany to the city with instructions to prepare the Passover meal for him, he told them that they were to follow a man who would meet them with a pitcher of water. He would lead them to a house with a large upper room furnished with rugs, where they were to prepare the meal. We owe this valuable piece of information to the Gospel of Mark (Mark 14:13-15), which rests on a tradition going back to John Mark. Matthew only relates that Jesus sent the two disciples with directions to inform someone in the city, "The Master saith — 'My time is at hand; I keep the Passover at thy house with my disciples.' " (Matthew 26:8) Theodore Zahn was one of the first to put forward the view that the house of the last meal of Jesus with his disciples was identical with that of John Mark's mother, in which the disciples met together with the believers from Galilee.[1]

Although Schweitzer says the house was that of John Mark's mother, he does not remind us that Mark's mother was the sister of Barnabas. Since Barnabas had by then sold all that he possessed, it is likely that he stayed with his sister when in Jerusalem, especially if she had a house with a room big enough for all the disciples to meet in. Perhaps the reason why none of this is clearly stated in the New Testament is because the disciples wished to keep their meeting place a secret at a time when they were being persecuted for their beliefs.

It might be asked why no mention of Barnabas is made in the descriptions of the Last Supper in the four accepted Gospels, since clearly he would have been the host to any gathering of men in his sister's house. Either mention of him was made, but has been removed, or else he simply was not present. It is possible that he was unable to be there because he was in prison. It is recorded that a man named Barabbas, with a company of men, attacked a group of pro-Roman Jews in the fighting which took place shortly before the feast of the Passover. Although the leader of these Jews was killed, Barabbas was captured and put in jail. Heinrich Holtzman, who examined the records of this fighting in detail, says that among those arrested was "the famous Barabbas who was certainly a patriot and a political 'prophet' and was tried at almost the same time as Jesus."[2] Since Barnabas was a Levite and one of Jesus's foremost disciples, he could well have been a chief of one of the divisions of the Zealots. These four divisions, as we know from the Dead Sea Scrolls, were an integral part of the Essene community and were committed to freeing the land of its foreign aggressors and their supporters. Only a band of Zealots could have been capable of an organised attack on the pro-Roman Jews at that time, and thus it may well be that Barabbas and Barnabas were one and the same person. It is quite possible that, along with its other amendments, the Pauline Church either eradicated, or at least altered, Barnabas's name when he was mentioned in connection with an event which was not a part of Paul's story. They could not adopt this procedure every time Barnabas was mentioned in the books of the New Testament since, as the Acts of the Apostles indicates, without the support which Barnabas gave Paul in the early days of the Church, Paul may well have had no place in the history of Christianity at all.

There is scant record of what happened to the close followers of Jesus after he had disappeared. It appears that many of them scattered after his supposed crucifixion. After some time they began to regroup in Jerusalem. How many of the twelve disciples and seventy closest followers came back is not known. It is certain, however, that those who did were men of faith, sincerity, and courage, and possessed a very deep love for Jesus. Barnabas's eminence as a man who had been close to Jesus made him a prominent member of this small group of disciples. They continued to live as Jews and practice what Jesus had taught them, observing the law of the prophets, which Jesus had come "not to destroy, but to fulfill." (Matthew 5:17) That the teaching of Jesus could ever be regarded as a new religion did not occur to any of them. They were sincere practicing Jews and were distinguished from their neighbours only by their faith in the message of Jesus. In these early days, they did not organise themselves as a separate sect and did not have a synagogue of their own. There was nothing in the message of Jesus, as understood by them, to necessitate a break with what was clearly the continuance and revivifying affirmation of the guidance which Moses had brought. The conflict between the Jews and the followers of Jesus was started by those Jews who had adapted Moses's message to suit their own ends, and who feared, quite correctly, that to support the followers of Jesus would inevitably lead to their losing the wealth, the power and the position which they enjoyed. The pact which the upper echelon of Jews had made with the Romans, to safeguard their vested interests and the privileges they had enjoyed for centuries, had necessitated their departing even further from the guidance they had been given. This group of Jews actively supported the Romans in the persecution of those whose actions and words threatened to expose what they had done. Thus it was that a follower of Jesus accepted Jesus while a Jew rejected him. It could not have been an easy time for the early followers of Jesus. On the one hand, they were hounded by the Romans who regarded them as a threat to their political power, and on the other hand they were pursued by the Jews who feared that their own "religious authority" would be undermined by them.

In the years that followed, the gulf between the Jews who refused to acknowledge Jesus and those who followed him began to widen. During the siege of Jerusalem in 70 A.D., the followers of Jesus left the city; and, by the time of the *Bar Coachaba* rebellion in 132 A.D.

The questions of the origin of Jesus, his nature and relation to God, which were later to become a source of much contention, were not raised among the first followers of Jesus. That Jesus was a man who was a prophet and one who had been given many gifts by God, was accepted without question. Nothing in the words of Jesus or the events in his life on earth had led them to modify this certainty. According to Aristides, one of the earliest apologists, the worship of the early Christians was more purely monotheistic than even that of the Jews.

It was into this circle of sincere followers that Paul of Tarsus walked. He had never met Jesus, nor had he been well acquainted with any of Jesus's closest disciples. He had the reputation of being one of the greatest enemies of Jesus. He watched over the stoning of Stephen. Stephen had been "full of faith and the Holy Ghost," (Acts 6:5) and one of the growing number of people who had joined the followers of Jesus after his disappearance. When Paul's own teacher, the famous Gamaliel, tried to protect Stephen, he too was stoned to death. It is recorded that Paul, who was then called Saul, was responsible for "a great persecution against the Church" at that time, and that he "made a havock of the Church, entering into every house and haling men and women and committed them to prison." (Acts 8:1-3) Paul himself admitted that:

> you have heard. . . how that beyond measure I persecuted the Church of God and wasted it — and profited in the Jews' religion above many of my equals in mine own nation, being more exceedingly zealous of the traditions of my fathers.
>
> (Galatians I:13-15)

And, as it is related in Acts 9:41:

> Saul yet breathing out threatenings and slaughter against the disciples of the Lord, went unto the high priest, and desired of him letters to Damascus to the synagogues, that if he found any of this way, whether they were men or women, he might bring them bound unto Jerusalem.

It was on this journey to Damascus that Paul is said to have met Jesus in a vision and become one of his followers as a result.

Not long before all these events took place, it is recorded that Paul had desired to marry a woman called Popea, who was the attractive but ambitious daughter of the high priest of the Jews. She possessed haunting beauty and an intriguing mind. She liked Paul, but she rejected his offers of marriage and went to Rome as an actress. Starting on the stage, she climbed step by step until she reached Nero's bed. Ultimately she married him and so became the Empress of the Roman Empire. Paul therefore had good reason to resent both the Jews and the Romans. Paul's conversion coincided with his being rejected by Popea. He must have been under considerable emotional and mental strain at the time. It is possible that this crisis in his life had some bearing on this sudden change from his being one of the greatest supporters of the Jewish Law to one of its greatest enemies.

After his conversion, Paul stayed with the followers of Jesus who were in Damascus and "straight away, he preached Christ in the synagogues, that he is the son of God." (Acts 9:20) As a result, he began to taste the persecution in which he himself had so recently been involved. If he actually used the term "son of God" to describe Jesus, then it was probably this which helped to anger the Jews. The idea of God having a child ascribed to Him was abhorrent to them, since they firmly believed in the Unity of God.

Paul then left Damascus and, instead of seeking out the company of the other followers of Jesus, went into the Arabian desert where he remained hidden for three years. It may well have been here that he began to formulate his own version of what Jesus had taught. This involved a rejection of the Jewish Law, which in turn meant his turning away from the fact that throughout his life Jesus had remained a practising Jew, and always sought to uphold the teachings which Moses had brought before him.

It was after this long period of withdrawal in the desert that Paul came to the apostles in Jerusalem. The sudden arrival of Paul caused more suspicion than surprise. The stories of his persecution of the followers of Jesus must still have been fresh in their minds. Could a leopard change its spots? It seems that the disciples had no reason to accept him into their circle. Not only had he been their persecutor, but also he now claimed to know what Jesus had taught, although he had never even seen him and had spent little time, if any, with those who had been with him. Instead of trying to learn from those who had been so intimately connected with Jesus while he was on earth, Paul wanted to teach them. Paul later justified this approach in his epistle to the Galatians where he states:

> I certify you brethren that the Gospel which was preached of me is not after man. For I neither received it of man, neither was I taught it, but by the revelation of Jesus Christ.
> (Galatians I:10-12)

Thus, Paul claimed to have an access to Jesus which had been denied to the closest followers of Jesus while he was on earth. The teaching which Paul claimed he had been given did not tally with what the apostles had heard from the very lips of Jesus. It is understandable that they were therefore suspicious of his conversion and considered his "revelations" unreliable. Many probably suspected that he was no more than a spy, posing as a follower of Jesus.[3] The dispute as to whether Paul should be accepted was therefore a bitter one and its outcome must have seemed a foregone conclusion. Barnabas, however, who according to tradition had been Paul's class fellow under Gamaliel, intervened and spoke in favour of Paul. Against their unanimous opposition, he succeeded in having Paul accepted by the followers of Jesus. This indicates the degree of influence which Barnabas had over the apostles, and therefore also points to the degree of intimacy which he must have enjoyed with Jesus when he was on earth. Paul must have realised that he had been accepted by virtue of Barnabas's authority and not because of his own efforts. He probably felt dissatisfied as a result. This may well have been one of the main reasons why he decided to return to Tarsus, his home town, shortly afterwards, although it is also recorded that he left because his life was in danger.

The persecution of the followers of Jesus, not only by the Romans, but also by the Jews, forced many of them to disperse throughout the land. Some of the apostles made their way to Antioch where they hoped to escape any further persecution by Paul and his followers. Founded by Seleucus Necator, Antioch had grown in size until by then it was the third largest city of the Roman Empire after Rome and Alexandria. It had once been the capital of the Greek kingdom and had grown into a centre of trade and commerce. With the accumulation of wealth, the people began to lead a life of luxury and decadence and so acquired the reputation of being a city of loose living. It was here that this small group of strangers, dressed in rags, began to lead a god-fearing life with simplicity and honesty. Those who had grown tired of an immoral life began to gather around them, but the majority of those who met them regarded them with contempt and ridicule and nick-named them "Christians". For a very few people, it might have been a term of respect, but to a large number of people it was used as a term of hatred and abuse. Up until this point, the followers of Jesus had always been known as Nazarenes. The root of this word in Hebrew means "to keep" or "to guard." Thus the adjective indicated their role as keepers and guardians of the guidance which Jesus had brought. Libanius records that the Jews in Antioch used to pray three times a day: "Send the curse of God upon the Nazarenes." Prophery, another historian, who always opposed the Nazarenes, described their way of life as a "barbarous, new and strange religion." Celsus records that, according to Jerome, the Christians were called "Greek imposters and deceivers" because they wore the same Greek cloaks which the priests of the Greek temple wore.

Despite the opposition they faced, people continued to visit these strange newcomers and their number increased. Encouraged by this interest, the disciples in Antioch sent word to Jerusalem asking the apostles there to send a man to help spread the truth and teaching of Jesus among the pagans who surrounded them. The disciples selected Barnabas as the most suitable person for this task, and thus Barnabas became the first missionary in Christian history. Barnabas came to

Antioch and met with unexpected success. Due to his efforts, "much people was added unto the Lord," (Acts II:24) for "he was a good man, and full of the Holy Ghost and faith." After a year, he decided the time had come to extend his activity beyond Antioch. He was sure that Paul would make a good helper and with this in view he went to Tarsus and brought Paul back with him.[4] Thus, again, Paul came face to face with some of the people who had suffered persecution at his hands, and again he met with hostility and opposition. Once more, the importance of and respect for Barnabas can be assessed by the fact that he had his way, and Paul was received into the community. Perhaps Barnabas was looking to the best in his former class-mate and felt that if Paul's zeal and enthusiasm, which had made him such a thorough persecutor, could only be rechannelled, he would make an outstanding and invaluable follower of Jesus.

Not all the apostles shared this view, and Peter came out in open opposition to Paul. As well as the hostility kindled by Paul's past actions, there was a difference of opinion over two other issues. They could not agree to whom the teaching of Jesus should be taken and what should be taught. Peter held that Jesus had come to revivify the guidance given to the Jews and that, therefore, what he had taught could only be preached among the Jews. On the other hand, there was Paul who not only believed in spreading the truth to everyone, Jew or otherwise, but also asserted that he had been given additional instruction from Jesus after his disappearance. He felt that any necessary adjustments should be made to adapt the teaching according to the apparent demands of time and situation. Barnabas held the middle position between the two. He held that they should only teach what they had been taught by Jesus, but felt that they should bring this guidance to anyone who would benefit from it and was receptive to it, Jew or non-Jew. Both Barnabas and Peter regarded the guidance they had been given as a continuation and an extension of Judaism. They could not accept Paul's teaching where it differed from what they themselves had heard from Jesus. They believed that Paul's new doctrine was in the main a purely personal creation of his own. Albert Schweitzer, in his book *Paul and His Interpreters*, says that "Paul never appealed to the sayings and commands of the Master."[5]

It is likely that Barnabas hoped that the two extremes would mellow, and that Paul, especially, by keeping company with the followers of Jesus, would forsake his own ideas in favour of their own knowledge of what must still have been a fairly complete understanding and embodiment of what Jesus had taught. It is clear how important Barnabas's support was to Paul at this stage, since Barnabas shielded and protected him against the unanimous opposition of the Apostles. It is probably for this reason that this part of Barnabas's life is recorded with such detail in the Acts of the Apostles. The relationship between Barnabas and Paul is indicated in Acts 13: 1-2:

> There was in the church that was at Antioch certain prophets and teachers as Barnabas, and Simeon that was called Niger and Lucius of Cyrene and Manaen, which had been brought up with Herod the Tetrarch, and Saul. As they ministered to the Lord, and fasted, the Holy Ghost said: "Separate me Barnabas and Saul for the work whereunto I have called them."

In the list of these followers, Luke mentions Barnabas first and Paul last. Having been selected to work together, they set out, accompanied by John Mark, who was Barnabas's nephew, to spread the teaching of Jesus in Greece. James, son of Mary by Joseph, was left at the head of the followers of Jesus. Peter also stayed behind.

It is recorded in the Acts of the Apostles that, in spite of being stoned in some places, these two missionaries were on the whole successful. Their reputation as men of Truth spread far and wide. When they reached Lucaonia and healed a cripple in Lystra, it was rumoured that:

> . . .the gods are come down to us in the likeness of men. And they called Barnabas, Jupiter and Paul, Mercurius. Then the priests of Jupiter. . . brought oxen and garlands unto the gates, and would have done sacrifice with the people. Which when the apostles, Barnabas and Paul, heard of, they rent their clothes and ran in among the people crying out. And saying: Sirs, why do ye these things? We

also are men of like passions with you, and preach unto you the Living God, which made heaven and earth and the sea and all things that are thereon.

(Acts 14:11-15)

·If this reaction by the inhabitants of Greece was typical, it is an indication of some of the practical difficulties which must have faced Barnabas and Paul. A true Jew would have immediately recognised the teaching of Jesus as a reaffirmation of what Moses had taught. But to many a pagan, it must have seemed new and strange and perhaps a little complicated. Most of the pagans still believed in a multitude of gods who, it was thought, mixed freely with human beings, mated with them, and took part in every sphere of human life. To the common people of Greece, any description of Jesus must have seemed like a description of one of their gods, and they were probably quite ready to accept Jesus in this capacity. There was always room for one more god. However, the actual teaching of Jesus negated all their gods, since it affirmed the Divine Unity. This could not have been received with favour by many of these idol worshippers. Furthermore, the code of behaviour which was an integral part of Jesus's guidance, would have necessitated an immediate and far-reaching change in the way of life of anyone who decided to follow it unless, of course, that person was already a practising Jew, which these pagans were clearly not. The Jews, who were regarded as a nation of money-lenders, were not at all liked by those who were not Jews. Toland, in his book *The Nazarenes*, says that:

> . . .amongst the Gentiles, so inveterate was the hatred of the Jews that their observing of anything, however reasonable or necessary, was sufficient motive for a Gentile convert to reject it.[6]

To anyone not as sincere and steadfast as Barnabas, the task of establishing Jesus's way of life in Greece without making any compromises must have seemed overwhelming. To Paul, who had already displayed his tendency to change what teaching he did know, it must have now seemed absolutely necessary to make what adjustments were needed to make Jesus's teaching palatable to the common people. Greece was now part of the Roman Empire. The Roman gods bore a marked resemblance to the Greek ones and belief in them only served to support the same misconceptions which a belief in the Greek gods entailed. Paul had previously spent some time in Rome and was a Roman citizen. It is possible that his own reasoning had been influenced by his contact with the Roman way of life. He was well aware of the strong hold which the Graeco-Roman religions had on the common people within the Roman Empire. It is clear that he seems to have felt that it would not be possible to change their ways without making changes too. Barnabas, on the other hand, as it is recorded of Jesus in Matthew 5:18, knew that his Creator did not wish His Law to be diminished or changed "one jot or one tittle." He therefore held firm to the guidance he had been given.

At this stage in the spread of Christianity, the main source of contention was not of a metaphysical nature. The subtle arguments and fine distinctions of the intellectuals were a development which was to come later. The issues over which Barnabas and Paul disagreed were those which affected a human's everyday existence and way of life. Paul wished to avoid making any abrupt changes in those customs which the Greeks had probably taken for granted before his and Barnabas's arrival in Greece. He therefore wished to abandon the commandments transmitted through Moses as to what meat it was lawful to eat and how the animal was to be sacrificed. He also wished to relinquish, where it seemed expedient, the commandment established by Abraham regarding the necessity of circumcision. Faced by the practical difficulty of establishing and implementing these aspects of Jesus's teaching, the difference between Paul and Barnabas must have been emphasised rather than diminished.

However, at this stage, these differences were probably not that marked. Both Paul and Barnabas were faced with the practical challenge of establishing Jesus's way of life. The teaching of the affirmation of the Divine Unity was essential to this, but initially it was necessary to establish a pattern of behaviour which was probably different in many ways to the one which the pagans had been used to. Clearly, this new way of doing things could only be learned and assimilated into the texture of everyday life gradually. No pagan community could have adopted overnight the whole course of action which Jesus embodied. From what records there are, it seems that Barnabas and Paul never stayed for very long in any one place. They could not have transmitted the whole of Jesus's teaching in a short space of time. They must, therefore, have taught what seemed to be the most important parts first, with the intention of returning later and supplementing what they had shown the people with further instruction. Whereas Barnabas intended to transmit the whole teaching of Jesus, Paul was prepared to dispense with many of its aspects altogether, since, according to the new doctrine he was developing, they were no longer necessary. Thus, on their return to Jerusalem, they must have defended their actions each for a different reason. Despite their descriptions of the miracles they had performed together, this underlying difference remained, and finally there was a parting of the ways.

It is said that they fell out with each other because Paul refused to take John Mark with them on any future mission, while Barnabas insisted that John Mark should continue to accompany them. It is recorded in Acts 15:39-40 that "the contention was so sharp between them, that they departed asunder one from the other — and so Barnabas took Mark and sailed unto Cyprus," which was Barnabas's birth-place. The fact that John Mark accompanied Barnabas clearly indicates that his beliefs were the same as his uncle's. This was probably one of the reasons why Paul had no desire to keep his company. Hardly any mention of Barnabas is made in the Bible after this point.

It is interesting that Barnabas, who, it is recorded in the Acts, was chosen by the Holy Ghost, was rejected by Paul. Perhaps Paul felt that he no longer needed Barnabas. In his early days as a Christian, no one would have relied on him once they knew that he had not been with Jesus. Now that he had become established among the community, this was no longer the case. His reputation was such that perhaps he felt he could go out and preach his doctrine without fear of being rejected, and without the restraining hand of Barnabas to check him, whenever he deviated from what Jesus had taught.

Furthermore, Paul was a Roman citizen. He must have learned the language of Rome. He probably spoke Greek. It was the official language of the area in which he was born. The epistles he later wrote to the Christian communities in Greece must have been written in their native tongue. This meant that he could travel in Greece and probably Italy without any difficulties over language. Barnabas, on the other hand, spoke neither of these two languages. John Mark, who spoke Greek, had accompanied him on the first missionary journey into Greece to act as his interpreter. If Barnabas were to go there by himself, he would not be able to make himself understood. Thus Paul's refusal to travel with John Mark may have been a round about way of ensuring that Barnabas would refuse to travel with him. Commenting on their parting in his *History of Christianity in the Apostolic Age*, McGiffert says:

> That Barnabas. . . whose right to work among the Gentiles had been recognised in Jerusalem. . . should have drawn back and separated himself from them is very strange. Barnabas was not in full sympathy with Paul's doctrine of the Christian's complete liberty from all laws of whatever kind. . . The separation of Paul and Barnabas is stated by the author of the Acts to be the result of a disagreement concerning Mark, but the real reason lay deeper than that. . . The man who stood closest to Paul and was most intimately associated with him during the early years of his Christian career was Barnabas, who was a member of the Church in Jerusalem in its primitive days. . . His friendship meant much to Paul and doubtless contributed in no small degree to his credit and influence with the Christians. Barnabas stood sponsor for Paul in the early days when the memory of his persecuting career was fresh in the mind of the Church.[7]

The change in Barnabas's attitude towards Paul could only have come about as a result of his experiences while travelling with Paul. Any hopes that Paul would change his views and become a true follower of Jesus must have been dispelled by what happened on that first missionary journey. Perhaps too Barnabas realised the futility of trying to spread a guidance, which had only been intended for the Jews, among the Gentiles, and, seeing the folly of this course of action, left it. Before he had attempted it, spreading Jesus's message among the Gentiles had seemed a viable proposition. But, having actually tried it, experience had proved that it was not possible. His experience in Antioch had seemed far more successful because there the Gentiles had been coming to the followers of Jesus and asking to be accepted as Christians. Whereas, when he and Paul went to Greece, it was they who had been asking the Gentiles to become Christians.

There is no record of what happened to Barnabas after he returned to Cyprus, but it is known that, like so many who held to a new prophet's teaching, he died as a martyr. In spite of the fact that Barnabas is blocked out from many of the pages of the Bible, it is evident that he acquired an integral position in the history of Christianity and cannot be forgotten. He was willing openly to affirm and teach what he had learned from Jesus in the early days of the Church, when even some of those who were nearest to Jesus were afraid to acknowledge their association with him. Barnabas's loyalty to Jesus is accepted as a fact by friends and foes alike. It was his sister's house where Jesus had his last Passover meal, and it must have remained a meeting place for the followers of Jesus after he had disappeared. The influence of Barnabas over the Apostles and other followers of Jesus has been established from the Bible itself. He is called a prophet, a teacher, and also an Apostle by Luke whose unquestioned loyalty was to Paul. Above all, he is remembered as a man who was not prepared to compromise or change Jesus's message.

After Barnabas had left for Cyprus, Paul continued with what he had begun. Although he had now been with many of the early Christians long enough to be accepted as one of them, he was still conscious of the weakness of his position. He might now be called an Apostle of Jesus, yet this did not alter the fact that he had never met Jesus in his life. Although he claimed to have had access to Jesus by revelation, he still needed someone who had lived with Jesus to accompany him on his journeys among the Gentiles. The company of an eyewitness would provide him with invaluable support and serve to back up his arguments with additional authority. He therefore persuaded Peter to join him.

That these two, who had opposed each other so vehemently in the past, should now come together is perhaps surprising. However, the situation had changed. Paul was now accepted by many as a Christian and was no longer regarded as a possible spy or persecutor. Celsus, a Greek philosopher and a bitter critic of the Christians, said that the root of the disagreement between the two in Antioch had been Paul's jealousy of Peter's popularity. Obviously, Paul's jealousy would by now have dwindled with his own increase in reputation, especially among the Gentiles. The persecution of the Christians also probably played its part in drawing them together. The persecution by the Romans and those Jews who supported them was quite severe by now. Peter had already demonstrated his weakness when, under pressure or faced by immediate danger, he denied his being a companion of Jesus at the time of Jesus's supposed trial and crucifixion. He was probably now more willing to fall in line with Paul's approach to Jesus's message, since changes here and there might mean less persecution.

Thus the situation in these early days was such that it seemed expedient to some to change and adapt the message of Jesus not only so that people who were not Jewish would accept it, but also so that it would not offend or apparently threaten those in authority in the land. This policy of obeying rulers indiscriminately, whether their laws were in accord with those of the Creator of the Universe or not, is evident in Peter's first Epistle 3:13-18:

Submit yourselves to every ordinance of man for the Lord's sake: whether it be to the king, as supreme; or unto governors, as unto them that are sent by him for the punishment of evildoers, and for the praise of them that do well. For so is the will of God, that with well-doing ye may put to silence the ignorance of foolish men: as free, and not using your liberty for a cloak of maliciousness, but as the servants of God. Honour all men. Love the brotherhood. Fear God. Honour the king. Servants, be subject to your master with all fear; not only to the good and gentle, but also to the froward.

Paul travelled West with Peter. Without the sincerity and restraining influence of Barnabas, he must have met with little opposition to his new doctrines and adapted ways of conduct and behaviour. In Romans 16:20-21, he says:

> Yes, so have I strived to preach the Gospel, not where Christ was named, lest I should build upon another man's foundation: but as it is written:
> To whom he was not spoken of, they shall see:
> And they that have not heard shall understand.

If Paul had been spreading the original teaching of Jesus, then "another man's foundation" would have been the same as his. They would both have been involved in building the same structure. The people who were hearing about Jesus, or rather Christ, for the first time from Paul's lips, had no means of comparing his account with that of the Apostles who still held to Jesus's teaching. Paul's version was the only one to which they had access.

Paul was helped a great deal in spreading his message by a learned Jew from Alexandria called Appolos. He was very successful in spreading the ideas of Paul among people. Paul, it was said, planted and Appolos watered. Ultimately, even Appolos could not accept all the innovations of Paul, and, like Barnabas, parted company with him.

Paul deviated further and further from the teaching Jesus had embodied, and laid more and more emphasis on the figure of Christ whom he claimed had appeared to him in visions. His defence against those who accused him of changing the guidance Jesus had brought was — that what he preached had its origin in a direct revelation he had received from Christ. This gave Paul Divine Authority. It was by virtue of this "authority" he claimed, that the blessings of the Gospel were not limited to the Jews, but to all who believed. Furthermore, he asserted that the requirements of the Law of Moses were not only unnecessary, but also contrary to what had been directly revealed to him from God. In fact, he said, they were a curse. Thus, Paul incurred not only the wrath of the followers of Jesus, but also that of the Jews, since he was contradicting both of their prophets. It is clear why he chose to spread his teaching among people who hated the Jews and who had not heard the truth about Jesus.

Paul justified his new doctrine with the use of this analogy:

> Know ye not, brethren, (for I speak to them that know the law) how that the law hath dominion over a man as long as he liveth? For the woman which hath an husband is bound by the law to her husband so long as he liveth; but if the husband be dead, she is loosed from the law of her husband. So then; if, while her husband liveth, she be married to another man, she shall be called an adulteress: but, if her husband be dead, she is free from that law, so that she is no adulteress, though she be married to another man. Wherefore, my brethren, ye also are become dead to the law by the body of Christ; that ye should be married to another, even to him who is raised from the dead, that we should bring forth fruit unto God.
>
> (Romans 7:1-4)

This analogy clearly indicates that Paul made a distinction between Jesus and "Christ". According to his reasoning, the law which had bound Jesus and his followers was no longer necessary, since Jesus had died. Now they were no longer "married" to Jesus, but to Christ, who had brought another law. It was, therefore, necessary to follow Christ and not Jesus. Thus, anyone who held to Jesus's teaching had gone astray. It was with the use of this reasoning that he assembled his doctrine of redemption and atonement, a theory which Jesus had certainly never taught. It was a great success, since, in so many words, it preached that a man could do what he wanted and not face the inevitable consequences of his actions, provided that, at the end of the day, he said: "I believe in Christ." However, the basic premise on which Paul's reasoning was based is false, since Jesus was neither crucified nor resurrected. His doctrines of redemption and atonement are fallacious.

Paul's reasoning had two major consequences. It not only resulted in further changes being made to what Jesus had taught, but also prepared the way for completely changing people's ideas of who Jesus was. He was being transformed from a man to a conception in people's minds. Divinity had been attributed to Jesus even when he was on earth by some of those who marvelled at his words and miracles, and who, mistakenly, considered him to be more than a prophet. Some of his enemies had also spread the rumour that he was the "son of God", hoping to rouse the orthodox Jew's anger against him for associating himself with God. Thus, even before he disappeared, there had been a tendency to obscure his true nature and ascribe godhood to Jesus. This imaginary figure of Christ, who apparently had the power to annul what Jesus had previously taught, was clearly no ordinary mortal, and, inevitably, became confused by many with God. Thus, this imaginary figure became an object of worship, and was associated with God.

This shift of emphasis from Jesus as a man to the new image of Christ, who was divine, enabled the intellectuals in Greece and Rome to assimilate into their own philosophy what Paul and those who followed him were preaching. Their view of existence was a tripartite one, and, with the Pauline Church's talk of "God the Father" and the "Son of God", it only needed the inclusion of the "Holy Ghost" to have a Trinity which matched theirs. With the passage of time, these two pictures merged into one, and the doctrine of Trinity was born. Not only the philosophical ideas prevalent in Greece at that time coloured the teaching, but also the very language of Greece itself influenced the expression of the teaching, trapping and limiting its meaning. Greek could contain the philosophy of the Greeks, but was neither vast nor supple enough to carry what Jesus had said. Thus, even a true follower of Jesus who spoke fluent Greek could not have expressed the totality of Jesus's teaching in this language. It had to be reworded. When the time came to translate the Hebrew Gospels into Greek, these limitations were made permanent, and finally sealed, when nearly all the Gospels in Hebrew were destroyed.

Although Paul never actually preached the divinity of Jesus, nor the doctrine of Trinity, his manner of expression and the changes he made opened the door to both these misconceptions, and prepared the way for their becoming established doctrines in Europe. It was these doctrines which lead to Mary being put in the impossible position of being regarded as the "mother of God".

It appears that Paul rationalised his actions by holding that there was no link between the period in which Jesus had lived and the period in which he himself now lived. Times had changed and the conditions which now prevailed were such that the teaching of Jesus was out of date and could no longer be applied. It had therefore become necessary to find a new basis for ethics. Paul took stock of the conditions which existed then and taught what they seemed to require him to believe:

> All things are lawful unto me, but I will not be brought under the power of any.
> (I Corinthians 7:12)

Paul not only rejected both Moses and Jesus, but asserted that he was a law unto himself. Many people, obviously, could not accept this. Paul responded by saying:

> For if the truth of God hath more abounded through my lie unto His Glory; why yet I am also judged a sinner?
> (Romans 3:7-8)

It would seem from this statement that, although he knew he was lying, Paul felt that the means justified the end, but it is not understood how truth would abound through a lie. According to this reasoning, if the man Jesus was equated with God, what objections could a follower of Jesus have?

Paul produced a religion which encompassed different contradictory elements. He took the unitarianism of the Jews and added to it the philosophy of the pagans. This admixture was combined with some of what Jesus had taught and some of what Paul claimed Christ had revealed to him. Paul's theology was based on his personal experience interpreted in the light of contemporary Greek thought. Jesus was deified and the words of Plato were put in his sacred mouth. The theory of redemption was the child of Paul's brain, a belief entirely unknown to Jesus and his disciples. It was based on the belief in "original sin", the "crucifixion", and the "resurrection", none of which have any validity. Thus, a synthetic religion

71

was produced: Christianity — mathematically absurd, historically false, yet psychologically impressive. In the magnificent temple of the religion which Paul helped so zealously to erect, he built doors on all sides. The result was that people who came across his brand of Christianity for the first time, when they entered its temple, were given the impression that they were paying homage to the same deity that they had worshipped all along, whether they were Jew or Gentile. As the basic misconception introduced by Paul evolved and became established, many a man who thought that he was following Jesus followed Paul without knowing it.

There is, therefore, some justification for Heinz Zahrnt calling Paul a "corrupter of the Gospel of Jesus"[8] and Werde describing him as "the second founder of Christianity." Werde says that, due to Paul:

> . . .the discontinuity between the historical Jesus and the Christ of the Church became so great that any unity between them is scarcely recognisable.[9]

Schonfield wrote:

> The Pauline heresy became the foundation of Christian orthodoxy and the legitimate Church was disowned as heretical.[10]

Thus Barnabas became the arch-heretic.

To the followers of Jesus, the path of Truth, like the geometrical straight line, had length but no breadth. They did not agree to change the teaching of Jesus merely because it seemed expedient. To them what Jesus had taught was the Truth and the whole Truth. Barnabas and his followers continued to preach and practise the Christianity they had learned from Jesus himself. They were always and still are to to be reckoned with as a force. From among them came saints and scholars respected by every sect of Christianity.

The followers of Jesus and Barnabas never developed a central organisation, yet, due to the devotion of their leaders for the Truth, their number increased rapidly. These leaders were wise and learned men who loved and feared God. They went into the deserts and mountains. Small communities formed around each saint. They were independent of each other, largely due to the rough terrain which surrounded them. Their lack of a structured organisation was a source of strength because it was not so easy for their persecutors to pick them up. Paul's version of Christianity spread through Greece and then Europe, while these men of God spread with their knowledge to the south and, eventually, right across North Africa. The communities they formed retained the lifestyle of Jesus. Those who still embodied Jesus's teaching must have transmitted much of their knowledge directly from person to person. Behaviour was imitated and the doctrine passed on orally. They continued to affirm the Divine Unity. Thus, there are records of various sects who lived in the early centuries after Jesus's disappearance, such as the Ebionites, the Cerinthians, the Basilidians, the Carpocratians, and the Hypisistarians, who refused to worship God as a father. They revered Him as the Almighty Ruler of the Universe, the Highest of all with no one equal to Him.

By now, many different written accounts of Jesus's life and teachings were in use. Jesus had spoken in Aramaic, a dialect of Arabic, which was not commonly written. The first Gospels were therefore recorded in Hebrew. In these early days, none were formally accepted or rejected. It was up to the leader of each Christian community to decide what books he would use. Depending on whom they had been taught by, each sect went to a different source. Those who followed Barnabas's example went to one source, those who followed Paul to another.

Thus, quite soon after Jesus's disappearance from earth, there was a definite and widening divergence between the followers of Jesus and the Pauline Church, which was later to become known as the Roman Catholic Church. Differences between the two were not only evident in life-style and belief, but were also clearly delineated geographically. As the Pauline Church grew more established, it became increasingly hostile to the followers of Jesus. It aligned itself more and more with the rulers of the Roman Empire, and the persecution which to begin with had been directed at all who called themselves Christians, now began to fall mainly on those who affirmed the Divine Unity. Attempts began to be made to change their beliefs and forcefully to remove those who refused to do so, together with the books they used. Most of the early martyrs were unitarians. The more the doctrine of Trinity became accepted, the more its adherents opposed those who affirmed the Divine Unity. By the time the Emperor Julian came to power, this infighting had reached such a stage that he said: "No wild beasts are so hostile to man as Christian sects in general are to one another."

Naturally, those who deviated from the teaching of Jesus were prepared to change the Scriptures too, and even introduce false writings in order to support their opinions. Toland, in his book *The Nazarenes*, records these words of Iranius, who was one of the early unitarian martyrs:

> In order to amaze the simple and such as are ignorant of the Scriptures of Truth, they obtrude upon them an inexpressible multitude of apocryphal and spurious scriptures of their own devising.

Toland continues:

> We know already to what degree imposture and credulity went hand in hand in the primitive times of the Christian Church, the last being as ready to receive as the first was to forge books. . . This evil grew afterwards not only greater when the Monks were the sole transcribers and the sole keepers of all books good or bad, but in process of time it became almost absolutely impossible to distinguish history from fable, or truth from error as to the beginning and original monuments of Christianity. . .
>
> How immediate successors of the Apostles could so grossly confound the genuine teaching of their masters with such as were falsely attributed to them? Or since they were in the dark about these matters so early how came such as followed them by a better light? And observing that such Apocryphal books were often put upon the same footing with the canonical books by the Fathers, and the first cited as Divine Scriptures no less than the last, or sometimes, when such as we reckon divine were disallowed by them. I propose these two other questions: Why all the books cited

as genuine by Clement of Alexander, Origen, Tertullian and the rest of such writers should not be accounted equally authentic? And what stress should be laid on the testimony of those Fathers who not only contradict one another but are also often inconsistent with themselves in their relations of the very same facts?

Toland goes on to say that when these questions are asked of the "wooden priests and divinilings," instead of meeting the arguments, they begin to call those who raise the questions "hereticks or concealed atheists." He continues:

This conduct will make them suspect all to be a cheat and imposture, because men will naturally cry out when they are touched in a tender part. . . No man will be angry at a question who is able to answer it. . .

Finally Toland asks:

Since the Nazarenes or Ebionites are by all the Church historians unanimously acknowledged to have been the first Christians, or those who believed in Christ among the Jews with which, his own people, he lived and died, they having been the witness of his actions, and of whom were all the Apostles, considering this, I say how it was possible for them to be the first of all others (for they were made to be the first heretics), who should form wrong conceptions of the doctrines and designs of Jesus? And how came the Gentiles who believed on him after his death by the preaching of persons that never knew him to have truer notions of these things, or whence they could have their information but from the believing Jews?[11]

Chapter 6

EARLY UNITARIANS IN CHRISTIANITY

The Apostolic Christians, as the followers of Jesus and Barnabas came to be known, produced a number of scholars and saints whose piety and learning is respected and admired even today. Apostolic, or, as it is generally known, Antiochene, exegesis of the Scriptures was historical, and, unlike what is now the orthodox approach, looked not for a hidden allegorical meaning in the text, but accepted the plain meaning of the words spoken by the inspired prophet. They were also critical of holding some parts of the Bible to be of more value than the others. They insisted on the One-ness of God and abhorred any dogma which to the slightest degree savoured of tri-theism. They emphasised the historical Jesus and avoided the use of the term "Son" when talking of him. They endeavoured to live as Jesus had lived and to behave as he had behaved. Many of them lived in North Africa. Some of the most important of these followers of the followers of Jesus were:

Iranaeus (130-200 A.D.)

By the time Iranaeus was born, the Antiochene Christianity had spread right across North Africa and up into Spain and the South of France. Mention is first made of him carrying a petition on behalf of Pothinus, the Bishop of Lyons, to Pope Elutherus in Rome. In this petition, a request was made to the Pope to stop the persecution of Christians who did not agree with the doctrine of the Pauline Church. Iranaeus was still in Rome when he heard that all the dissenting Christians, including Bishop Pothinus, had been killed. On his return, Iranaeus succeeded Pothinus as Bishop of Lyons.

In 190 A.D. he himself wrote to Pope Victor to stop the

massacre of Christians who were being killed solely for their differences in belief. The story was again repeated and he himself was murdered in 200 A.D. for espousing the cause of Christians who did not follow the Pope.

Iranaeus believed in One God and supported the doctrine of the manhood of Jesus. He bitterly criticised Paul for being responsible for injecting the doctrines of the pagan religions and Platonic philosophy into Christianity. Iranaeus quoted extensively from the Gospel of Barnabas. It was after reading the writings of Iranaeus that Fra Marino became interested in this Gospel, which in turn led to his discovery of the Italian manuscript of the Gospel of Barnabas in the Papal library.

Tertullian (160-220 A.D.)
Tertullian belonged to the African Church. He was a native of Carthage. He believed in the Unity of God and identified Jesus with the Jewish Messiah. He opposed Pope Callistus for teaching that capital sin was forgiven after doing canonical penance. He stressed the unity of the heart with existence.

He wrote: "Common people think of Christ as a man."

It was he who introduced the term "trinitas" into Latin ecclesiastical writings when discussing this strange new doctrine. The term trinity is not once used in the inspired Scriptures.

Origen (185-254 A.D.)
Origen was an Egyptian by birth. Perhaps he was born in Alexandria. His father, Leonidas, founded a centre of learning and appointed the famous theologian Clement as its head. Origen received his education here. The Pauline Church did not approve of the beliefs held by Leonidas, who followed Apostolic Christianity and refused to accept the interpretations and innovations of Paul. He was murdered in 208 A.D. Origen was so affected by this event that he too wished to offer himself as a martyr, but was prevented from doing so by his mother.

His teacher, Clement, finding his life to be in danger, fled from Alexandria. His father was dead, his teacher had gone, and Origen felt obliged to step into the breach. As the new head of the school, he soon acquired a reputation for learning and courage. Owing to his piety and excessive zeal, he mutilated himself, following the words of Matthew 19:12:

> There are some eunuchs, which were so born from their mother's womb: and there are some eunuchs, which were made eunuchs of men: and there be eunuchs, which have made themselves eunuchs for the kingdom of heaven's sake. He that is able to receive it, let him receive it.

In 230 A.D. he was ordained a priest in Palestine, but Bishop Demerius deposed and exiled him. He found refuge in Caesarea in 231 A.D. Following the example of his father, he started a centre of learning in Caesarea and this school also became very famous.

Jerome, the author of the famous Vulgate Bible, the first Latin translation of the Greek Bible, supported Origen to begin with, but later began to believe in the doctrine of Trinity and became his enemy. Jerome had tried to have Origen condemned by the Church, but because of Origen's popularity, Bishop John did not dare to do so. In fact, Jerome himself was exiled. However, Jerome succeeded in 250 A.D. Origen was condemned by the Council of Alexandria. He was put in prison and subjected to a prolonged torture which resulted in his death in 254 A.D. The reason given for his imprisonment was that he rejected the doctrine of Trinity and preached the Unity of God. He believed that God was supreme and that Jesus was not equal to Him, but was His slave.

Origen wrote about six hundred tracts and treatises. He has been described as "one of the most appealing characters in Church History." From his youth to his last hour, he showed an uncommon fearlessness. He was conscientious and patient. He had all the qualities of a true teacher and those whom he taught loved him. His power of discrimination, creative energy and catholicity of knowledge were almost unparalleled among the Christians.

Diodorus
Diodorus was a Bishop of Tarsus. He is regarded as one of the most important leaders of the Antiochene branch of Christianity.

He held that the world is subject to change, but that the

change itself is a condition which implies a beginning and requires one to assume that there is a constancy behind it. Moreover, the variety of existence and the wisdom displayed in the very process of change itself points to the underlying unity of origin and shows the presence of a Creator and a Providence. There could only be one such Creator.

Diodorus emphasised the complete manhood of Jesus who had a human soul and human flesh.

Lucian (Died in 312 A.D.)

Lucian's reputation for fear of God was no less than his fame as a man of learning. He had knowledge of both Hebrew and Greek. He remained outside the communion of the Church from 220 to 290 A.D. His purity and profound knowledge attracted a large number of people and soon his school became a nursery of what later became known as Arian doctrine. Arius was one of his pupils.

Lucian believed in the grammatical and literal exegesis of the Scriptures. He opposed the tendency to look for symbolic and allegorical meanings in them and believed in an empirical and critical approach to them. The existence of this controversy demonstrates the fact that by now people were beginning to rely more and more on the Scriptures and less and less on the oral transmission of what Jesus had taught. It is an indication of how quickly the teaching of Jesus in its totality was lost.

Lucian was a great scholar. He revised the Septuagent. He eliminated many of the changes which had been made to some of the Gospels when they were translated into Greek, and produced the four Gospels which, according to him, were true Gospels. These Gospels were not the same as the four Gospels commonly accepted by the Pauline Church today.

He believed that Jesus was not equal to God and that he was subordinate to Him. It was for this that he incurred the enmity of the Pauline Church, and after many tortures he was put to death in 312 A.D.

Arius (250-336 A.D.)

The life of Arius is so much intertwined with the life of

Emperor Constantine that it is not possible to understand one without knowing the other. The story of how Constantine first became involved with the Christian Church begins in Rome.

Constantine became jealous of his eldest son and heir, Crispus. The young prince had become very popular because of his good looks, his charming manner and his bravery on the field of battle. To make sure of his position as Emperor, Constantine had him murdered. The death of Crispus cast a gloom over the whole realm. It was known that the step-mother of Crispus had wanted her own son to succeed Constantine. She therefore had a motive for killing Crispus. Constantine accordingly put the blame for his crime on her, and killed her by immersing her in a bath full of boiling water. He hoped to mitigate one crime by the other. The result, however, was just the opposite of what he had planned — the supporters of the dead queen joined forces with the followers of his dead son, and both sought revenge. In desperation he turned to the priests of the Roman temple of Jupiter for help, but they told him there was no sacrifice or prayer which could absolve him from the two murders. It became so uncomfortable to be in Rome that Constantine decided to go to Byzantium.

On his arrival there, he renamed the city after himself, and called it Constantinople. Here he met with unexpected success from the Pauline Church. They said that if he did penance in their Church his sins would be forgiven. Constantine made full use of this facility. His hands were not only stained with the blood from two murders, but were also full of the problems of governing his empire. Having salved his conscience with his confession, the life to come ceased to worry him, and he turned his attention to the affairs of the Empire. He saw the possibilities of using the Church to his own ends provided that he could win its loyalty to him, so he gave the Church his full support. With this unexpected backing, the Church became a strong force almost overnight. Constantine made full use of her. The country around the Mediterranean was dotted about with Christian churches and the Emperor utilised them to great advantage in the wars he was fighting. Many of the priests carried out very useful intelligence work for him, and their help was an important factor in his efforts to unite Europe and the Middle East under him. Partly as a token of his gratitude and partly in order to diminish the power of the Roman priests in the temple of Jupiter who had refused to support him, Constantine encouraged the Christians to open a church in Rome. However, Constantine did not become a Christian himself, for many of his subjects still believed in Jupiter and the other gods in the Pantheon of Rome. In order to allay any suspicions they might have, he made a number of decisions which seemed to prove that he too worshipped the Roman gods. Everything appeared to be going very well when the old controversy between the Pauline and Apostolic Churches again flared up.

The leader of the Apostolic Church, which continued to affirm belief in One Reality, was at this time a presbyter known to history as Arius. He was a Libyan by birth. He gave new strength to the Apostolic Church. He followed the teaching of Jesus implicitly, and refused to accept the innovations introduced by Paul. "Follow Jesus as he preached" was the motto of Arius. His importance can be gauged by the fact that his name has become a synonym for unitarianism even today.

The Pauline Church received a violent jolt from Arius. He was no mere "bustling schemer" as his enemies would have people believe, and even they were forced to admit that he was a sincere and blameless presbyter. At a time when the oral tradition which had kept the teaching of Jesus alive was beginning to weaken, and when the understanding of what had been written down was starting to diminish, Arius revived both and renewed them with his vigour and wisdom. He remained aloof from the alliance which the organised Church had made with the Emperor Constantine.

Arius was the disciple of the greatest critic of the Pauline Church at that time, the venerated martyr, Lucian of Antioch, who was known for his great learning and who, like his predecessors, was killed for holding views not approved of by the Pauline Church. Thus Arius was fully aware of the dangers involved in entertaining a belief which differed from those acceptable to this Church. Although his early life is hidden in mystery, it is recorded that in 318 A.D., he was in charge of the Church of Baucalis in Alexandria. It was the oldest and one of the most important of the city's churches.

From the scanty record which is available, it is known that he was tall and thin. He would have been handsome but for his general emaciation, the deadly pallor of his face and a downcast look which was imparted by the weakness of his eyesight. His dress and demeanour were those of a dedicated ascetic. He wore a long coat with short sleeves. His hair hung in a tangled mass from his head. He was usually silent, but, if occasion arose, would break into fierce and exciting words. There was a sweetness to his voice and he had an earnest but winning manner about him which fascinated those who came into contact with him. He was regarded as one of the most remarkable presbyters in Alexandria, and was held in high esteem by anyone who met him:

> His fame soon spread, even outside Alexandria, as an earnest worker who led a strict and ascetic life, a powerful preacher who dealt boldly and frankly with the great principle of faith. He was gifted with great conversational powers and charm of manner. He was also capable of injecting others with the enthusiasm which he himself felt. Like all the great religious leaders of the world, he was fanatically sincere and the doctrine he preached was vital and fecund.[2]

It is also known that he had the following of not less than seven hundred of the Christian ladies of Alexandria.[2]

Up until this time, a Christian's faith was not the result of compulsion. There were differences between sects, sometimes deep and bitter, but whatever belief an individual held was based on his own personal conviction and sincerity. In this period after Jesus's disappearance from earth, saints and martyrs had gladly given up their lives rather than compromise their belief. The swords wielded by those in authority over the land had been used in an attempt to dispel such beliefs and certainly not to enforce them. When Constantine made his first alliance with the Church, there was a dramatic change in the situation. Although he remained Pontifex Maximus, and continued in his capacity as head of the pagan state religion, he began to openly support the Christian Church, probably making little distinction between the Pauline and the Apostolic branches. This sign of favour put Christianity in a new light and it became virtually the only official cult of the Roman Emperor. For many people, Christianity had suddenly become a matter of policy and expediency. Some of those who held back soon joined with the aid of a little governmental pressure. Thus many of the conversions to Christianity ceased to come from the heart, but were the result of an entirely different kind of conviction. Christianity had become a mass movement.[3] However, it was a movement which re-emphasised the split between the Pauline Church and the Apostolic Church. Those who became Christians out of expediency naturally chose the less rigorous approach of the Pauline Church. The Apostolic Church welcomed only those who sincerely wished to follow the way of Jesus.

Constantine, who at this stage neither understood nor believed in Christianity, saw the political advantage of having a united Church which would obey him, and whose centre would be based in Rome, and not in Jerusalem. When the members of the Apostolic Church refused to comply with these wishes, he tried to compel them by means of force. This pressure from without, however, did not produce the desired result. A number of the Apostolic Christian communities still refused to accept the overlordship of the Bishop of Rome. They recognised this move as a political ploy by a foreign ruler, and as something entirely apart from the teaching of Jesus.

The first revolt came from among the Berber communities of North Africa. It was led not by Arius but by a man named Donatus. On the whole the Berbers have always retained certain basic beliefs, the strongest of which was their belief in the Divine Unity. They could believe in Jesus as a prophet, but never as God. Since Jesus had never said anything about Rome being the centre of his teaching, they could not entertain such an idea, let alone attribute it to him retrospectively. In 313 A.D. Donatus was chosen from among these people as their bishop. For forty years he remained the leader of their Church which continued to flourish in opposition to the Bishop of Rome. According to Jerome, "Donatism" became the religion of nearly all North Africa within a generation, and neither force nor argument could change it.

The Bishop of Rome tried to install one of his own bishops in Carthage to replace Donatus. His name was Cacealian. The prestige of Constantine was such that, in the conflict which ensued, both parties appealed to him. It appears that they thought that whoever won his support would have no further battles to fight. This attempt to win the patronage of Constantine brought with it a very important change in the history of Christianity. For the first time it had become possible for schism and unorthodoxy to become an offence punishable by secular law. This secular coat of armour stood at the disposal of whoever could prove himself to be orthodox, and could then be used against those who differed from this new standard of orthodoxy. Constantine decided in favor of Cacealian. The populace of Carthage gathered around the office of the Roman pro-consul and denounced Cacealian. Constantine was annoyed by their action, but nevertheless appointed a tribunal under the Bishop of Rome to hear the case of the two parties. Donatus was not present and no one was there to argue his case. The decision went against him in absentia. The Apostolic church in Africa refused to accept the *ex parte* verdict of the Roman Bishop. Constantine was scandalised that the "ministers of God were wrangling amongst themselves like ordinary litigants."[4] In spite of his disappointment, he set up a new tribunal at Arles. The two parties were told to travel there by different routes, in order to prevent any clashes before the hearing took place. The Donatists lost again. The decision was that "the bishops found themselves dealing with dangerous men who had no respect for authority or tradition. They were fit only for condemnation."[5] This was no more acceptable to the North African Christians than the previous rulings. As it was, they had little respect for the Roman pro-consul and the other imperial officials. For generations now the Christians had suffered persecution at their hands, and regarded them as emissaries of Satan. Formerly, they had been persecuted because they were Christians. Now they were to be persecuted because they were not the right kind of Christians. The North

African Christians could not accept that the officials of the Roman Empire had become servants of God overnight, merely because they sought to enforce a ruling of the Pauline Bishop of Rome. Up until this point, Donatus had been their bishop. He now became their popular leader.

Very little is known about this remarkable man. The books he wrote and his precious library of manuscripts were all burned by the Roman soldiers. They performed these deeds in the name of the Roman Christian Church, which, with the support of a pagan Emperor, was now beginning to grow in importance and strength. Thus, little is known about his background, his personal appearance, his friends and the events in his life. It is known that Donatus was a fine orator and a great leader of men. He was met with such enthusiasm wherever he went that these times were remembered long after he had died. His followers used to swear by his "white hairs". He seems to have personified the popular loathing for the worldly ecclesiasts who were sure they would do well both in this life and the next if they performed the correct maneuvers. His integrity and honesty were recognised by friend and foe alike. He was known as the religious reformer "who purified the Church of Carthage from error."[6] He was regarded by the people as a worker of miracles and a saint wiser than Daniel. He stood as firm as a rock against all attempts to erode and alter the original teaching of Jesus.

Constantine wrote a letter to the two Churches urging them to forget their differences and to unite under the Church favoured by him. This letter is significant in that Constantine regarded himself as being superior to the Church, whatever its form, and any reference to Jesus was conspicuous by its absence.[7] The letter had no effect on anyone, and no progress was made in enforcing the decision of the tribunal which had met at Arles.

In July 315 A.D. the Emperor returned to Rome. It was necessary to go to Milan to suppress the Frankish incursions which had begun in the north of Italy. When he again had some time at his disposal, he appointed a commission to travel to Africa, examine the situation and settle the dispute. When the commission arrived, it was boycotted, and such a violent riot took place that its members were forced to return to Italy without having achieved anything. This disquieting news reached Constantine in 316 A.D. He decided to go to North Africa in person and himself give a clear ruling as to exactly how the Supreme Deity should be worshipped.

It is interesting that Constantine considered it within his competence to pass such a judgement. In the letter which he wrote to the two Churches in Africa, he concluded:

> What more can be done by me, in accord with my constant practise and with the very office of a prince, than after expelling error and destroying rash opinion, to cause all men to argue together to follow true religion and simplicity of life, and to render to Almighty God the worship which is His due.[7]

It is clear that once the example of Jesus was forgotten or ignored "true religion" became a matter of opinion, and there was no opinion that Constantine favoured more than his own. It was only by approaching Christianity in this manner that Constantine could take such a keen interest in the internal affairs of a religion which he did not yet follow. Constantine regarded himself as a man who spoke with greater authority than the leaders of the Churches, and seems to have regarded himself more as God's own vicar than as an ordinary mortal. The Pauline bishops who had sat on the tribunal at Arles appear to have been of the same opinion as Constantine. They claimed that their devising was recorded "in the presence of the Holy Ghost and His angels."[8] Yet when their ruling was ignored, it was to the Emperor that they turned for help.

As it happened, Constantine did not make the journey to Africa he had planned. The Donatists had become so strong, he was told, that it was inadvisable to take part personally in the dispute between Donatus and Cacaelian. For should his personal intervention meet with failure, it would be a great blow to his prestige. Instead, he issued a decree condemning Donatus and drawing his attention to "the advantage of worshipping the Supreme Deity in the proper manner."[9] When it was ignored, "a most severe law" was dispatched to Africa: the churches held by the Donatists were to be confiscated, and their leaders were to be sent into exile. Cacaelian at first tried to bribe the leaders of the Donatist Church, but without success. They defied the imperial command, ignored his bribes and made his offers of money publicly known. Cacaelian was branded as "a man more cruel than a butcher and more brutal than a tyrant."[10]

The Church of Rome, which had by now adopted the epithet "Catholic" to indicate the universality of its approach in the worship of God, appealed to the Donatists to unite. The appeal had no effect, and Donatus refused to hand over his churches to Cacaelian. Finally, the Roman army came into action. There was a mass slaughter of people. Dead bodies were thrown into wells, and bishops were murdered in their churches. However, the surviving Donatists remained firm, and if anything, their movement became stronger than before. They named their Church the "Church of Martyrs". These events widened the rift between the Donatists and the Catholic Church even further. Since the Catholic Church was working in alliance with the pagan magistrates and their soldiers, the Catholics were called schismatics and their churches were identified as places of "hated idolatry".

Constantine, who was a good administrator, realised the futility of trying to restore religious harmony and unity by force. Deciding that discretion was the better part of valour, he left the people in North Africa to themselves. However, it was these events and their consequences which played a large part in his later making the decision to call the famous Council of Nicea.

Before returning to the story of Arius, who at this point was just beginning to make his voice heard, it would be of interest to give a brief history of the Donatists up until the coming of Islam: once Constantine had turned his attention away from North Africa to other parts of his Empire, the persecution of the Donatists lessened considerably, and their numbers again began to increase rapidly. They became so powerful that when the Emperor had a church built for the Catholics of North Africa in 330 A.D., the Donatists took possession of it. The Emperor was enraged, but could do nothing except promise the Catholics sufficient money to build another church for themselves. The Donatist movement spread even to Rome. They too had a Bishop of Rome, but he was regarded as being a rank below the Bishop of Carthage and Nicomedia.[11]

Donatus acquired sovereign authority at Carthage. He was regarded by the masses as a being superior to other mortals. He was never called a bishop, but was known as "Donatus of Carthage". Augustine once complained that the Donatists reacted more sharply to an insult against Donatus than to a blasphemy against Jesus, a fact which is easily explained by the strong and unkind language which many of the Catholics used when talking about Donatus.

When the reign of Constantine ended, the Donatists continued to work for the independence of their Church and to oppose any interference from the Emperor or his officials in matters of religion. They were not, however, narrow-minded sectarians. Augustine himself observes that the Donatists did not oppress the Catholics even when they outnumbered them. The Catholics, who were always ready to claim toleration for themselves, were not prepared to grant it to the Donatists when once more the imperial forces were sent to subdue these fearless people. However, despite this continued persecution, the Donatists refused to allow the Emperor to alter the way they worshipped God. In their opinion, "the Catholics were evil priests working with the kings of the world. Relying on royal favours, they had renounced Christ."[12]

After the death of Donatus, the people of North Africa continued to follow his example, and for three hundred years his teaching of what Jesus had brought was followed by them. When Islam came to them, they embraced it, so well-prepared were they for what was, after all, an extension and reaffirmation of the guidance they had been following.

There was another movement similar to that of Donatus which took place simultaneously, yet quite independently of it, in the south of Egypt. Constantine was just about to make another attempt at unravelling the tangled skein of North African Christianity in 324 A.D., when his attention was drawn to Egypt, a country which was seething with discontent and revolt. When the persecution of the Christians by Diocletian was at its height, many of them had compromised themselves to avoid it. A priest called Meletius was now saying that those priests who had publicly renounced Christianity should be prevented from reassuming their clerical functions. He felt that they should also be stopped from attending all the assemblies of pure worship unless they demonstrated sufficient proof of their penitence. Peter, who was patriarch of Alexandria at that time, advised a more lenient course. The majority of the people, however, supported Meletius. When Alexander came on the episcopal throne, he banished Meletius to the mines.

When Meletius returned, many followers gathered around him. He ordained bishops, priests and deacons and was responsible for building many churches. They refused to submit to their persecutors. Meletius called his Church the "Church of the Martyrs", as opposed to the followers of Alexander who called themselves Catholic and followed the Pauline version of Christianity. After the death of Meletius, Alexander forbade his followers to hold their assemblies of worship. In opposition to this order, they sent a deputation to Constantine. It was only with the help of Eusebius of Nicomedia that they were allowed to see the Emperor. Their presence in his court was yet another factor which led to his calling the Council of Nicea. Eusebius was a friend of Arius, and it was through this meeting that contact was made between the Arian and Meletian movements.

The movement led by Arius took place against the background of these two Churches of Martyrs. Anything written in favour of Arius or any independent assessment of his movement has virtually been destroyed. Nearly all the books covering Arius which still exist have been written by his enemies. It is, therefore, impossible to give a full account of his life. Connecting the pieces of information which still exist the following picture emerges: Peter, the Bishop of Alexandria, ordained him a deacon but later excommunciated him. Achillas, Peter's successor, again ordained him a priest. Arius became so popular that when Achillas died, he had every chance of taking his place. However, Arius had no desire to be involved in any kind of election, and so it was Alexander who was chosen to sit on the episcopal throne. A complaint was made against Arius because of what he preached. His rival became his judge, and eventually Arius was again excommunicated.

Up to this point, there had been a great latitude in the beliefs of the Christians. The doctrine of Trinity was now accepted by many of those who called themselves Christians, but no one was sure what it actually meant. Some blindly affirmed it; others, like Meletius and Donatus, strongly rejected it, and those who fell between these two poles were at liberty to explain the doctrine in the way they thought best. After more than two centuries of discussion, no one had been able to state the doctrine in terms which were free from equivocation. Arius stood up and challenged anyone to define it. Alexander was completely taken aback. The more he tried to explain it, the more confused he became. Arius, by the use of reason, and relying on the authority of the Scriptures, proved the doctrine to be false.

Arius began his refutation of Alexander's explanations with reference to Jesus: if Jesus was in reality the "son of God", he argued, then it followed that the father must have existed before the son. Therefore, there must have been a time when the son did not exist. Therefore, it followed that the son was a creature composed of an essence or being which had not always existed. Since God is in essence Eternal and Ever-existent, Jesus could not be of the same essence as God.

Arius always appealed to reason and logic, and since Alexander could not furnish any reasonable counter-arguments, he always ended up by losing his temper. Given the premises, Arius would say: "Where is the fault of my deduction and where does my syllogism break down?" By the year 321 A.D., Arius was a popular rebellious priest, profoundly confident and certain of what he believed.

After receiving this personal set-back, Alexander called a provincial synod to pronounce judgement on the doctrine of Arius. About one hundred Egyptian and Libyan bishops attended. Arius boldly maintained the stand he had taken, and with great ability stated his case: there was a time when Jesus did not exist, whereas God existed even then. Since Jesus was created by God, his being was finite and so he could not possess the attribute of Eternity. Only God is Eternal. Since Jesus was a creature, he was subject to change like all other rational creatures. Only God is unchanging. Thus, he asserted that Jesus was not God. As well as his appeal to logic, Arius backed up his arguments with numerous verses from the Bible which nowhere teaches the doctrine of Trinity. If Jesus said: "My father is greater than I,"[13] then to believe that God and Jesus were equal, argued Arius, was to deny the truth of the Bible.

The arguments of Arius were irrefutable, but Alexander, by virtue of his position, excommunciated him. However Arius had such a large following that he could not be ignored by the Pauline church, especially since many of the Eastern Bishops did not accept Alexander's decree. The controversy which had been simmering for nearly three hundred years came to a boil. Alexander was troubled and annoyed that so many of the Eastern bishops supported Arius, whose greatest ally was Eusebius of Nicomedia. He and Arius were old friends, since both had been students of Lucian, a man who had been universally respected for his purity and learning. It is possible that Lucian's martyrdom in 312 A.D. helped to strengthen the friendship and the resolve which these two shared.

There is a letter which Arius wrote to Eusebius in Constantinople after his excommunication by Alexander, and which still exists. Arius complains of his persecution by Alexander, who was trying to expel him from Alexandria as an impious atheist because he and his friends did not subscribe to the outrageous doctrines which the bishop professed: "We are persecuted because we say that Jesus has a beginning, while God had no beginning." [14] As a result, Arius received increased support from Eusebius who had much influence, not only with the common people, but also in the imperial palace itself. In spite of this backing, Arius appears always to have inclined towards reconciliation rather than opposition, so far as discipline within the Church was concerned.

Unfortunately, the record of this dispute is very scanty, but there are a few letters in existence which show that Arius' intention was solely to keep the teachings of Jesus pure and free from alteration, and not to cause disruption among the Christians. On the other hand, the letters written by Alexander show that the Bishop was always using intemperate language against Arius and his supporters. In one letter he writes: "They are possessed of the Devil who dwells in them and goads them to fury; they are jugglers and tricksters, clever conjurors with seductive words; they are brigands who have lairs for themselves wherein day and night they curse Christ . . . they make proselytes through the agency of loose young women of the town." [15] The use of such violent and outrageous language by the Patriarch raises the suspicion that he too must have been aware of the weakness of his case.

Eusebius hotly resented the tone of the Patriarch of Alexandria. He summoned the synod of Eastern bishops and laid the whole matter before them. The result of this gathering was a letter, which was sent to all the bishops of East and West, begging them to induce Alexander to take back Arius into the Church. Alexander, however, wanted Arius's total surrender. Arius returned to Palestine and continued to hold services for his followers. Alexander issued a long letter addressed to "all his fellow workers of the Catholic Church," in which he again attacked Arius. He also made a pointed reference to Eusebius, mentioning him by name and accusing him of believing "that the welfare of the Church depended on his nod." [16] He added that Eusebius supported Arius, not because he sincerely believed in Arian doctrine, but in order to further his own ambitious interests. Thus the ecclesiastical controversy degenerated into a personal conflict between the Eastern and Western bishops.

The questions in issue spread from the circle of the bishops out to the common people. Gregory of Nyssea writes:

> Every corner of Constantinople was full of their discussions: the streets, the market place, the shops of the money changers, the victuallers. Ask a tradesman how many obols he wants for some article in his shop, and he replies with the disquisition on generated and ungenerated being. Ask the price of bread today and the baker tells you: "The son is subordinate to the father." Ask your servant if the bath is ready and he makes an answer: "The son arose out of nothing." "Great is the only Begotten," declared the Catholics, and the Arians rejoined: "But greater is He that begot." [17]

People would ask women whether a son could exist before he was born. The debate in the higher ecclesiastic circle was equally hot and bitter. It is recorded that "in every city, bishops were engaged in obstinate conflict with bishops. People were against people. . . and came into violent collision with each other." [18]

As far as Constantine was concerned, things were going from bad to worse. He was obliged to intervene and addressed a letter to both Alexander and Arius. He said that his consuming passion was for unity of religious opinion, since it was the best guarantee of peace in the realm. Deeply disappointed by the events in North Africa, he had hoped for better things from the "bosom of the East" whence had arisen the "dawn of Divine Light". He then continues:

> But Ah! Glorious and Divine Providence, what a wound was inflicted not alone on my ears but on my heart, when I heard that divisions existed among yourselves even more grievous than those in Africa; so that you, whose agency I hoped to bring healing to others, need a remedy worse than they. And yet, after making a careful enquiry into the origin of these discussions, I find that the cause is quite insignificant and entirely disproportionate to such a quarrel . . . I gather that the present controversy originated as follows: for when you, Alexander, asked each of the presbyters what he thought about a certain passage in the Scriptures or, rather, what he thought about a certain aspect of a foolish question; and you, Arius, without due consideration, laid down propositions which never ought to have been conceived at all, or if conceived ought to have been buried in silence, dissensions arose between you — communion was forbidden, and the most people, torn in twain, no longer preserved the unity of a common body.

The Emperor then exhorts them to let both the unguarded question and the inconsiderate answer be forgotten and forgiven:

> The subject never ought to have been broached, but there is always mischief found for idle hands to do and idle brains to think. The difference between you has not arisen on any cardinal doctrine laid down in the Scriptures, nor has any

new doctrine been introduced. You both hold one and the same view. Reunion, therefore, was easily possible.

The Emperor went on to quote the example of pagan philosophers who agree to disagree on details while holding the same general principles. How then, he asked, can it be right for brethren to behave towards one another like enemies because of mere trifling and verbal differences. Such conduct in his opinion was:

> vulgar, childish, and petulant, ill-fitting priests of God and men of sense . . . It is the wile and temptation of the Devil. Let us have done with it. If we cannot all think alike on all topics, we can at least all be united on great essentials. As regards the Divine Providence, let there be one faith and one understanding, one united opinion in reference to God.

The letter concludes:

> Restore me then my quiet days and untroubled nights that I may retain my joy, the gladness of peaceful life. Else I must groan and be defused wholly in tears, and no comfort of mind till I die. For while the people of God, my fellow servants, are thus torn asunder in unlawful and pernicious controversy, how can I be tranquil of mind? [19]

This letter demonstrates the profound ignorance of the Emperor, not only of Christianity, but also of any religion, since it assumes that it is the same whether a man worships God as he pleases or in the manner which God indicates to him. To say that the controversy between Alexander and Arius was merely a verbal quarrel or an insignificant and non-essential point is absurd. To regard the difference between the two as "trifling" clearly shows that Constantine did not understand what he was talking about. A certainty in the Divine Unity, on the one hand, and a belief in a Trinity of God, on the other hand, could not be more fundamentally opposed. The letter indicates that Constantine was not concerned with the nature of Reality, but with his own peace of mind. It is not surprising that his letter achieved nothing. It was carried to Alexandria by Hosius of Cordoba. After a short stay, he returned empty-handed to report the failure of his mission to the Emperor.

While this was going on, Constantine clashed with his brother-in-law, Licinus, on the battle-field, and Licinus was killed. Licinus had been a supporter of Arius, and his death further weakened the position of Arius in the Emperor's court. However, Constantine realised that it is possible to win a war and yet lose the peace. Since the failure of Hosius's mission, the situation in the East had become very unsettled. The songs and arguments of Arius had resulted in blood being shed in Alexandria, and unrest had spread throughout the eastern parts of the Empire. There was already turmoil in North Africa. Constantine realised that his friends in the Pauline Church were not powerful enough to dispel any of this trouble. His experience in dealing with the North Africans, which had partly resulted in his coming east after almost burning his boats in Rome, seemed to have taught him a lesson: he should not take sides openly. So he decided to call a meeting of Christian bishops in order to settle the matter once and for all. His position as a pagan, he said, was a great advantage since by virtue of his not belonging to any sect, he would make an impartial judge. This would resolve the problem which had faced the bishops up until then, for they had not been able to agree on any one Christian to preside over such a meeting as their arbitrator. This gathering of the bishops under Constantine is known today as the Council of Nicea.

The invitations were despatched, and all expenses were paid for by Constantine from the state treasury. Apart from the leaders of the two contending parties, the majority of those who were invited were not on the whole very knowledgeable. No one from the Church of Donatus was asked to attend, although Cacaelian, Donatus's chief opponent, was invited. Among the more important bishops who participated in the council were:

Eusebius of Caesaria, who is the father of ecclesiastical history. His book is the chief repository of traditions which connect the fourth century with the first of the Christian era. Apart from his knowledge, the degree of his influence rested on the fact that he alone of the Eastern prelates could tell what was going on in the mind of the Emperor. For he was the interpreter and nominal chaplain and confessor of the Emperor. He was at heart an Arian, and enjoyed the support of most of the bishops in Palestine.

Eusebius of Nicomedia, who came from an aristocratic family, and who had been a follower of Lucian at the same time as Arius. His spiritual eminence was universally recognised. Thus, there were two important men of God in this age who bore the same name, a fact which has caused much confusion in some of the minds of the historians of this period. Eusebius of Nicomedia was the most resolute supporter of Arius. He was called "the great" by the followers of Arius. Miracles were attributed to him. Originally, the Bishop of Beyruth, he was later transferred to Nicomedia, the capitol of the Eastern Empire. He had been a good friend of the Emperor's brother-in-law and rival, Licinus, and thus exercised an influence on Constantina, the sister of Constantine. Licinus had recently fought the Emperor and lost his life. After the death of her husband, Constantina went to stay in the Imperial Palace. Thus, through her and through his own distant relationship with the Imperial family, he kept a hold on the court which he never lost. It was to be through his influence that the Emperor accepted Christianity in the Church of Arius, and finally died a believer in the Divine Unity.

Athanasius, who was a young and fiery supporter of the Trinitarian school of theology. Alexander, who was growing old, and who had been routed so many times before by Arius, decided to send Athanasius to Nicea as his representative, instead of going there himself.

Hosius, who was the Chief Councillor of the Emperor. His importance lay in the fact that he represented the Pauline Church in the West where the Emperor's influence was weakest. Hosius was recognised as a profound scholar of theology in his own right. In history he is known as the venerable old man who was called "holy" by Athanasius. His high character was known to everyone. His importance had increased due to his intimacy with the Emperor.

Apart from these few, the Council was composed of persons with a reputation of piety, but not of learning, men whose hearts were pure, but whose tongues were not always very articulate:

Spiridem, who was one of the rough and simple, almost illiterate bishops that formed the majority of the bishops in the Church at that time. A closer study of him will help illustrate the kind of men they were. He was a shepherd who had suffered persecution and yet remained firm in his faith. His knowledge of the politics of religion was superficial. He had been appointed bishop because many miracles had been attributed to him. After becoming a bishop, he did not change his rough and ready rural attire. He always walked on foot. The other "princes" of the Pauline Church did not like him, and were anxious that he should not reach Nicea in time for the Council. When Spiridem received his invitation from the Emperor, he realised that he would have to travel by mule if he was to arrive in time. He set out with one attendant, unlike other bishops who went with a whole retinue. They travelled on two mules, one white, the other piebald. One night they were staying in an inn when there also arrived those bishops who were not sure whether Spiridem was the right kind of person to take part in the deliberations of the Council. Early the next morning, while Spiridem was still asleep, they chopped off the heads of his two mules and departed. When he awoke, he asked his attendant to feed and saddle the mules. The attendant discovered the dead animals and reported the loss to Spiridem. Spiridem told the attendant to put the head of each mule near the dead body it had been a part of. In the darkness, the attendant put each head next to the wrong animal. As soon as he had done this, the mules got up alive, and they continued on their journey. After a while, they overtook the bishops, who thought they had left Spiridem well behind and were sure that he would not reach Nicea in time. Their surprise was even greater when they found that the white mule had a piebald head, and the piebald, a white head. [20]

Patammon, who was a hermit.

Oesius, who was known only for his puritanical zeal.

Myser of Nicholas, whose name is preserved, especially by Church historians, by virtue of the fact that when Arius was speaking, he boxed his hears.

Thus, the Council was composed largely of bishops who held their faith earnestly and sincerely, but without much intellectual knowledge of the grounds on which they maintained it. These men were suddenly brought face to face with the most agile and most learned exponents of Greek philosophy of the age. Their way of expression was such that these bishops could not grasp the significance of what was being said. Incapable of giving rational explanations of their knowledge or entering into arguments with their opponents, they were to either stick to their beliefs in silence or to agree to whatever the Emperor decided.

All the delegates reached Nicea a few days before the Council was scheduled to start. They collected together in small groups where the questions in issue were publicly debated with earnestness and with feeling. In these gatherings, which took place either in the gymnasium or in some open space, the Greek philosophers placed their darts of argument and ridicule with great effectiveness. This caused no small confusion among the delegates.

At last the day arrived, and everyone gathered for the inauguration of the Council which was to be by the Emperor himself. The chamber prepared for the meeting was a long, oblong hall in the palace. In the centre of the room were placed copies of all the known Gospels, which at that time numbered about three hundred. Every eye lay upon the Imperial throne, which was carved in wood and richly covered in gilt. It was placed at the upper end of the hall between two rows of seats which faced each other. The deep silence was disturbed by the faint sounds of distant procession. It was approaching the palace. Then the officers of the court came in one by one. At last a signal from without announced that the Emperor was close at hand. The whole assembly stood up, and for the first time set their wondering gaze on Constantine, the Conqueror, the August, the Great. His towering stature, his well-built frame, his broad shoulders, and his handsome features were all in keeping with his grand position. His expression was one that many thought him to be the manifestation of Apollo, the Roman sun-god. Many of the bishops were struck by the dazzling, albeit barbaric, magnificence of his dress. His long hair was crowned with the imperial diadem of pearls. His scarlet robe blazed with precious stones and gold embroidery. He was shod in scarlet shoes, then worn only by the Emperor and now worn by the Pope.

Hosius and Eusebius sat on either side of the Emperor. Eusebius started the proceedings with an address to the Emperor. The Emperor replied with a short speech translated from Latin into Greek which very few understood, including the Emperor, whose knowledge of Greek was sparse. With the meeting under way, the flood-gate of the controversy was opened wide. Constantine with his broken Greek concentrated all his energy on one point, which was to achieve a unanimity of decision. He informed everyone that he had burned all the petitions which he had received from different parties a few days earlier. He assured them that since he had not read any of them, he had an open mind and was not inclined one way or the other.

The representative of the Pauline Church wanted to put three "parts" of God on the Divine Throne, but could produce arguments from the Bible in favour of only two. In spite of this, the third "part" of God, namely the Holy Ghost, was declared to be the third person of the Trinity, although no reasons were given in support of this innovation. The disciples of Lucian, on the other hand, were sure of their ground, and forced the Trinitarians to shift from one impossible position to the next.

The Trinitarians found it difficult to define a Christian in such a way as to exclude Arius and the other unitarians from their definition, especially since belief in the doctrine of the Trinity, which they asserted was the distingusihing factor between the two parties, was never actually mentioned in the Gospels. They said that the "Son" was "of God". The Arians replied that they themselves were "of God" since it is written in the Bible, "All things are of God".[21] Therefore, if this argument was used, then it also proved the divinity of all creatures. The Pauline bishops then argued that Jesus was not only "of God", but also "of the Essence of God". This distinction roused opposition from all the orthodox Christians since, they said, these words were not to be found in the Bible. Thus, this attempt to prove that Jesus was God, instead of uniting the Christians, further divided them. In desperation, the trinitarians argued that the Bible says that, "Jesus is the eternal image of the Father and True God."[22] The Arians replied that the Bible also says, "We men are the image and glory of God." [23] Therefore, if this argument was used, not only Jesus but all men could claim to be Divine.

The discussion continued, not only in the meeting hall but also within the Imperial Palace: Helena, the Queen mother, supported the Pauline Church. She was a political animal, and administrative expediency ran in her blood. On the other hand, Constantina, the sister of the Emperor, was a believer in the Divine Unity and supported Arius. In her opinion, Arius followed the teaching of Jesus. She hated politics and loved and feared God. The debate spread throughout the court. What had started as a Council, had also developed into a palace intrigue, in which the imperial eunuch and the palace cook also played a significant role. The Emperor, a master of strategy, remained aloof from the two factions, and kept everyone guessing. Being a pagan, he did not belong to any of the sects. This was the strongest point in his favour.

As the debate continued, it became evident to both parties that no clear-cut decision would be reached on the floor of the Council. However, they still both desired the support of the Emperor since, for the Pauline Church, it would mean an increase in power, and for the North African Church an end to persecutuion. In order to keep the favour of Constantine, all the bishops present agreed to make some changes in the religion. Princess Constantina had advised Eusebius of Nicomedia that the Emperor strongly desired a united Church, since a divided one endangered his Empire. However, if no agreement was reached within the Church, he might lose patience and withdraw his support for Christianity altogether. Should he take this course of action, the situation of the Christians would be even worse than before, and the teaching itself would be endangered even further. Counselled in turn by Eusebius, Arius and his followers adopted a passive role, but disassociated themselves from the following changes which the Council agreed to: since worship of the Roman Sun-god was very popular throughout the Empire at this time, and the Emperor was considered to be the manifestation of the Sun-god on earth, the Pauline Church therefore:

> —Declared the Roman Sun-day to be the Christian Sabbath;
> —Adopted the traditional birthday of the Sun-god, the twenty-fifth of December, as the birthday of Jesus;
> —Borrowed the emblem of the Sun-god, the cross of light, to be the emblem of Christianity;
> —And, decided to incorporate all the ceremonies which were performed at the Sun-god's birthday celebrations into their own ceremonies.

It must have been very comforting to Constantine to see the gulf which existed between Christianity and the religion of the Empire narrowed so considerably. The Church must have gone up in his estimation, and the likelihood of his support of the Church, once apparently weak, was now much firmer.

Finally, the dogma of Trinity was accepted as a fundamental doctrine of Christianity. It is possible that at this stage some of its adherents still had direct experience of the Divine Unity and affirmed it. For them, the doctrine of Trinity was no less than the means by which they attempted to describe what they witnessed. Since the language of Unity which Jesus had used was by now lost, they had resorted to using the terminology of neo-Platonic philosophy which, although it was not really adequate for the purpose, was all that they had left to indicate what they knew. However, this perspective was only open to very few people. "I pass over in silence," wrote Apuleius, "those sublime and Platonic doctrines understood by very few of the pious, and absolutely unknown to every one of the profane." [24]   Plato said that, "To discover the Creator was difficult, but to explain it to the vulgar is impossible."[25] Pythagoras said, "To tell of God among men of prejudicial opinion is not safe. To tell the truth or falsehood is equally dangerous."[26]

Although the use of this terminology was justified by some of those who were attempting to express the nature of the Divine Unity, in fact the attempt was doomed to failure. There was no way in which the Greek concept of "theos", which was not based on any revealed message, could successfully encompass the superior teaching revealed to Jesus. It was only the innovations made by Paul and his followers that made this marriage even seem possible in the first place. For those who could not grasp the ideas of the Greek philosophers there was only added confusion. This was the case with the majority of people who came into contact with the doctrine of Trinity. The confusion they fell into led to endless speculation, as the course which the Council itself had so clearly demonstrated. It is understandable how the doctrine came into being and why it was accepted, informally to begin with, and then officially at the Council of Nicea. It is also clear, on account of the confusion which the doctrine caused, why Arius insisted on returning to the source of Christianity for guidance, rather than resorting to the thinking of the Greek philosophers, which did not stem from the revelation of the prophet Jesus.

Once these changes had been secured at the Council of Nicea, the next step away from Jesus's teaching was made possible, and what is today known as the Nicene Creed was drawn up and attested to in writing by those present with the full support of the Emperor Constantine. It enshrined the view of the trinitarians and had the following anathema appended as a direct rejection of Arius's teaching:

> But as for those who say, "There was when he was not, and, before being born he was not, and that he came into existence out of nothing," or who assert that the Son of God is of a different hypostasis or substance, or is created, or is subject to alteration or change — these the Catholic Church anathematises.

Of those who signed the creed, some believed in it, some did not know what they were putting their names to, and some, the majority of the delegates in the Council, did not agree with the doctrine of Trinity, but, nevertheless, signed with mental reservation, to please the Emperor. One of them said: "The soul is nothing worse for a little ink."[27] Referring to this statement, Professor Gwatkin moans that it was not a pleasant scene for a historian. Perhaps this is because Professor Gwatkin does not write as a historian, but as an advocate who accepts a brief to plead a weak case!

These were the people who decided, under a pagan Emperor, what should be the test for an orthodox Christian. The result was as much a surprise to the trinitarians as to the Arian party. No one had expected the turn events would take. The idea of a universal test was a revolutionary change. It was not liked by anyone. The insertion of a direct condemnation of Arianism was a still more serious step. Even those who had consented to attesting the creed, did so with misgiving. When it came to signing in support of a term not found in the Scriptures, and without the authority of Jesus or his companions, they told themselves that they had signed under duress. The Council which had begun with such a fanfare had in reality completely failed to achieve anything.

The one person who knew what he was doing was the Emeror. He knew that a creed which was based not on conviction but on votes could not be taken seriously. One could believe in God, but could not elect Him by the democratic method. He knew how and why the bishops had signed the creed. He was determined not to create the impression that he had forced the bishops to sign against their convictions. So it was decided to take resort to a miracle of God to affirm and support the decision of the Council: the pile of the Gospels — the written record of Jesus's teaching — still lay in the middle of the hall where they had been placed at the beginning of the Council. According to one source, there were at least 270 versions of the Gospel at this time, while another states there were as many as 4,000 different Gospels. Even if one accepts the most conservative record, the number must have been quite overwhelming for a literate Christian of that time. The drawing up of a creed which contained ideas not to be found in the Gospels and, in some cases, in direct contradiction of what was in the Gospels, must have made matters more confusing for some people, while the continued existence of the Gospels must have been very inconvenient for others.

It was decided that all the different Gospels should be placed under a table in the Council Hall. Everyone then left the room and the door was locked. The bishops were asked to pray for the whole night that the correct version of the Gospel might come onto the top of the table. In the morning, the Gospels acceptable to Athanasius, Alexander's representative, were found neatly placed on top of the table. It was decided that all the Gospels remaining under the table should be burned. There is no record of who kept the key to the room that night.

It became a capital offence to possess an unauthorised Gospel. As a result, over a million Christians were killed in the years following the Council's decisions. This was how Athanasius tried to achieve unity among the Christians.

On their return from the Council, the bishops soon picked up the threads of the dispute which they had left on being summoned by the Emperor. The battle resumed and the old conflict continued. They forgot that they had signed the creed. The supporters of Arius did not hide the fact that they did not consider the creed to be an affirmation of true Christianity. Only Athanasius was perhaps loyal to it, but even his supporters had their own doubts. In the West the creed was almost unknown.

Saint Hillary was still a stranger to the Nicene Creed thirty years after the Nicene Council took place. He wrote:

> We anathematise those we defended. We condemn either the doctrine of others in ourselves or our own in others, and, reciprocally tearing one another to pieces, we have become the cause of each other's ruin. The translation (of the creed) from Greek to Latin was imperfect, for the Greek terms of Platonic philosophy, which had been consecrated by the Church, failed to express the mysteries of the Christian faith. Verbal defects in Scriptures might introduce into the Latin theology a long train of errors or perplexity. [28]

Sabinas, one of the early bishops of Thrace, describes all those who assembled in Nicea as being ignorant simpletons. He brands the faith they declared there as having been set forth by ignorant persons who had no intelligence in the matter. Socritus, the historian, compares the two combatants to armies engaged in battle at night, neither knowing the meaning of the words used by the other. Dr. Stanley writes that if Athanasius, when young, had adopted the moderation which he showed in his old age, then the Catholic Church would not have been divided, and much bloodshed would have been avoided.

Thus the Council, instead of bridging the gulf between the Christian sects, succeeded in widening it, and the bitterness between them was not diminished, but increased. Such was the temper of the Church, that, withstanding reason and persuasion, it learned the efficacy of force, and the first major bloodbath of the Arians began. The Goths and the Lombards were "converted" by the same means. The fearful loss of life, which was the result of the Crusades, followed. During the Thirty Years War in Europe, it was established that even belief in the Trinity was not enough: the Church had to be obeyed. By the time of the Reformation, the situation was such that Luther's actions were not even directed towards any real attempt to return to the true teaching of Jesus, but demonstrated a mere struggle for power.

Returning to the events which took place immediately after 325 A.D., we find that Bishop Alexander died in 328 A.D. A stormy election for the Bishopric of Alexandria followed. The Arians and Meletians put up a strong resistance, but Athanasius was declared, elected, and consecrated as a bishop. His election was disputed. Those who opposed his election complained of persecution, political intrigue and even magic.

Meanwhile, at Constantine's court, Constantina, his sister, who feared and loved God, continued to voice her opposition to the killing of the Christians. She never tried to hide the fact that she thought Arius represented true Christianity. She also opposed the treatment of Eusebius of Nicomedia who had been banished by the Emperor for his beliefs. At long last, she had her way, and Eusebius was allowed to come back. His return was a great blow to the Athanasian faction. The Emperor gradually began to lean towards the side of Arius. When he received news that the election of Athanasius was being disputed, he summoned the new Bishop to the capital. Athanasius, however, made excuses and did not go to

Constantinople. In 335 A.D., a Council was held in Tyre to celebrate the thirtieth year of Constantine's reign. Here Athanasius was obliged to attend. He was accused of episcopal tyranny, and the atmosphere was so charged with feeling against him that he left the Council without waiting to hear what decisions would be made. He was condemned. The bishops then gathered in Jerusalem where the condemnation of Athanasius was confirmed. Arius was taken back into the Church and allowed to receive communion.

The Emperor invited Arius and his friend Euzous to Constantinople. The peace between Arius and the Emperor was virtually complete, and to further this, the bishops again officially condemned Athanasius. In desperation, Athanasius decided to try and face the lion in his own den. He came in person to Constantinople, and audience was granted to him by the Emperor. Eusebius of Nicomedia was present on this occasion. He well knew that the decision made in Nicea had gone against Arius for political reasons. So, instead of starting an ecclesiastical debate which the Emperor would not have understood anyway, he accused Athanasius of hindering the supply of corn to the capital. This caught Athanasius completely by surprise. He discovered that someone else could also play the game at which he was so expert. The charge was easily proved and Athanasius was sent away to Trier in Gaul. Arius was appointed the Bishop of Constantinople. He died soon after, however, from poisoning, in 336 A.D. The Church called it a miracle, but the Emperor suspected murder. He appointed a commission to investigate the death which had taken place in such a mysterious manner. Athanasius was found to be responsible, and was condemned for the murder of Arius.

The Emperor, greatly moved by the death of Arius, and doubtlessly influenced by his sister, became a Christian. He was baptised by Eusebius of Nicomedia. He died only a year later in 337 A.D. Constantine, who had spent so much of his reign persecuting those who affirmed the Divine Unity, died in the faith of those he had killed.

Arius played an important part in the history of Christianity. He was not only largely the means by which Constantine finally accepted Christianity, but also represented those people who have attempted to follow the teaching of Jesus implicitly. At a time when this guidance was beginning to be seriously eroded, and when the memory of Jesus as a man who embodied his message was beginning to fade, Arius stands out as a man who was not prepared to accept this course of events with complacency.

He believed that God is absolutely One, and that there-fore this belief is absolutely simple. He believed that God is alone ingenerate, alone eternal, alone without beginning, alone good, alone almighty, alone unchangeable and unalter-able, and that His Being is hidden in eternal mystery from the outward eye of every creature. Arius opposed any idea of the manhood of God.

He earnestly pressed in favour of following Jesus im-plicitly. He was willing to recognise in him every attribute compatible with the isolation and Unity of God, but refused to compromise with any idea which led to a belief in mul-tiple Divinity. Thus, he felt bound to reject any dogma which accepted the divinity of Jesus. Since ingenerateness is the very essence of Divinity, there could be no son of God in any strict or primary sense.

If the act of generation is attributed to God, he said, it destroys the singularity of God. It also ascribes to God cor-poreality and passion which are attributes of man and imply that the Almighty is subject to necessity, which He is not. Thus, on every ground, it is impossible to ascribe the act of generation to God.

Arius also stated that since Jesus is finite, he is other than God, Who is Eternal. It is possible to visualise a time when Jesus did not exist, which again demonstrates that he is other than God. Jesus is not of the Essence of God, but a creature of God, essentially like other creatures, albeit definitely unique among men on account of his prophethood. Instead of sharing the Divine Essence, he does not even comprehend his own. He must depend, like every other creature, on the help of God's grace, while God is dependant on nothing. Like all mankind, he has free will and a nature capable of leading him to acts which are either pleasing or displeasing to God. However, although Jesus was potentially capable of acting in a manner displeasing to God, his own virtue kept him from doing so.

These basic tenets of Arius's belief have survived right up to the present day, and are still the foundation of the belief of many Unitarian Christians.

After Constantine's death in 337 A.D., the next Emperor, Constantius, also accepted the faith of Arius, and belief in the Divine Unity continued to be officially accepted as the orthodox Christianity. A conference held in Antioch in 341 A.D. accepted monotheism as the true basis of Christianity. This ruling was confirmed by another Council that was held in Sirmium in 351 A.D., again with the concurrence of the Emperor then in power. Thus, the teaching Arius had held to was accepted by an overwhelming majority of Christians. St. Jerome wrote in 359 A.D. that "the whole world groaned and marvelled to find itself Arian." [29] In the years that followed, the trinitarians grew in number, but, in 381 A.D., the official religion of the Emperor in Constantinople was declared to be that of Arius. However, the doctrine of Trinity gradually came to be the accepted basis of Christianity in the West. The phenomenon of "councils" meeting and passing "official" resolutions demonstrates how far even the orthodox Christianity in Europe had departed from what Jesus had taught. He himself had never resorted to this kind of organisation, which was usually to be found within the courts of the rulers.

In 387 A.D., Jerome completed his famous Vulgate Bible. This was the first Latin translation of some of the Scriptures which had been translated into Greek from the Hebrew texts. It included what is known today as the Old Testament. It was this Bible which became the basis of all other Bibles translated into other languages, and which was adopted by the Roman Catholic, and later the Protestant, Churches as their official book. Once it had become established, all other Gospels and Scriptures not included in Jerome's selection were almost completely destroyed by these two Churches at one stage or another. Thus, all contact with the real Jesus continued to be gradually lost.

The next important figure is that of Pope Honorius. A

contemporary of the Prophet Muhammad, peace and blessings of Allah be on him, he saw the rising tide of Islam, whose tenets very much resembled those of Arius. The mutual killing of Christians by each other was still fresh in his memory, and perhaps he thought that what he had heard of Islam might be applied in healing the differences between the Christians. In his letters, he began to support the doctrine of "one mind" within the doctrine of Trinity. He argued that if God had three independent minds, the result would be chaos. The logical conclusion pointed to the belief in the existence of One God.

The Council of Chalcedon in 451 A.D. had ruled that Christ's natures were indivisible. This influenced Honorius in concluding that there was a single will in Christ. He therefore argued that Christ took to himself a human nature free from the curse of original sin. According to this view, Christ had human will. Thus, belief in One God was indirectly affirmed within Pauline Christianity. That this kind of controversy had arisen at all is an indication of the degree to which Paul's innovations had taken hold of and confused people's minds. Pope Honorius died in October 638 A.D. In the same year, Emperor Heraclius officially accepted the doctrine of Honorius and issued an order that "All the Emperor's subjects are to confess the one will of Jesus." [30] The Synod of Constantinople which also took place in 638 A.D. supported the doctrine as "truly agreeing with Apostolic preaching."[31] The doctrine of Honorius was not officially challenged for about half a century. In 680 A.D., forty-two years after his death, a council was held in Constantinople and Pope Honorius was anathematised, since he "did not extinguish the flame of heretical teaching in its first beginning but fostered it by negligence," and, therefore, "allowed the immaculate faith to be stained."[32] This decision, whereby a Pope was denounced by his successor with the support of the Church, is unique in the history of the Papacy.

The Pauline Church, or rather, the Roman Catholic Church, as it came to be known, grew in size and power. This was largely due to its associations with the Roman Emperors. The more it compromised itself with those in authority, the more identified it became with them. During the eight centuries which followed the Council of Nicea, the Roman Catholic Church became firmly established with her headquarters not in Jerusalem, but in Rome. She acquired vast amounts of land and property in and around this city. They were known as the "Gift of Constantine". It became very dangerous for anyone to differ from the Roman Catholic Church, which came to have the support of the imperial army, as well as its own power. After 325 A.D., over a million Christians were killed for not subscribing to the doctrine of the Catholic Church. These were indeed Dark Ages, and few people in Europe dared to openly affirm the Unity of God.

While the Catholic Church was busy eliminating these dissenters who were branded as "heretics", the Muslims began to make themselves known on the periphery of the Christian world. Nearly all the followers of Jesus in North Africa recognised Islam as a further message from their Lord, which directly followed and superceded the guidance by which they had been living. They became Muslims. Only the "Christianity" of Europe remained.

The leaders at the Vatican must have seen the marked similarity between Islam and the unitarianism preached by Arius. Both believed in One God. Both accepted Jesus as a prophet who, nevertheless, was still a man. Both believed in the Virgin Mary and in the immaculate conception of Jesus. Both accepted the Holy Spirit. Both rejected the divinity which had been attributed to Jesus. So the hatred for the Arians was turned against the Muslims. Looking with this perspective, the Crusades cease to be an isolated phenomenon of Church history, but become an extension of the massacre of the Arians by the Pauline Church.

During this period, the Church did not ignore any opposition from within itself. A body known as the Inquisition was organised to investigate and eliminate any traces of "deviation" from the established doctrines of the Church. The exact record of how many people were murdered by this group is not known, but certainly a great number suffered and perished at their hands.

With the event of the Reformation, and the subsequent establishment of Protestant Churches, which also became very powerful, the doctrine of Trinity became even more firmly established, even though the Protestants and the Roman Catholics bitterly opposed each other over other issues such as the validity of the document which authorised the "Gift of Constantine". Some scholars took a closer look at the deed and discovered that it was a forgery. Since then, the Vatican has ceased to boast of it. The famous Thirty Years War between the Protestants and the Catholics was yet another indication that these Churches' battles were not fought with the intention of establishing the true guidance of Jesus in the land. Like the Pauline Church's agression towards the followers of Arius and later the Muslims, this war clearly demonstrated that what the Church wanted was power. In all these three events, the Church was fighting in order to establish its own existence as an institution, and not in order to spread what Jesus had taught.

As Islam continued to expand, a grand strategy was formulated to attack the Muslims both from the East and the West. It was hoped to join forces with a legendary Indian Christian king and, with his aid, conquer the whole world. In his efforts to reach India, Columbus discovered America, and Vasco de Gama discovered a new route to India. Both these discoveries turned out to be very profitable ventures financially. The Christians did not discover their legendary king nor did they eliminate Islam, but they colonised much of the world, and their leaders and traders became very wealthy as a result.

Despite the tremendous power of the Roman Catholic and Protestant Churches, they could not stamp out belief in the Divine Unity. Whether it became known as Arianism or Socianism or Unitarianism, it has survived within the Christian movement right up to the present day, as the following short biographies of its most outspoken adherents demonstrate.

Chapter 7

LATER UNITARIANS IN CHRISTIANITY

Michael Servetus (1511-1553)

Michael Servetus was born in Villanueva in Spain in 1511. He was the son of a local judge. He lived at a time when there was unrest in the established Church, and in a period when everyone was questioning the nature of Christianity. In 1517, when Servetus was six years old, Martin Luther started his revolt against the Roman Catholic Church. This resulted in his being excommunicated, and he became a leader of the new reformed "protestant" religion. This movement, known today as the Reformation, spread like wild fire, and even those who did not agree with Luther were forced to take notice of him. As well as this conflict, there was another closer to home: although the Muslims and the Christians in Spain had enjoyed better relations in the past, the results of the Crusades in the East caused the Christians to direct their anger against the Muslims in Spain. The organisation known as the Spanish Inquisition set about converting all people who were not Christian to Roman Catholicism. Any laxity in observing the outward rites of the Church resulted in severe punishment, if not death.

As he grew older and more informed, the young Servetus was appalled by the shedding of so much blood. There was a large settlement of Muslims and Jews in the country, and they were spared the sword only if they publicly confessed their faith to be that of the Roman Catholics and affirmed the formula of the Trinity. Imagine his excitement when, upon examining the Bible more closely, he found that the doctrine of Trinity was nowhere a part of its teaching. He further discovered that the Bible did not always support what was being taught by the Church. He was only twenty years old when he decided to tell the world the truth as he had found it, for it followed from this discovery that if the Christians accepted that there was only One God, then all cause for strife between the Christians and the Muslims would be ended, and both communities could live together in peace. This sensitive but inexperienced youth, his imagination fired with enthusiasm, felt that this end would most easily be achieved with the help of the leaders of the Reformation, who had, after all, already broken away from the Catholic Church. The new Protestant Churches would become unitarian, and with their help the Christians, the Muslims and the Jews would be able to live together in peace. A world of toleration would become a possibility, based on One God, the "Father" of the family of mankind.

Servetus was too young to realise that the minds of the leaders of the Reformation were still trapped in the same false metaphysics. He was to find that both Luther and Calvin would have nothing to do with his belief in the Unity of God. They feared that the Reformation would go too far. A number of ceremonies of the Catholic Church were abolished, but they were afraid to rediscover the original teaching of Jesus, since this would have added to their difficulties and entailed a diminishing of their own power and reputation. Perhaps they were unaware of how far the practises of the Roman Catholics had deviated from the life which Jesus lived. Certainly, they took great pains to contain the reformed religion within the frame-work of Catholic orthodoxy. Their quarrel was not so much with the theology of Rome as with its organisation, and particularly over the question as to who should rule the Church. The beliefs of Servetus posed a threat to both of these organisations, and so, ironically, his appeal to the Reformists only caused them to join forces with the Catholic Church in order to protect their common interest. None of this was fully grasped by the young Servetus.

He had every hope in the leaders of the Reformation, for he was convinced that Roman Catholicism was not the religion of Jesus. His studies had shattered his belief in the doctrine of Trinity and resulted in his believing that there was One God and that Jesus was one of His prophets. His conviction had been strengthened by his witnessing of the coronation of Charles V of Spain by the Pope. In 1527, Charles V invaded and sacked Rome. At first, he imprisoned the Pope, but then realised the expediency of having the Pope as an ally. A captive Pope would hardly influence the people in the way he wanted, so he restored some measure of freedom to him. To demonstrate the good terms they were on, he decided to have a coronation at the hands of the Pope. Strictly speaking, it was not necessary. It was like having a church wedding after a civil ceremony. The king's predecessors had discontinued this practise, but he felt that he was now powerful enough, and the Pope weak enough, to revive it. The ceremony was not held in Rome, but in Bologna, since, according to the popular belief, "where the Pope is, there is Rome." Servetus witnessed the gorgeous spectacle and it filled him with revulsion for the Catholic Church. Describing the event, he wrote:

> With these very eyes I saw him (the Pope) bourne with pomp on the shoulders of princes, making with his hand the sign of the cross, and adored in the open streets by all the people kneeling to such a point that those who were able to kiss his feet or slippers counted themselves more fortunate than the rest and declared that they had obtained many indulgences, and that on this account the infernal pains would be remitted for many years. Oh vilest of all beasts, most brazen of harlots.[1]

Thus Servetus's hopes were directed towards the leaders of the Reformation. He felt sure that if he could bring the error of the doctrine of the Trinity to their notice, then they would abandon their belief in this dogma. This misconception was to cost him his life. He left Spain and resided in Toulouse where he studied medicine and eventually took his doctor's degree in 1534. In the years that followed, he soon became a working physician, but, during all this time, his interest was directed towards re-establishing pure Christianity. He did not stay long at any one place, but travelled far and wide in search of people who were open-minded enough to listen to what he was sure was the true Christianity as taught by Jesus.

He went to Basle to meet the then famous Oeclompadius, who was one of the leaders of the Reformation. He had several meetings with him and the talk mainly centered on the two natures of Christ. Servetus denied the belief that Jesus pre-existed the creation of the world. He pointed out that the Jewish prophets always spoke of the "Son of God" in the future tense. However, he found that his views were not acceptable to the Protestants in Switzerland, and he left Basle in 1530. This was a great shock to him, since he had hoped that, unlike Catholic France, the Protestants would give a patient ear to what he had to say about Jesus and his teaching. He went to Strasbourg only to find that he could not earn a living there. Due to his ignorance of the German language, he was unable to practice medicine, and so he was forced to go to Lyons. Servetus also conducted a lengthy correspondence with Calvin throughout this period after his departure from Spain, but without any favourable reponse from Calvin, who was not altogether interested in trying to embody the teaching of Jesus, but who did want to remain leader of his movement.

Since all his attempts to influence people by personal contact had failed, Servetus printed his views in a book which he called *The Errors of Trinity*. It was published in 1531. In the same year, he published another book called *Two Dialogues on Trinity*. The two books took the whole of Europe by storm. No one had ever written such a daring book within living memory. The result was that the Church hounded Servetus from one place to another. Servetus was forced to change his name, but not his views. From 1532 up until his death, he lived under an assumed name. Servetus still appeared to have a childlike faith in Calvin, who, after reading the books, developed a deep dislike for this presumptuous young man who dared teach him theology. Servetus continued to write to Calvin and the leader's anger increased when he found that Servetus refused to accept his views. The leaders of the Protestant movement feared that it might suffer a set-back if the views of this young enthusiast became known to the people. The reformers also feared that persecution by the Catholic Church might increase if the Protestant doctrine deviated too far from the Catholic doctrine.

Thus, Servetus, instead of converting the Protestants to his views, forced them to embrace the dogma of Trinity even more zealously. Luther, for instance, publicly condemned him in 1539.

Throughout this time, Servetus continued to practice as a doctor, and became a very popular physician. In spite of the fact that a doctor's profession is very time-consuming, Servetus found time to supervise the printing of a Bible. It was published in 1540. Servetus wrote a preface to it in which he questioned whether a text of Scripture could have more than one meaning. Calvin wrote and replied in the affirmative, but Servetus disagreed with him. Today the Calvinist Church accepts the very principle of interpretation which Calvin alleged was one of the greatest offences of Servetus against orthodoxy. Servetus stated that he was following the views held by the early apostles who belonged to the Antiochene school of Christianity.

It is refreshing to discover that at the height of this bitter controversy, Servetus found refuge and peace in the house of his old friend, Peter Palmier, who was then the Roman Catholic Archbishop of Vienna. He lived there for thirteen years, enjoying the freedom to practice medicine, and he became quite renowned as a physician. He was one of the first people in Europe to write about the principle of the circulation of the blood. He also wrote a book on geography. In spite of his literary attainments, the issues facing Christianity always held the centre of his attention. He continued to write to Calvin, still hoping to win him over to his views, but Calvin firmly rejected the beliefs expressed in his letters. Servetus refused to accept the *obiter dicta* of Calvin. Calvin, who was at that time recognised as the foremost thinker of the Protestant religion, felt he was justified in expressing annoyance with Servetus for daring to challenge his rulings in matters of religion. Servetus refused to accept Calvin as an indisputable authority on religion. Calvin wrote back in anger and Servetus replied in turn with sarcasm. Servetus then wrote another book called *The Restoration of Christianity,* and sent an advance copy of the manuscript to Calvin. When the book was published, it was found to have seven chapters, the first and last of which were devoted entirely to the doctrines of Christianity. The fifth chapter contained copies of thirty letters which had passed between Servetus and Calvin. It exposed the fact that, whatever merits Calvin might possess, he lacked what is known as Christian meekness. The book resulted in Servetus being condemned yet again, both by the Catholic and Protestant Churches. They united in their efforts to have the book completely destroyed, and were so thorough that not more than two copies are known to exist today. A facsimile of the book was published in 1791, but copies of this book were also destroyed. In a letter written in 1546, Calvin threatened Servetus, saying that if he ever came to Geneva he would not allow him to escape with his life. Servetus did not seem to believe him, but Calvin was as good as his word. When Servetus later came to Geneva and went to see him, still convinced that a meeting of minds was possible, Calvin had him arrested by the Roman Catholics and thrown into prison on a charge of heresy.

Servetus had become so popular as a physician that he succeeded in escaping from the prison with the help of some of his former patients. He decided to go to Naples. His route lay through the city of Geneva. He thought he had disguised himself sufficiently to escape detection, but he was wrong. While passing through the city, he was recognised and arrested once more. This time he did not escape. At his trial, he was found guilty of heresy. Some of the judgement ran as as follows:

> Servetus confesses that in his book he called believers in the Trinity, Trinitarians and Atheists. He called this Trinity a diabolical monster with three heads. . . He called the infant baptism an invention of the devil and sorcery. . . This entails the murder and ruin of many souls. Moreover, he wrote a letter to one of the ministers in which, along with other and numerous blasphemies, he declared our evangelical religion to be without faith and without God, and that in place of God we have a three-headed Cerberus. Addressing Servetus, the Court says that you had neither shame nor horror of setting yourself against the Divine Majesty of the Holy Trinity, and so you have obstinately tried to infect the world with your stinking heretical poison. . . For these and other reasons desiring to purge the

> Church of God of such infection and cut off the rotten
> member. . . we now, in writing, give final sentence and con-
> demn you, Michael Servetus, to be bound and taken to the
> Chapel and there attached to a stake and burned with your
> book to ashes. And so you shall finish your days and give
> example to others who would commit the like.[2]

On the 26th of October, 1553, Servetus was fastened to the trunk of a tree fixed in the earth, his feet just touching the ground. A crown of straw and leaves sprinkled over with brimstone was placed on his head. Bundles of wood inter-mingled with green oaken faggots still in leaf were piled around his legs. His body was then bound to the stake with an iron chain and a course twisted rope thrown around his neck. The wood was then lit. The fire tormented him, but did not burn him severely. Seeing this, a few onlookers felt compassion for him and added more fuel in order to end his misery. According to one eye-witness, Servetus was writhing for about two hours before he died. A copy of *The Errors of Trinity* had been tied to his waist before the wood was lit. It is said that the book was rescued by someone, and that the half-burnt book still exists. Celsus relates that the constancy of Servetus in the midst of the fire induced many to go over to his beliefs. Calvin made it an express subject of complaint that there were so many people who cherished and revered his memory. As Castillo, a follower of Servetus, said: "To burn a man is not to prove a doctrine."[3] In later years, the people of Geneva were to remember him by erecting a statue, not to Calvin, but to the man he was responsible for burning alive.

Cowper was moved to write these lines:

> They lived unknown
> Till persecution dragged them into fame
> And chased them up to heaven. Their ashes flew
> No marble tells us whither. With their names
> No bard embalms and sanctifies his song.
> And history so warm on meaner themes
> Is cold on this.[4]

Servetus's death was by no means an isolated incident. This kind of thing was happening throughout Europe at this time, as the following passage from Motley's *Rise of the Dutch Republic* indicates:

> Upon the 15th of February 1568, a sentence of the Holy Office condemned all the inhabitants of the Netherlands to death as heretics. From this universal doom only a few persons, especially named, were excepted. A proclamation of King Philip II of Spain, dated ten days later, confirmed this decree of the Inquisition, and ordered it to be carried into instant execution. . . Three millions of people, men, women and children, were sentenced to the scaffold in three lines. Under the new decree, the executions certainly did not slacken. Men in the highest and the humblest positions were daily and hourly dragged to the stake. Alva, in a single letter to Philip II, cooly estimates the number of executions which were to take place immediately after the expiration of Holy Week at "eight hundred heads."[5]

A few excerpts from *The Errors of Trinity,* which caused such violent actions, follow. Servetus writes:

> The philosophers have invented a third separate being truly and really distinct from the other two, which they call the third Person, or the Holy Spirit, and thus they have contrived an imaginary Trinity, three beings in one nature. But in reality three Gods, or one threefold God, are foisted upon us under the pretence, and in the name of Unity... For with them it is very easy, taking the words in their strict sense, for three beings to exist, which they say and yet strictly, simply, and really, so different or distinct yet one is born of another, and one is breathed out of the others, and yet all these three are shut up in one jar. Since I am unwilling to mis-use the word Persons, I shall call them the first being, the second being, and the third being, for in the Scripture I find no other name for them. . . Admitting therefore these three, which after their fashion they call Persons, they freely admit a plurality of beings, a a plurality of entities, a plurality of Essences, a plurality of substances, and taking the word God strictly, they will have a plurality of Gods.

He continues:

> If this is so, then why the Tritorites are blamed, who say that there are three Gods, for they also contrive three Gods or one threefold one. These threefold Gods of theirs form one composite substance. And although some will not use the word implying that the three have been put together, yet they do use a word that they are constituted together, and that God is constituted out of three beings. It is clear therefore that they are Tritorites and we have a threefold God. We have become Atheists, men without any God. For as soon as we try to think about God, we are turned aside to three phantoms, so that no kind of unity remains in our conception. What else is being without God but being unable to think about God, when there is always present to our understanding a haunting kind of confusion of three beings, by which we are forever deluded into supposing that we are thinking about God. . . They seem to be living in another world while they dream of such things for the kingdom of heaven knows none of this nonsense and it is in another way unknown to them, that Scripture speaks of the Holy Spirit.

He adds:

> How much this tradition of the Trinity has alas, alas! been the laughing stock of Mohammedons only God knows. The Jews also shrink from giving adherence to this fancy of ours, and laugh at our foolishness about the Trinity, and on account of its blasphemies, they do not believe that this is the Messiah promised in their Law. And not only the Mohammedons and the Hebrews, but the very beasts of the field, would make fun of us, did they grasp our fantastic notion, for all the workers of the Lord bless the One God. . . .This most burning plague, therefore, was added and superimposed, as it were, on the new gods which have recently come, which our fathers did not worship. And this plague of philosophy was brought upon us by the Greeks, for they above all men are most given to philosophy; and we, hanging upon their lips, have become philosophers, and they never understood the passages of the Scriptures which they adduced with regard to this matter.

Servetus also stressed what he believed to be the true nature of Jesus:

> Some are scandalised at my calling Christ the prophet, because they happen not themselves to apply to him the epithet, they fancy that all who do so are chargeable with Judaism and Mohametism, regardless of the fact that the Scriptures and ancient writers call him the prophet.[6]

Michael Servetus was one of the most outspoken critics of the established Church of his time. It earned him the singular distinction of being burnt to death by the Catholics with the aid of the Protestants. He combined within himself all that was best in the Renaissance and the Reformation, and came near to fulfilling the ideal of his age which was to produce a "universal man" with "pansophic" knowledge. He was proficient in medicine, geography, Biblical scholarship and theology. The diversity of his learning gave him a breadth of vision which was denied to men who were less educated than he. Perhaps the most significant part of his life was his clash with Calvin. It was certainly a personal conflict, but it was more than that. It was a rejection of the Reformation which was prepared to alter the form and not the content of a decadent Church. It cost him his life, but although Servetus is dead, his belief in the Divine Unity still lives. He is still regarded by many as "the founder of modern Unitarianism."

Not everyone who shared the beliefs of Servetus also shared his fate, as is shown by the following letter by Adam Neuser, who was his contemporary. It was addressed to the leader of the Muslims in Constantinople, Emperor Selim II. It is included in "Antiquities Palatinae" which is now in the Archives at Heidelberg.

> I, Adam Neuser, a Christian born in Germany and advanced to the dignity of Preacher to the people in Heidelberg, a city where the most learned men at this day in Germany are to be found, do fly for refuge to your Majesty with a profound submission conjuring you for the love of God and your Prophet, on whom be the peace of God, to receive me into the number of your subjects and those of your people that believe in God. For by the grace of the Omnipotent God, I see, I know, and I believe with my whole heart that your Doctrine and your Religion are pure,

121

clear, and acceptable to God. I am firmly persuaded that my Retreat from among the idolatrous Christians will engage many persons of Consideration to embrace your Belief and your Religion, especially since many of the most learned and most considerable amongst them are herein of the same sentiments with me as I shall inform your Majesty by word of mouth. As to what concerns myself I am certainly one of those of whom it is said in the thirteenth chapter of the Al Coran: The Christians show us more good will than the Jews; and when their Priests and Bishops, provided they are not imprudent and opinionated, understand the commandments which the Prophet of God gave, and thereby acknowledge the truth, they say with tears in their eyes, O God! We hope from our Hearts that since we believe the same things that the good people do, Thou wilt also make us enter into the communion: For why should not we believe in God and in Him who is manifested to us by the Truth?

Certainly, O Emperor! I am one of those that read the Al Coran with joy. I am one of those that desire to be of your People and I give testimony before God that the Doctrine of your Prophet, upon whom be the peace of God, is of undoubted Truth. For this reason I most humbly supplicate your Majesty for the love of God and of your Prophet to be graciously pleased to hear me' and know after what manner the God of Mercy hath revealed this Truth to me.

But first of all your Majesty ought to be entirely persuaded that I have not recourse to your protection as some Christians are accustomed, who because of their crimes, thefts, murders, or adultries, cannot live with safety among the people of their own Religion. For I had resolved above a year ago to fly for Refuge to you, and was advanced in my way as far as Presburg but not understanding the Hungarian language I could go no further and against my will was constrained to return to my country which I should not have ventured to do if I had fled for any crime. Besides nothing constrains me to embrace your Religion, for who could force me to it being unknown to your people, and at so great a distance from them?

So your Majesty ought not to place me in the number of those Christians who being conquered and made prisoners by your subjects embrace your Religion but not with good will and who so soon as they find occasion run away and renounce the true faith. Wherefore I again supplicate your Majesty to lend attention to what I am going to say and to be informed of the true course of my retreat to your Dominion.

Being promoted to the dignity of Preacher in the famous University of Heidelburg by the Elector Palatine who next to the Emperor is the most powerful prince in Germany, I began to weigh maturely within myself the divers dissensions and divisions of our Christian religion: for so many persons as there are amongst us there are so many opinions and sentiments. I began with abstracting from all the Doctors and Interpreters of the Scriptures who have wrote and taught since the days of the Prophet Jesus Christ. I tied myself only to the commandments of Moses and to the Gospel. Then I called upon God inwardly with a most religious application and prayed him to shew me the right way that I may not be in the danger to mislead myself and my hearers. Then it pleased God to reveal to me the "Articles of the Invocation of the One Only God", upon which Article I composed a book in which I prove that the Doctrine of Jesus Christ did not consist in asserting that he was himself a God as the Christians falsely allege: but that there is only one God who has no son consubstantial with him. I dedicated this book to your Majesty and I am very sure that the most able men amongst the Christians are not capable of refuting it. And wherefore indeed should I associate to God another God like unto him? Moses had forbid it and Jesus Christ never taught it. Afterwards fortifying myself from day to day by the grace of God, and understanding that the Christians abuse all the benefits of Jesus Christ as formerly the Jews abused the brazen serpent . . . I concluded that nothing pure is to be found amongst the Christians and that all they have is falsified. For they have perverted by their false interpretations almost all the writing of Moses and the Gospel which I have shewn in a book wrote with my own hand and which I shall present to your Majesty. When I say that the Christians have falsified and corrupted the commandments of Moses and the Gospel I mean only the words and the sense. For the doctrine of Moses, of Jesus and of Mahomet agree in everything and are not contrary to anything . . . the Al Coran gives a very advantageous testimony to Moses and Jesus Christ. But it insists principally upon the Christians corrupting the commandments of Moses and the Gospel of Jesus Christ by their false interpretations. Indeed if the Word of God was faithfully interpreted there would be no difference amongst the Jews, Christians and Turks. Thus what the Al Coran so often repeats is true. The doctrine of Mahomet destroys all the false interpretations of the Scriptures and teaches the true sense of the Word of God . . .

After that by the grace of God I understood there was but one only God, that I had observed that the doctrine of Jesus Christ was not taught as it ought to have been, that all the ceremonies of the Christians were very much different from their first institutions. I began to think I was the only man of my opinion in the World. I had not seen Al Coran and among us Christians there was care taken to spread in all parts such infamous and scandalous reports against everything that concerns the doctrines of Mahomet that the poor people who are made to believe things as so many truths are seized with horror and run out of themselves at the very name of Al Coran. Nevertheless by the effect of Divine Providence that book fell into my hands for which I give thanks to God. To God I say who knows that in my prayers I invoke him for your Majesty and for all those that belong to you. I sought all effects of ways to impart the knowledge of these truths to my Auditors and in case they would not receive this doctrine I resolved to ask leave of the Electors to abandon my charge and retire to you. I began to attack by way of dispute in all the churches and in the schools some points of our doctrine and obtained what I wished: For I brought the matter to such a point that it was known to all the States of the Empire and I drew several learned men to my side. The Elector (fearing an invasion from the Emperor Maximillian) . . . deposed me . . . [7]

This letter fell into the hands of Emperor Maximillian. Neuser was arrested along with his friends who included two men called Sylvan and Mathias Vehe. They were thrown into prison. On the 15th of July 1570 Neuser escaped only to be retaken. He escaped a second time but was again arrested. Their trial continued for two years. It was decided to cut off the head of Sylvan. At this point, Neuser again escaped. This time he reached Constantinople and embraced Islam.

Francis David (1510-1579)

Francis David was born in Kolozsar, Transylvania, in 1510. He was a brilliant student, winning a scholarship to Wittenberg where he trained for the Catholic priesthood for four years. On his return to Kolozsar, he was appointed as rector of a Catholic school. He then accepted Protestantism, left the Catholic school and in 1555 became the rector of a Lutheran school. When the split in the Reform movement between Luther and Calvin took place, David joined the Calvinist party. The Reformation was still young and in this atmosphere the spirit of enquiry was not yet completely inhibited. Discussion was allowed on every aspect of Christianity. The Reformed Church had not yet adopted a fixed doctrine and there was room to think freely. In this situation, it was possible to advocate a freedom of belief in which each individual was only accountable to God.

The two dogmas which caused most confusion in the minds of the general public, and which defied rational explanation, were those of the Divinity of Jesus and the Trinity. David's mind was troubled by these inexplicable articles of faith. He could not see why anyone who believed in these mysteries without trying to understand them was considered to be a better Christian. He was not prepared to follow a faith blindly. Gradually he reached the conclusion that Jesus was not Divine, and affirmed belief in the existence of One God.

This belief already had strong adherents in Poland. The leaders of this group were two: Blandrata, the court physician, and a man called Socianus. While David was still formulating his idea of faith, King John of Transylvania fell ill and called Blandrata to treat him. David met Blandrata during his stay there and this confirmed his acceptance that belief in One God was the true basis of Christianity. In 1566, David produced a confession of faith which showed the position of the dogma of Trinity in the light of what the Bible actually said. In it he disowned the scholastic concept of Father, Son and Holy Ghost. Blandrata, for his part, published a paper in which he formulated seven propositions refuting these doctrines both positively and negatively. In the same year, on the recommendation of Blandrata, King

John appointed David as his court preacher. As such, David became spokesman for the unitarian party in the national debates called by the king to clarify the religious issues of that time. He was an incomparable public speaker, one who, as a contemporary said of him, "seemed to have the Old and New Testament at his tongue's end." [8]

The major debates during John's reign were at Gyuala-fehervat in 1566 and 1568, and at Nagyvarad in 1569. The first debate was inconclusive. The king, however, was impressed by the arguments of Blandrata and David. So, in 1567, a decree of toleration was passed. It declared that

> in every place the preachers shall preach and explain the Gospel according to his understanding of it, and if the congregation likes, so far so good; if not, no one shall compel them, and they shall keep the preacher whose doctrine they approve. None shall annoy or abuse the preacher . . . or allow anyone to be imprisoned or punished . . . on account of his teaching, for faith is the gift of God. [9]

The second synod in 1568 was called in order to establish whether the doctrines of the Trinity and the eternal deity of Jesus were taught in the Scriptures. David, who was a very powerful and convincing speaker, could not be disproved. When his opponents realised that they were losing the debate, they resorted to abuse, which only served to help convince the king that David's arguments were genuine. The debate lasted for ten days. It established unitarianism as a popular faith and David as its champion.

During this time the writings of Michael Servitus, which had been almost completely destroyed, were smuggled into Transylvania and were translated into the local language. They were widely read and served to strengthen the unitarian movement in Eastern Europe.

The third synod, held in Hungary in 1569, was, in the judgement of one Hungarian historian, "the decisive debate" which produced the "final triumph of Unitarianism." [10] The king himself presided over it, and it was attended by all the highest ranking civil and military officials of the kingdom. David's arguments were these:

The view of Trinity held by the Pope in Rome is really a belief in four or five gods: one substance, God, three separate persons, each of whom are said to be God, and one man, Christ, who is also regarded as being God. According to Francis David, God is only One, the Father, from Whom and by Whom is everything, and Who is above everything, Who created everything through the word of his wisdom and the breath of His mouth. Outside of this God, there is no other god, neither three, neither four, neither in substance, neither in persons, because the Scripture nowhere teaches anything about a triple God.

The Church's God-Son who was supposed to have been born of the substance of God from the beginning of eternity is nowhere mentioned in the Scriptures, nor is a God-Son who would be the second person of the Trinity descended from heaven and become flesh. This is only human invention and superstition and as such is to be discarded.

Jesus did not create himself — the Father gave him his eminence. The Father had him begotten by the Holy Spirit. The Father sanctified him and sent him into the world.

The relationship of Christ with God is only of a kind which God gave him, God remaining in his Divine Sovereignty above everyone else.

There is no difference in time before God — for God everything is in the present tense — but the Scriptures nowhere teach that Jesus was born from the beginning of eternity.

The debate lasted for five days. It was again conclusive. In his final address, the king ordered that the unitarians be given full liberty of conscience. Melius, the leader of the Lutheran party, was warned not to play the pope, nor burn books, nor to use force to convert the people.

David afterwards summed up the debate in these words:

> I followed the line of Scripture, but my opponents hid it in a bag; they turned light into darkness when they made three of the Father God and two of Christ. Their religion is self-contradictory to the extent that even they cannot present it as a whole. Nevertheless, they will see that even against their will God will prove His Truth. [11]

The result of this debate was that nearly the whole city

of Kolozsar became believers in One God. This belief spread out into the countryside and became the faith of a large majority of the people there. Unitarianism became one of the four officially "received religions", that is, one protected by law. By 1571, there were almost five hundred unitarian congregations in Transylvania. It was in this year that King John died. Although the popularity of unitarianism continued to grow, the new king, King Stephen, did not share King John's tolerance, and he reversed the policy of the freedom of conscience initiated by his predecessor. Life was made difficult for those who affirmed the Divine Unity, and, to make matters worse, David fell out with both Blandrata and Socianus. David was an uncompromising unitarian and could not bear anything to be associated with God, even indirectly. Socianus made a distinction between adoration and invocation directed towards Jesus. One could not invoke him, but one could adore him. David could not tolerate this. Even the Polish unitarians found the distinction too subtle, since little difference could be perceived between the two. In common thought and daily practise, this distinction tended to become blurred, and, during the course of worship, it could not be honestly said whether a person was adoring or invoking.

The Roman Catholics enjoyed the support of the new king, and the division between the leaders of the unitarian movement gave them additional strength. In a Diet at Torda in 1571, a general complaint was made that some pastors were guilty of innovations. This was repeated in Diets of 1573, 1576, and 1578, and the complaints made became more specific until they were pointedly made at Francis David. Blandrata had in the meanwhile become increasingly friendly with the king and appreciated the reputation and wealth this association brought. In 1578, he openly opposed David, and advised David not to pursue his beliefs any more. David, however, was not prepared to abandon his convictions merely to save his skin. Blandrata, after a lifelong struggle to establish belief in the Divine Unity, had become infirm and old and wanted a rest. He did not want to invite fresh trouble on himself or his friends. They knew that what David was doing was very dangerous, and felt that matters would be made much easier for them all if he followed their example.

David remained unmoved. He not only continued to preach, but also began to write and distribute leaflets containing his beliefs, despite opposition. Blandrata invited Socianus to Transylvania in order to persuade David to change his views and accept the distinction which he made between the adoration and the invocation of Jesus. Socianus came and stayed as David's guest. His persuasion was to no avail, but it was agreed that David should summarise his beliefs in writing, and that they should then be presented to a synod of the Polish Unitarian Church. David did this, making the following four points:

The strict command of God is that no one should be invoked save God the Father, Creator of heaven and earth.

Christ, the teacher of Truth, taught that no one is to be invoked besides the heavenly Father.

True invocation is defined as that which is paid to the Father in spirit and in truth.

The forms of simple prayer are directed not to Christ, but to the Father.

Socianus wrote against these views, and David responded again in writing in support of his views. The discussion became heated and then gradually bitter and personal. The result was that Blandrata and David were now open enemies. This gave the Catholic king the support he needed and the order was given to place David under house arrest and to allow no one to see him. David found out about the order before it had been executed. He immediately began to preach in as many places as was possible, in churches, and in the public square, and openly told the people the reason for his impending arrest. He declared: "Whatever the world might try to do, it will nevertheless become clear to the whole world that God is One." [12]

After his arrest, David was taken before a Diet, and Blandrata acted both as the chief prosecutor and also as chief witness for the prosecution. The strain on David was so great that he fell ill. He had to be carried about in a chair for he could hardly move his arms and legs. He was condemned to life imprisonment, and was put in the dungeon of a castle built on the summit of a high hill. No one knows how much he suffered during the five months he was there. He died in November 1579 and was given the burial of a criminal in an unknown grave.

After his death, a poem was found written on the wall of his cell. Part of it reads:

Twice ten years I have loyally served my country
And to the Prince my fidelity hath been proven.
Ask you the crime that the Fatherland hates so?
This alone is it: "One God not three" I have wor-
    shipped.

The last lines of the poem are:

Nor lightening, nor cross, nor sword of the Pope,
    nór death's visible face,
No power whatever can stay the progress of Truth.
What I have felt I have written, with faithful heart
    I have spoken.
After my death the dogmas of untruth shall fall. [13]

Although David died, his movement continued; and indeed, for many years, the Transylvanian unitarians were referred to as "of Francis David's religion." Today his arguments are accepted as "plain, straightforward and scriptural. The verdict of all reasonable men is given in favour of David." [14] Blandrata who had played such a great part in David's death became very popular with the Catholics and the king. He became so rich that his heir was not prepared to wait for his natural death and murdered him. Although the persecution of the unitarians continued, it did not, as is usual, produce the result which the persecutors desired to achieve. David was soon sanctified as a Martyr and his example provided the unitarians with an inspiration which survived generations of organized persecution.

The number of unitarians in Transylvania diminished considerably, but began to increase in the south of Hungary which was under Turkish rule, for the Muslim rulers were enjoined by the Qur'an to allow the followers of other faiths to live in peace, provided that they did not interfere with the practices of Islam. Thus, under Turkish rule, all Christians enjoyed a freedom which did not exist in any of the Christian countries. They were even allowed to practice their personal laws. Taking advantage of this freedom, for instance, a Calvinist bishop had a unitarian hanged for heresy. Another unitarian brought this act to the notice of the Turkish governor in Buda. He ordered the Calvinist bishop to appear before him, and after a trial, the bishop and his two assistants were sentenced to death as murderers. The unitarian minister interceded on behalf of the condemned bishop, saying that he had not sought revenge, but only that such incidents should be prevented from happening again. So the culprits were not hanged, but a heavy fine was imposed on them instead.

The unitarians enjoyed peace under the Turkish government for nearly a century. They had about sixty churches in the country ruled by the Turks. With the decline of the Turkish rule, however, this freedom of belief also declined, and the people were again forced to become Roman Catholics. Those who refused were violently persecuted. By the end of the nineteenth century, however, it no longer became possible to persecute people openly, and the number of unitarians again began to increase. The unitarian movement still survives in Eastern Europe today, and David's influence is still to be found in the hearts of this growing brotherhood.

There is some speculation as to how much contact Francis David had with the Muslims. Certainly, his beliefs come very close to Islam, and at least in one place in his writings he openly refers to the Qur'an in support of these beliefs:

> It is not without reason said in Qur'an that Jesus can give no assistance to those who worship him because they would have him pass for God contrary to the doctrine taught by him. . .so they are worthy of blame who teach that we ought to worship and invoke Jesus; he himself having taught that the Father is to be invoked. . .God is not threefold but One. [15]

Of all the abuses which were hurled at David, however, he was never called a Muslim, perhaps because both the Calvinists and the Catholics feared that to say this would have brought the then powerful Turkish rulers to the aid of the unitarians. The apparent ignorance of the Turkish rulers with regard to the unitarian movement, whose beliefs were so close to their own, can perhaps be ascribed to the degeneration of their own Islam. One of the main criticisms of David was that if his views were accepted, then the distinction between Judaism and Christianity would tend to disappear, and the latter would relapse into the former. Even Blandrata openly taunted David by saying that he was returning to Judaism. He never refuted any of David's arguments, but attempted to discredit him by playing on the popular sentiment against the Jews, and appeared to have forgotten that each new prophet came to reaffirm and extend the teaching of the prophet before him. Francis David's importance lies in the fact that by his affirmation of the Divine Unity he reaffirmed Jesus's position in the prophetic tradition without denying in any way the prophets who came before and after him. Further, he reminded people that true faith and trust in God together with a life lived according to the example and teaching of Jesus were sufficient for this life and the one after it. [16]

Lelio Francesco Maria Sozini (1525 – 1562)

Lelio Sozini was born in 1525, and he became a jurist whose legal studies led him to researches in Hebrew and the Bible. When he was a young man, he left Bologna and moved to the area around Venice where a degree of religious freedom existed which was unknown to other parts of Italy. The writings of Servetus had found their way there and influenced many. Among those who embraced his belief, writes Wallace in his *Anti-trinitarian Biography,* there were "many persons of distinguished rank and eminent attainments in the city of Venice." [17] Since these opinions were not openly tolerated by the Senate, those who held them began to meet in secret. Their intention was to study the truth of Christianity and to re-establish the teaching of Jesus in its purity. Lubinietski in his *History of the Reformation in Poland*, writes:

> They came to the conclusion that there is but one God. Jesus was truly a man. He was conceived by the operation

of the Holy Ghost in the chaste womb of a virgin. The doctrine of Trinity and the divinity of Jesus were the opinions introduced by pagan philosophers.[18]

Lelio met these people and, writes Wallace, "soon became enamoured of these views and embraced them with all the ardour and ingenuousness of a youthful mind bent upon the pursuit and acquisition of religious truth."[19] A gnostic called Camillo influenced him especially. A new vista opened up before him. Up until then, his mind had been inhibited by the rigid dogmas of the established church. He now felt a new freedom which he had not experienced before. His life had taken on a new meaning, and he wished to devote himself to the search for truth. It is known that the number of the members in the Secret Society of Vinecenza, as it is known today, was over forty. When the existence of this society was ultimately discovered, some of its members were arrested and put to death, while others were fortunate enough to make their escape and find asylum in other countries. Other known members of this society besides Lelio Sozini, were Ochinus, Darius Sozini (Lelio's cousin), Alciati and Bucalis. There is a strong tradition that the last two of these men ultimately embraced Islam. Dr. White, in his Brompton lectures, called the disciples of Sozini "followers of the Arabian prophet."[20]

While the existence of this society was still a secret, Lelio Sozini's attention was drawn to two men outside it. One was Servetus and the other was Calvin. Servetus had the courage openly to declare his belief in the Divine Unity, whilst Calvin had made himself known as a force to be reckoned with in the Reformist circles of Europe.

Sozini decided to see Calvin first. When Sozini met him, he was utterly disappointed to find that Calvin was as hidebound as any Roman Catholic priest. This feeling soon changed to one of disgust when he discovered that Calvin himself had helped to have Servetus arrested. From then on, Sozini relied on the example of Servetus and the inspiration of Camillo in his extensive studies of the accepted doctrines of the established church.

In 1559 he went to Zurich and spent the last three years of his life deep in reflection and study. He died in 1562 when he was thirty-seven years old.

Fausto Paolo Sozini (1539 — 1604)

Fausto Paolo Sozini, Lelio Sozini's nephew, was born in 1539. His uncle handed down to him all that he had acquired during his short but useful life. At the age of twenty-three, young Fausto Sozini, or Socianus as he became popularly known, became an heir not only to Lelio's inheritance, but also to the light of Camillo and the learning of Servetus. His most precious legacy, however, was the great number of manuscripts and exegitical notes left by his uncle.

Socianus received his early education in Sienna where he was born. On coming of age, he visited Lyons and Geneva. He returned to Italy in 1565. He went to Florence and entered the service of Isabella de Medeci. He received both position and honour from her hands. After her death, he left Italy and settled in Basle. Here, the young scholar soon attracted the attention of all those who were interested in the study of theology. He published a book for private circulation anonymously, as it was very dangerous to openly differ from the teaching of the Church.

His book reached the hands of Blandrata who was the court physician in Poland. At this stage, Blandrata had the courage, vision, ability, and ambition to free the minds of the common people from the stranglehold which the established church had on them. The religious toleration of the rulers of Poland had made the country an attractive place for all those who wanted to discuss their religion freely, and who did not wish to follow the obtuse dogmatism of the Church. Blandrata invited Socianus to Poland, and his offer was gladly accepted. In the free and congenial atmosphere that Socianus found there, he was at liberty to write in his own name without fear of persecution by the Church. Though his own person was safe, his property in Italy was confiscated. Socianus married a Polish woman and severed all connections with his native land.

The rulers of Poland did not believe in the doctrine of Trinity, but they were still groping in the dark. They did not know what steps to take to produce a positive dogma. The presence of Socianus fulfilled this need and clearly gave satisfaction to the rulers and the people alike. The knowledge which his uncle had passed on to him, together with the fruits of his own study, fused together in Socianus' intellect, and his writings had a powerful impact on the established church.

In its anger, the Church had him arrested and he was condemned to be burnt alive. However, popular support for Socianus was so great that the court decided to subject him to the ordeal by cold water, in order to give their judgement greater weight. This test, along with the ordeal by fire, had been adopted by the church, and given the name of *judicum dei*, the judgement of God, although it had never been part of Jesus's, or even Paul's, teaching. The outcome of the ordeal was said to be the immediate judgement of God. In the ordeal by cold water the accused was thrown into deep water. If he drowned, he was guilty. Knowing full well that Socianus could not swim, the officiating clergy threw him into the sea. He was saved from drowning, however, and lived until he died in 1604.

In 1605, his writings were collected together in a book. Since it was published in Rokow, it became popularly known as the Racovian Cathechism. Originally published in the Polish language, it came to be translated into almost all the languages of Europe. In time, his teaching spread everywhere, and his school of theology became known as Socianism. Harnack, in his *Outlines of the History of Dogma*, ranks Socianism along with Roman Catholicism and Protestantism as the last of the final stages of Christian Dogma. It is largely due to Socianus that Unitarians became a separate entity within modern Christianity. Harnack declared that Socianism had these characteristics:

It had the courage to simplify the questions concerning the reality and content of religion and to discard the burden of the ecclesiastical past.

It broke the contracted bond between religion and science, between Christianity and Platonism.

It helped spread the idea that the religious statement of truth must be clear and apprehensible if it is to have strength.

It tried to free the study of the Holy Scriptures from the bondage of old dogmas which themselves were not in the Scriptures. It was said by someone that "The Ignorance of the laity is the Revenue of the clergy." The teachings of Socianus did much to diminish both.

The Socian religion crossed Europe and spread to England. Bishop Hall of Norwich is recorded as bewailing the fact that "the minds of Christian men were seduced. . .through the infernal Socian heresy by Anti-trinitarians and New Arians so that the final destruction of Christianity was to be feared." [21] In 1638, brutal and organised persecution of the Socians started. Their College at Rokow was suppressed, and the followers of Socianus were deprived of all civil rights, and many people who affirmed the Unity of God were burnt alive. Thus, for instance, in 1639, Catherine Vogal, the wife of a jeweller in Poland was burnt alive at the age of eighty. Her crime was that she believed that God was One; that He was the Creator of the Seen and the Unseen worlds; and that God could not be conceived of by the human intellect. This is, of course, the pure metaphysics of Islam. Fuller writes that "such burning of heretics startled the common people. . .because of the hideousness of the punishment. . . and they were ready to entertain good thoughts even of the opinions of the heretics who sealed them so manfully with their blood." [22] Therefore, says Wallace, "James I indulged his propensity for incendiarism by the more harmless practice of burning their books." [23]

In 1658, the people were given the option of either accepting Roman Catholicism or else going into exile. The unitarians dispersed throughout Europe. They spread with their teaching, and continued to stay a separate entity for a long time.

In the writings contained in the Racovian Cathechism, Socianus struck at the very root of orthodox Christianity by denying the doctrine of atonement. Although he was ignorant of the fact that Jesus was neither crucified nor resurrected, and that therefore the doctrine is entirely without a foundation, Socianus was able to establish the absurdity of the doctrine on other grounds. Briefly speaking, the doctrine of atonement preaches that man is born in a state of sin because of the first wrong action of Adam, and that Jesus, by his (supposed) crucifixion, atones for this state of sin and all the wrong actions of all those who take baptism and follow him. According to orthodox Christianity, the Church is a religious fellowship, a society of divine origin which was founded by Christ through his atoning work for men. Only within its communion, it says, and by its office, can sinful men find the way to God. The Church was therefore considered to be more important and prior to the individual believer. Sozini denied all this. He was sure that a man could have direct access to God without the need for any intermediaries. To attain salvation, not baptism, but "Right Reason" was needed, and it was not necessary to blindly follow the Church. By denying this doctrine, Socianus brought the whole authority of the Church and its raison d'etre into question. It was largely because of this that both the Catholics and Protestants joined forces with such fervour to fight Socianism. Socianus refuted the doctrine of atonement on the following grounds:

Christ could not have offered an infinite sacrifice for sin since Christ, according to the Gospel narration, suffered only for a short time. The most intense suffering for a limited period is as nothing compared with the eternal suffering to which man was liable. If it is said that the suffering is greater in so far as he who suffers it is infinite, so also the power to endure the suffering is greater. But even the suffering of an infinite being cannot take the place of eternal suffering.

If it is granted that Christ did offer infinite atonement, then it is impossible to speak of the forgiveness of God or of man's gratitude to Him for granting His forgiveness, since a man who was baptised in the name of Christ automatically acquired atonement for his sins before God could remit the penalty for them. To follow the doctrine means that God's Law is no longer binding on His servants since the penalty for all his sins has already been paid in full. Therefore, a man is at full liberty to do what he likes. Since the offering of Christ was absolute and infinite, it included all. Therefore, universal salvation must follow. In other words, God has no right to add any further conditions to what He requires of man. The whole price has been paid, past, present and future; and, therefore, all debtors are now free. For, suppose a number of men had owed a great debt to an earthly creditor and someone had paid it all off; then what right would the creditor have to make further demands or conditions on these men who were no longer indebted to him?

The doctrine of atonement was also questioned by Socianus indirectly by his affirming that Jesus was not God, but a man. For there is no way that a man could atone for all the wrong actions of mankind. This fact in itself is enough to dispel this mythical doctrine.

Socianus asserted that Jesus was truly a mortal man. He was born of a virgin. He was separated from all other men due to the holiness of his life. He was not God, but he received inspiration from God. Thus, he had divine vision and divine power although he was not their author. He was sent by God with His supreme authority on a mission to mankind. Socianus supported these beliefs with a comprehensive citation and confident exegis of the relevant passages from the Scriptures. His subtle and able argument gave a rational meaning to the word of Christ. Jesus was not the Word made flesh. He was a man who achieved victory over wrong action in his life in the flesh. He did not exist before the world came into existence. It was permissible to invoke the help of Jesus in prayer as long as he was not worshipped as God.

Socianus affirmed that God is the supreme Lord of all. Omnipotence is not His only attribute, but rules every other attribute. There can be no question raised against God. The finite cannot be a measure of the infinite. Therefore, all human conceptions of the nature of God must be considered as inadequate grounds on which to base a critical judgement about Him. God's will is free and bound by no law that the human mind can formulate. His purpose and His will are hidden from the human mind. God's dominion comprises of a right and supreme authority to determine whatsoever He may choose, in respect of us all and all other things. He can read our thoughts even though they may be hidden in the innermost recess of our hearts. He can at pleasure ordain laws and determine both reward and punishment for the purity and the lapses in a man's intentions. Thus, man is an individual who has been given the freedom of choice, but who in fact is powerless.

Since there cannot be more than one being who possesses supreme dominion over all things, asserted Socianus, to speak of three supreme persons is to speak irrationally. The essence of God is one, not only in kind but also in number. It cannot in any way contain a plurality of persons, since an individual person is nothing else than an individual intelligent essence. Wherever there exist three numerical persons, there must necessarily in like manner be reckoned three individual essences. If it is affirmed that there is one numerical essence, it must be held that there is one numerical person.

The doctrine of Trinity was also refuted by Socianus on the grounds that it was not possible for Jesus to have two natures simultaneously. He said that two substances having opposite properties cannot combine into one person, and such properties are mortality and immortality: to have a beginning and to be without beginning, to be mutable and to be immutable. Again, two natures each of which is apt to constitute a separate person, cannot be huddled into one person. For, instead of one, there, of necessity, arise two persons and consequently they become two Christs, one divine and one human. The Church says that Christ is constituted of a divine and human nature as a man is of body and soul. Socianus replied that, in that case, this is widely different from the belief that the two natures in Christ are so united that Christ is thus constituted of a divine and a human body. In a man, body and soul are so conjoined that a man is neither soul nor body. For neither the soul nor the body separately constitute a person. Whereas, the divine nature by itself constitutes a person and therefore, of necessity, so must the human by itself also constitute a separate person.

Furthermore, said Socianus, it is also repugnant to the Scriptures themselves that Christ should have a divine nature: Firstly, God created Jesus. Secondly, the Scriptures say that Jesus was a man. Thirdly, whatever excellence Jesus had is testified by the Scriptures to be the gift of God. Fourthly, the Scriptures most clearly indicate that Jesus perpetually ascribes all the miracles not to himself or any divine nature of his own, but to the Father. Jesus himself confirmed the Divine Will.

The following excerpt from the Racovian Cathechism is to be found in Reland's "Historical and Critical Reflections upon Mahometanism and Socianism":

> The opinion of those who attribute divinity to Jesus Christ is not only repugnant to right reason but likewise to the Holy Scriptures, and they are in gross error who believe that not only the Father but also the Son and the Holy Ghost are three persons in one deity. . .The essence of God is most simple and absolutely one, and therefore it is a downright contradiction for one to generate another if they are three independent persons. And the poor little reason of our adversaries to the contrary to prove that the Father had begot a son of his own substance are ridiculous and impertinent. . .Always till the times of the Nicene Council and some time later as appears by the writings of those who lived then, the Father. . .alone was acknowledged for the true God, and those who were of the contrary mind, such as the Sabellians and the like were accounted heretics. . .The spirit of the Anti-Christ hath not introduced more dangerous error into the Church of Christ than this doctrine which teaches that there are three distinct persons in the most simple essence of God each of which is itself God, and that the Father. . .is not the only true God but that the Son and the Holy Ghost must be joined with him. There is nothing more absurd or more impossible and more repugnant to right reason. . .Also Christians believe that Jesus Christ died to merit salvation for us and to satisfy the debts which we contracted by our sins, yet this opinion is false, erroneous and most pernicious." [24]

Socianus said that one of the causes of the acceptance of the doctrine of Trinity was the influence of pagan philosophy as this passage from Toland's "The Nazarenes" indicates:

> The Socians and the other unitarians no less confidently assert that the Gentiles did likewise introduce into Christianity their former polytheism and deifying of dead men: thus retaining the name of Christianity but quite altering

the thing and suiting it as their interest or the necessity of their affairs required to all the opinions and customs anywhere in vogue from that time to this. [25]

It is clear why the writings of Socianus achieved such widespread acceptance. They not only took people back to a more accurate picture of who Jesus was and what he came for, but helped also to destroy much of the power which the Church had over people. The greatness of Socianus lies in the fact that he produced a theology which was at once logical and yet based on the Bible. It was therefore very difficult for his opponents to dismiss his writings. For instance, when, in 1680, the Reverend George Ashwell found that the books of Socianus were becoming very popular among his students, he decided to write a book on the Socian religion. His assessment of Socianus is interesting since it comes from the pen of an enemy:

> So great was the author and patron of this sect in whom all the qualities, which excite the admiration and attract the regard of men, were united; so that he charmed, as it were, by a kind of fascination all with whom he conversed, and left on the mind of all a strong impression of admiration and love. He so excelled in the loftiness of his genius and the suavity of his disposition, such was the strength of his reasoning and the force of his eloquence, so signal were the virtues which he displayed in the sight of all, which he...possessed...in an extraordinary degree; so great were his natural endowments and so exemplary was his life that he appeared to captivate the affection of mankind.

After saying all this, Ashwell concluded that Socianus was the "devil's great noose or snare." [26] Today many Christians do not share the same contradictory feelings about Socianus as the Reverend Ashwell. There is a dominant feeling of sympathy for Socianism and the brutal way it was suppressed, and there is a definite reaction against trinitarianism. Many thinking Christians affirm the beliefs of Socianus and deny the divinity of Jesus and all that it implies.

John Biddle (1615-1662)

John Biddle, the Father of Unitarianism in England, was born in 1615. He was a brilliant student and was described as a man who "outran his instructors and became tutor to himself." [27] He went to the University at Oxford in 1634, was made a B.A. in 1638 and an M.A. in 1641. After leaving Oxford he was appointed as a teacher in the Free School of St. Mary de Crypt in Gloucester. Here he began to re-examine his religious views, and began to doubt the validity of the doctrine of the Trinity. He was influenced by the thought of the European unitarians for the teaching of Socianus had by now made its way to England. A Latin version of the Racovian Cathechism had been sent to England with a dedication to King James. It was burnt by the hangman in public in 1614. Although the book might be burnt, its contents caught the interest of the public. Steps were taken to discredit it. John Owen, who was commissioned by the Council of State under Cromwell to refute the teaching of Socianus, is recorded as saying: "Do not look upon these things as things far off wherein you are little concerned, the evil is at the door; there is not a city, a town, scarce a village in England wherein some of the poison is not poured forth." [28]

These attempts to uphold the accepted dogmas of the church met with opposition. William Chillingworth, (1602-1644), condemned "the mischief of creeds which led to the persecution, burning, cursing, damning of men for not subscribing to the words of men, as the word of God." [29] Jeremy Taylor and Milton both affirmed that "the faithful pursuit of reason did not make a heretic. The mischief lay in the influences that perverted the will." [30] The debate spread, and more steps were taken by those in authority to protect the belief in the Trinity. In June 1640, the Conventions of Canterbury and York decided to prohibit the import, printing and circulation of Socian books. Priests were ordered not to preach the Socian doctrines, and everyone was warned that anyone who believed in these doctrines would be excommunicated. A number of authors and thinkers denounced this decision, but to no effect.

It was in this climate of reappraisal and fresh examination that Biddle's own views underwent a change, especially in connection with the doctrine of Trinity. He spoke freely about them and as a result was asked by the Magistrates to give them a written confession of faith in 1644. This he did in simple language: "I believe there is one Almighty Essence called God. So there is only One person in Essence."[31]

He also published a pamphlet at this time entitled "Twelve Arguments Refuting the Deity of the Holy Spirit." It was addressed "To the Christian Reader." In 1645, the manuscript of the "Twelve Arguments" was seized and Biddle was imprisoned. He was called to appear before Parliament but still refused to accept the Deity of the Holy Spirit. He reprinted the pamphlet in 1647. On the 6th of September of the same year, Parliament ordered that the pamphlet be burnt by the hangman, and this was done. On the 2nd of May, 1648, a "Severe Ordinance" was passed. It stated that anyone who denied the Trinity, or the divinity of Jesus or the Holy Spirit, would suffer death without the benefit of clergy.

A summary of the "Twelve Arguments", the cause of such extreme measures, follows:

1) He that is distinguished from God is not God.
   The Holy Spirit is distinguised from God.
   Therefore the Holy Spirit is not God.

Biddle further explained this syllogism with these words:

The major premise is quite clear inasmuch as if we say that the Holy Spirit is God and yet distinguished from God then it implies a contradiction. The minor premise that the Holy Spirit is distinguished from God is confirmed by the whole current of scripture. The argument that the Holy Spirit is distinguished from God if it is taken personally and not essentially is against all reason:

First, it is impossible for any man to distinguish the Person from the Essence of God, and not to frame two Beings or Things in his mind. Consequently, he will be forced to the conclusion that there are two Gods.

Secondly, if the Person be distinguished from the Essence of God, the Person would be some Independent

Thing. Therefore it would be either finite or infinite. If finite then God would be a finite thing since according to the Church everything in God is God Himself. So the conclusion is absurd. If infinite then there will be two infinites in God, and consequently the two Gods which is more absurd than the former argument.

Thirdly, to speak of God taken impersonally is ridiculous, as it is admitted by everyone that God is the Name of a Person, who with absolute sovereignty rules over all... None but a person can rule over others therefore to take otherwise than personally is to take Him otherwise than He is.

2) He that gave the Holy Spirit to the Israelites is Jehova Alone
Then the Holy Spirit is not Jehova or God.

3) He that speakest not for himself is not God.
The Holy Spirit speaks not for himself.
Therefore the Holy Spirit is not God.

4) He that is taught is not God.
He that hears from another what he shall speak is taught.
Christ speaks what he is told.
Therefore Christ is not God.

Here Biddle quotes John 8.26 where Jesus says: "Whatsoever I have heard from Him these things I speak."

5) In John 16.14 Jesus says: "God is He that giveth all things to all.'
He that receives from another is not God.

6) He that is sent by another is not God.
The Holy Spirit is sent by God.
Therefore the Holy Spirit is not God.

7) He that is not the giver of all things is not God.
He that is the gift of God is not the giver of all things.
He that is the gift of God is himself given.
The gift is in the power and at the disposal of the giver.
It is therefore absurd to imagine that God can be in the power or at the disposal of another.

Here Biddle quotes Acts 17.25: "God giveth to all, life, breath and all things."

8) He that changes place is not God.
   The Holy Spirit changes place.
   Therefore the Holy Spirit is not God.

Biddle further explained this syllogism in these words: "If God changes place then he would cease to be where he was before and begin to be where he was not before, which is against his Omnipresence, and His Deity. Therefore it was not God who came to Jesus but an Angel sustaining the Person in the Name of God."

9) He that prays to Christ to come to judgement is not God.
   The Holy Spirit does so.
   Therefore the Holy Spirit is not God.

10) In Romans 10.14 it reads, "How shall they believe in him of whom they have not heard. He in whom men have not believed, yet were disciples."
   He who is not believed in is not God.
   Men have not believed in the Holy Spirit, yet were disciples.
   Therefore the Holy Spirit is not God.

11) He that hears from God at the second hand, viz the Christ Jesus, what he shall speak has an understanding distinct from God.
   He that heareth from God what he shall speak is taught of God.
   The Holy Spirit does so.
   Therefore the Holy Spirit is not God.

12) He that has a will distinct in number from that of God is not God.
   The Holy Spirit has a will distinct in number from God.
   Therefore the Holy Spirit is not God.

Here Biddle quotes Romans 8.26-27 which reads: "Likewise the Spirit also helpeth...for we know not how to pray as we ought but the Spirit maketh intercession for us with groans unutterable...he maketh intercession for the saints according to the will of God."

Biddle also discussed the one verse in the New Testament which the established church quoted to support their view of Trinity. It is John 5.7 which reads: "For there are three that bear record in heaven — the Father, the Word, and the Holy Ghost; and these three are One." Biddle said the verse was contrary to common sense. It contradicted other verses in the scriptures, and it only signified union of consent and agreement but never of essence. Furthermore, the verse did not even appear in the ancient Greek copies of the gospel, nor in the Syriac translations, nor in the very old Latin editions. It seemed therefore that the verse had been interppolated, and was rejected as such by interpreters both ancient and modern.[32]

Despite the Act of 1648, Biddle published two other tracts, and would probably have been hanged for doing so had he not been helped by a number of independent members of Parliament. One of the works was called "A Confession of Faith Touching the Holy Trinity According to the Scripture." It was composed of six articles, each illustrated with passages from the Bible and supported with his arguments. In the preface, he boldly talked of the evils resulting from the belief in the doctrine of Trinity. He said that the arguments used by the trinitarians were "fitter for conjurers than Christians." [33]Here is an excerpt from Biddle's "Confession of Faith.":

> I believe that there is one most High God, Creator of Heaven, and Earth and the first Cause of all things and consequently the ultimate object of our Faith, and Worship. I believe in Jesus, to the extent that he might be our brother, and have a fellow feeling of our infirmities and so become more ready to help us. He has only human nature.
>
> He is subordinate to God. And he is not another God. There are not two Gods.
>
> The Holy Spirit is an Angel who due to his eminence and intimacy with God is singled out to carry His message."[34]

The other work Biddle published at this time was called "The Testimonies of Iraneus, Justin Martyr, Etc. Concerning One God and the Persons of the Holy Trinity."

After a long wait in prison, a magistrate stood bail for Biddle, and he was released. The name of the magistrate was kept secret since he feared for his safety. Biddle had not enjoyed his liberty for very long before he was again thrown into prison. The magistrate died soon after, and left a small legacy to Biddle. It was soon eaten up by the high costs of the prison, and for a while Biddle's food was reduced to a small quantity of milk taken in the morning and in the evening. His situation was eased when a London publisher employed him while still in prison as a proof reader for a new edition of the Septuagent, a Greek translation of the Bible. On the 16th of February 1652, the Act of Oblivion was passed and Biddle was set free. An English version of the Racovian Cathechism was printed in Amsterdam during the same year, and immediately became popular in England. Biddle printed a book on unitarianism in 1654, again in Amsterdam, and it was widely read in England. During this period of freedom, Biddle began to meet with other unitarians every Sunday to worship God in their own way. Those who attended did not believe in the concept of Original Sin and the doctrine of Atonement. On the 13th of December 1654, Biddle, who had recently published two cathechisms, was again arrested and sent to prison. He was forbidden the use of pen, ink and paper and was not allowed to have any visitors. All copies of his books were ordered to be burnt. He appealed, and was released on the 28th of May 1655.

It was not long before Biddle again clashed with the authorities: A public debate was taking place. The speaker commenced the dispute by asking if there was anyone present who denied that Christ was God most High. Biddle promptly and firmly declared, "I deny it." When he supported this statement with arguments which his adversaries could not refute, it was decided to halt the proceedings and to continue on another day. Biddle was then reported to the authorities, and before the day fixed for the debate was again arrested and put in prison. To begin with, Biddle was denied the services of a lawyer, perhaps because it was doubtful whether there was a law in force at that time under which he could be convicted. His friends who were well aware of this decided to approach Cromwell directly. They drew up a petition and sent it to him. Before it could reach him the petition was so altered and disfigured that its authors had to openly disown it as a forgery.

Cromwell, who was at his wits end, found a way out of this difficult situation by banishing Biddle to the Scilly Islands on the 5th of October 1655. He was to remain in custody in the Castle of St. Mary's for the rest of his life and would be paid an allowance of one hundred crowns per annum. During his captivity there, Biddle wrote a poem a few lines of which follow:

> The conclave met, the judge was set,
> Man mounted on God's throne;
> And they did judge a matter there,
> That rests with Him alone;
> A brother's faith they made a crime,
> And crushed thought's native right sublime. [36]

The more he suffered, the more convinced he became about the errors of the prevailing religion supported by the established Church. Thomas Firmin, who had helped Biddle in the past, continued to help him by providing him with money which made his life in prison as comfortable as it could be. Meanwhile sympathy for Biddle increased far and wide. The more he suffered, the more popular his creed became. The government asked Dr. John Owen to counteract the effect of Biddle's teaching. After holding a survey in which he discovered that a large number of Englishmen were unitarians, he published a reply to Biddle in 1655. In a way Cromwell's actions helped Biddle: Supported by the allowance, Biddle was out of reach of his enemies and could spend his time in contemplation and prayer. He remained a prisoner in the Castle of St. Mary's until 1658; when, due to the increased pressure for his release, he regained his freedom.

As soon as he had come out of prison, he began to hold public meetings in which he examined the Scriptures to demonstrate the Unity of God and show the falsehood of the doctrine of Trinity. These meetings developed into regular unitarian worship according to their faith. This had never happened in England before.

On the 1st of June 1662 Biddle was again arrested together with some of his friends in the middle of one of their meetings. They were all put in prison and bail was refused. There was no statute under which they could be punished so they were prosecuted under Common Law. Biddle was fined one hundred pounds and condemned to lie in prison until it was paid. His fellow worshippers were fined twenty pounds each. Biddle was ill-treated in prison and kept in solitary confinement. This, together with the foul air of the prison brought on a disease which resulted in his death in less than five weeks. He died on the 22nd September 1662.

Biddle's death, together with the effects of the Act of Uniformity, passed in the same year, meant that public worship which followed the pattern established by Biddle could not take place. Under the Act 2,257 priests were ejected from their "living." Their fate is unknown. But it is known that about 8,000 people died in prison for refusing to accept the doctrine of Trinity during this particular era in England. The author of a memoir of Biddle, written about twenty years after his death, preferred to remain anonymous for safety's sake. However, unitarianism continued as a school of thought and its adherents grew. The use of force to bring back people into the established Church only helped to win many people over to the beliefs of Socianus and Biddle, and many of the leading intellects of the age, including Milton, Sir Isaac Newton and Locke, affirmed the Divine Unity.

The degree to which the authorities attempted to stamp out unitarianism can be measured by the laws they passed: An act of 1664 condemned all persons convicted of refusing to go to an established church with banishment. Should such a person return, they would be hanged. There were also penalties for anyone who attended a religious meeting of five or more persons not authorised by the Church. Should anyone commit this offence a second time, they would be banished to America, and in case of return or escape would suffer death without benefit of clergy. The Test Act of 1673 provided that, apart from the punishment provided for in the Act of 1664, any person who did not receive the sacrament according to the usage of the Church of England would on conviction be no longer able to sue anyone or bring any action in the law courts. He could no longer be a guardian of any child, or executor, or the recipient of any legacy or deed or gift. Should anyone convicted under this law attempt to do any of these things, they were liable to a five hundred pound fine. In 1689 the Toleration Act was passed. However, toleration was denied to those who did not accept the doctrine of Trinity. The unitarians condemned the intolerance of the Toleration Act. Parliament replied by condemning unitarianism as an "obnoxious heresy." The penalty for this crime was the loss of all civil rights together with imprisonment for three years. However what Biddle had stood for could not be removed from men's hearts by statute alone, even though the laws prevented many from openly professing their faith. Those who felt they were unable to defy the law and openly denounce the doctrine of Trinity resorted to various expedients in order to quieten the reproaches of their conscience. Some quietly omitted those parts of the Athanasian Creed of which they did not approve. Some had it read by the parish clerk. One priest is said to have shown his disrespect for the creed by having it sung to a popular hunting tune. Another priest, before he read the doctrine of Trinity prescribed by law, said, "Brethren, this is the creed of St. Athanasius, but God forbid that it should be the creed of any other man." [37] However, on the whole those who believed in the Divine Unity did not generally dare to openly declare their faith.

Biddle was a laborious scholar, and his formulations were the result of profound study. He was convinced that he could best serve mankind by fearlessly bearing witness to the truth even if this meant reproach and persecution. He was prepared to accept poverty, the dungeon and exile. He wanted men to leave the churches which he regarded as corrupt, and to renounce all outward conformity to any profession of error. He had the courage of a martyr.

Milton (1608-1674)

Milton, who lived at the same time as Biddle and shared many of his views, was not as outspoken as Biddle, preferring to lead his life outside prison. In volume two of his "Treatise of True Religion" he says, "The Arians and Socians are charged to dispute against Trinity. They affirm to believe the Father, Son and Holy Ghost according to Scripture and the Apostolic Creed. As for terms of trinity, triunity, co-essentiality, tri-personality, they reject them as scholastic notions not to be found in scripture which by general Protestant maxim is plain and perspecuous abundantly to express its own meaning in the properest words belonging to so high a matter and so necessary to be known, a mystery indeed in their sophistic subtleties but in scripture a plain doctrine." [38]

In another book he was more direct. He said that the power exercised by Popes, Councils, Bishops and Presbyters was to be classified as among the rankest and most odious of tyrannies. He continued, "All imposition of ordinances, ceremonies and doctrines are an unwarranted invasion of Liberty." [39]

The poet did not openly defy the civil authority of the country, but he kept to himself as a protest against the bigotry and intolerance of the established church. Like a number of leading intellectuals, he stopped going to any church. Dr. Johnson said of Milton, "He has not associated with any denomination of Protestants. We know rather what he was not than what he was. He was not of the Church of Rome. He was not of the Church of England. Milton grew old without any visible worship. In his distribution of his hours there was no hour of prayer — his work and his meditation were an habitual prayer." [40]

It is clear that Dr. Johnson was not aware of a book written by Milton and discovered nearly a hundred and fifty years after his death in 1823. The manuscript was found in the old State Paper Office in Whitehall and was entitled "A Treatise Relating to God." Written while he was a Latin secretary to Cromwell, it was obviously not intended to be published during Milton's life.

In Book I, chapter two, Milton writes about the attributes of God and in particular the Divine Unity:

> Though there be not a few who deny the existence of God,
> 'for the fool hath said in his heart there is no God', Psalm
> 14.1, yet the Deity has imprinted upon the human mind

so many unquestionable tokens of Himself and so many traces of Him are apparent throughout the whole of nature that no one in his senses can remain ignorant of truth. There can be no doubt that everything in the world by the beauty of its order and the evidence of a determinate and beneficial purpose which prevades it, testifies that some supreme efficient Power must have pre-existed by which the whole was ordained for a specific end.

No one however can have right thoughts of God with nature, or reason alone as his guide, independent of the word or message of God...God therefore has made as full a revelation of Himself as our minds can conceive or the weakness of our nature can bear...Such knowledge of the Deity as was necessary for the salvation of man, He has Himself of His goodness been pleased to reveal abundantly ...The names and attributes of God either show His nature or His divine power and excellence.

Milton then lists some of the attributes of God: Truth, Spirit (I am that I am), Immensity and Infinity, Eternity, Immutability (I change not), Incorruptibility, Immortality, Omnipresence, Omnipotence, and finally, Unity, which he says "proceeds necessarily from all the foregoing attributes." Milton then lists the following proofs from the Bible:

Jehova, He is God, there is none besides Him.
(Deuteronomy 4.35)

Jehova, He is God in the heavens above and upon the earth beneath: there is none else. (Deuteronomy 5.39)

I, even I, am He and there is no God with Me.
(Deuteronomy 32.39)

...that all the people of the earth may know that Jehova is God and that there is none else. (I Kings 8.60)

...Thou art the God, even Thou alone, of all the kingdoms of the earth. (2 Kings 19.15)

Is there a God besides Me? Yea, there is no God.
(Isaiah 44.8)

I am Jehova and there is no God besides Me.
(Isaiah 45.5)

There is no God else besides Me...there is none besides Me.
(Isaiah 45.21)

I am God and there is none else. (Isaiah 45.22)

Commenting on the above verse, Milton says, "that is, no spirit, no person, no being beside Him is God for "none" is a universal negative."

> I am God and there is none else. I am God and there is none like Me. (Isaiah 46.9)

Milton continues,

> ...what can be plainer, what more distinct, what more suitable to general comprehension and the ordinary forms of speech, for the purpose of impressing on the people of God that there was numerically One God and One Spirit in the common acceptation of numerical unity? It was in truth fitting and highly agreeable to reason that the first and consequentially the greatest commandment to which even the lowest of the people were required to pay scrupulous obedience should be delivered in so plain a manner that no ambiguous or obscure expressions might lead his worshippers into error or keep them in suspense or doubt. Accordingly, the Israelites under the law and their prophets always understood it to mean that God was numerically one God besides whom there was none other, much less any equal. For the schoolmen had not as yet appeared who through their confidence in their own sagacity, or more properly speaking on arguments purely contradictory, impunged the doctrine itself of the Unity of God, which they pretended to assert. But as with regard to the omnipotence of the Deity, it is universally allowed, as has been stated before, that he can do nothing which involves a contradiction: so it must always be remembered in this place that nothing can be said of the One God which is inconsistent with his Unity, and which assigns to him at the same time the attributes of unity and plurality. Mark 13.29-32: "Hear O Israel, the Lord our God is one Lord." To which answer the scribe asserted, "Well, Master, thou hast said the truth: for there is One God; and there is none other than He." "

Milton then goes on to discuss the nature of the Holy Spirit. The Scripture he says is silent, on its nature, in what manner it exists, and from whence it arose. He continues,

> It is exceedingly unreasonable not to say dangerous that in a matter of so much difficulty believers should be required to receive a doctrine represented by its advocates

as of primary importance and of undoubted certainty or anything less than the clearest testimony of Scriptures, and that a point that is confessedly contrary to reason should nevertheless be considered as susceptible of proof from human reason only or rather from doubtful and obscure disputations.

Milton then draws the following conclusions from his knowledge of the Bible: The Holy Spirit is not omniscient. The Holy Spirit is not omnipresent. It cannot be said that because the Holy Spirit carries out the work of God, therefore it is part of God. If this was so then why is the Holy Spirit called the Comforter, who will come after Jesus, who speaks not of himself nor in his own name, and whose power therefore is acquired. (John 16.7-14) It therefore becomes clear that instead of accepting the term "Comforter" in its obvious sense as a prophet who will come after Jesus, to call him Holy Spirit and yet call him God creates a confusion which cannot be ended. [41]

Milton agrees with Arius that Jesus was not eternal. He says it was in God's power to create or not to create Jesus. He concludes that Jesus was born "within the limits of time." He is at a loss to find any passage of scripture which would support the "eternal generation of Jesus." The hypothesis that Jesus, though personally and numerically another, is yet essentially one with God is strange and repugnant to reason. This dogma does violence not only to reason but also to scriptural evidence. Milton agrees with the "Israelitish people" that God is One and only God. It is so evident that it requires no explanation, that God alone is the self-existing God; and that a being that is not self-existing cannot be God. He concludes,

> It is wonderful with what futile subtleties or rather with what juggling artifices certain individuals have endeavoured to elude or obscure the plain meaning of the passages of the Scriptures. [42]

Milton says that the Holy Ghost was inferior to both God and Jesus, since his duties were to carry messages from one to the other. On his own he could do nothing. He is subservient and obedient to God in all things. He is sent by God and is given nothing to speak of himself.

Milton felt he could not express these views openly, for to have done so would have been to endanger his own personal safety, and to expose himself to the same treatment that Biddle and many others had suffered. In 1611, that is within Milton's lifetime, two men called Mr. Legatt and Mr. Wightman, were burnt alive with the king's permission because they believed that there was no Trinity of persons, Father, Son and Holy Spirit, in the Unity of Godhead; that Jesus Christ was neither the natural true son of God, nor of the same substance, eternity and majesty with the Father in respect to his godhead; and that Jesus Christ was a man only and a mere creature, and not God and man together in one person. Milton's silence while he was alive was therefore an understandable one.

John Locke (1632-1704)

John Locke, who is best known for his treatises on the social contract, was also a man who held unitarian views but was afraid to openly declare them. At one point, he was forced to leave England on account of his political views. On his return, after the revolution of 1688, he made sure that he did not directly offend the powers of the Church, since he feared further persecution. Even his monograph supporting reason was not liked by the Church, and another tract written by him had to be published anonymously. However, it is known that he studied the teachings of the early disciples of Christ and could find no justification for the belief in Trinity. He was a close friend of Newton and obviously discussed this matter, which was so much in dispute in that age, with him. Le Clere, a friend of Locke and Newton, observes that no controversy was ever conducted with so much skill on the one hand or, on the other, with so much misrepresentation, confusion and ignorance. There is a tradition that the terms of the Toleration Act of 1689 were negotiated by Locke.

Sir Isaac Newton (1642-1727)

Newton's illustrious life has been summed up by Pope, the famous English poet, in these words:

> Nature and nature's laws lay hid in night
> God said, "Let Newton be." — and all was light. [43]

And yet Newton was another man who felt it unwise to profess his beliefs openly: In 1690, he sent John Locke a small
packet containing his remarks on the corruption of the text
of the New Testament with reference to John 5.7 and I Timothy 3.16. He hoped that Locke could help him have the
manuscript translated into French and published in France,
since he felt it would be too dangerous to print it in England.
It was called "An Historical Account of Two Notable Corruptions of Scripture." In 1692, an attempt was made to
publish a Latin translation of it anonymously. When he heard
of this, Newton entreated Locke to take steps to prevent
this publication, since he felt the time was not ripe for it.

In his "Historical Account", Newton says, referring to
John 5.7,

> In all the vehement universal and lasting controversy about
> the Trinity in Jerome's time and both before and long
> enough after it, this text of the "three in heaven" was
> never once thought of. It is now in everybody's mouth
> and accounted the main text for the business and would
> assuredly have been so too with them, had it been in their
> books.

He continues,

> Let them make good sense of it who are able. For my
> part I can make none. If it be said that we are not to
> determine what is Scripture and what not by our private
> judgements, I confess it in places not controverted, but
> in disputed places I love to take up with what I can best
> understand. It is the temper of the hot and superstitious
> part of mankind in matters of religion ever to be fond of
> mysteries, and for that reason to like best what they under-
> stand least. Such men may use the Apostle John as they
> please, but I have that honour for him as to believe that
> he wrote good sense and therefore take that to be his which
> is the best. [44]

According to Newton, this verse appeared for the first time
in the third edition of Erasmus's New Testament. He believed
that before the publication of this edition, the "spurious

text" was not to be found in the New Testament: "When they got the Trinity into his edition they threw by their manuscript, if they had one, as an almanac out of date. And can such shuffling dealings satisfy considering men?" He continues, "It is rather a danger in religion than an advantage to make it now lean on a broken reed."

In referring to I Timothy 3.16, Newton says: "In all the times of the hot and lasting Arian controversy it never came into play. . .they that read "God manifested in the flesh" think it one of the most obvious and pertinent texts for the business." [45]

Newton was opposed to the allegorical or double interpretation of the Old Testament. He did not regard all the books of the Scriptures as having the same authority. According to Whiston, Newton also wrote a dissertation upon two other texts which Athanasius had attempted to corrupt, but there is no trace of it today.

Finally, Newton also had this to say:

> The word Deity imports exercise of dominion over subordinate beings and the word God most frequently signifies Lord. Every lord is not God. The exercise of dominion in a spiritual being constitutes a God. If that dominion be real that being is the real God; if it be fictitious, a false God; if it be supreme, a supreme God. [46]

Thomas Emlyn (1663-1741)

Thomas Emlyn was born on the 27th May 1663. He went to Cambridge in 1678; and, having concluded his studies there, returned to Dublin, where he soon became a very popular preacher. This Presbyterian Minister preached his first sermon in 1682, and for the next ten years his reputation as a good preacher grew. In about 1702, a member of his congregation observed that Emlyn avoided certain well-known pulpit expressions and the arguments usually employed in support of the dogma of Trinity. This lead to his being questioned as to what he thought about the concept of the Trinity. Since he was asked so pointedly, Emlyn found himself bound to express his views openly and without reserve:

He admitted that he believed in One God. He declared

that God was Alone the Supreme Being and that Jesus derived all authority and power from Him alone. He added that if the congregation found his views obnoxious, he was quite willing to resign to enable them to choose a minister who supported their own opinions. The majority of the congregation did not want this, but the situation was such that he resigned, much to their sorrow. He was advised to go to England for a short while to let things calm down. This he did.

After staying in England for ten weeks, he returned to Dublin in order to collect and bring his family back to England. Before he could do so, he was arrested in 1703 and charged with being a heretic. It had been found that he was responsible for publishing a book on unitarianism entitled "An Humble Inquiry into the Scripture Account of Jesus Christ", and this provided the prosecution with the evidence they needed. The entire book if fundamentally based on the text in John 14.28 in which Jesus says, "The Father is Greater than I." Emlyn sought to establish that Jesus was a mediator between man and God. Thus, in a subtle way, he separated Jesus from God; and, in so doing, demolished the idea of the Trinity.

On account of the difficulty felt by his opponents in wording the indictment against him, trial was deferred for a few months, which he spent in prison. When the trial finally commenced, a "gentlemen of the long robe" informed him that he would not be permitted to defend himself, but that it was designed "to run him down like a wolf without law or game." [47] It is not surprising that he was convicted and found guilty of "writing and publishing an infamous and scandalous bible declaring that Jesus Christ is not the Supreme God." [48] He was given the choice of being imprisoned for one year, or of paying a fine of one thousand pounds. He was to remain in prison until the fine was paid. In the appeals which followed this sentence, he was dragged from court to court and paraded as a heretic before the public. This disgraceful treatment was described as being merciful for if he had been in Spain, he would have been burned alive. Due to a great deal of pressure on the government, the fine was reduced to seventy pounds. It was paid and Emlyn left the prison and Ireland. An eminent priest, commenting on the treatment meted out to heretics, declared that "the enlightening faculty of a dungeon and fine is very convincing."[49]

Emlyn thus joined the distinguished saints who dared deny the Trinity and support the faith in One and only One God. In the Divine revelation of Qur'an, the whole matter is made clear. He is supreme and there is no one like Him. No one else is mentioned as God. Unfortunately, it is not so in the Bible. Emlyn therefore tried to clear up this confusion in his book: God, according to Emlyn, "sometimes signified the most High, Perfect, and Infinite Being, Who is of Himself Alone, and owes neither His Being nor His Authority, nor anything else to another; and this is what is most commonly intended when we speak of God in ordinary Discourse, and Prayer, and Praise; we mean it of God in the most eminent sense."

Emlyn then went on to show that in the Bible, although the word "God" is employed, it is often used to signify persons who are invested with subordinate authority and power in comparison with the Supreme Being: "Angels are styled as God. . .'Thou hast made him a little lower than the Gods.' (Psalm 8.5); Magistrates are Gods. (Exodus 22.28, Psalm 82.1, John 10.34-35); sometimes a person is styled as God as Moses is twice called a God to Aaron, and afterwards a God to Pharaoh; and the Devil is also called the God God of this World, i.e. the Prince and mighty ruler of it, who by unjust usurpation and God's permission occupies this position. Now as He who alone is God in the former sense is infinitely above all these, so we find Him distinguished from all others who are called Gods."

To further clarify this distinction, Emlyn quoted Philo who describes the Supreme Being as "not only God of men but God of Gods." This is the highest and most glorious epithet given to Him in the Old Testament, when it is designed to make a most magnificent mention of His Greatness and Glory.

Since the Bible uses the term "God" to describe God and to describe beings inferior to God, Emlyn then proceeded to try and resolve the question: "In which of the

two senses is Christ said to be God in the Holy Scriptures?"
He concluded that Christ is an inferior being compared with
the God of Gods, (see I Corinthians 8.5). He reached this
conclusion by asking himself this crucial question: "Has Jesus
Christ any God over him, who has greater Authority, and
greater ability than himself, or not?" The reply to this question would decide the position of Jesus one way or the other.
If he had God above him, then he would not be the Absolutely Supreme God. Emlyn's reply was "Yes", and he provided three arguments to support his answer:

> Jesus expressly speaks of a God other than himself.
> He accepts His God to be above or over himself.
> He asks for perfection since he lacks those super-eminent
> and infinite perfections which belong only to God, the
> Supreme Being.

Emlyn felt that these three points had to be elaborated on
in a way which would be understood by the general public.
He decried the practice of those who wrote about the scriptures in a manner unintelligible to the people and yet who
expected them to believe in the dogma their writings described. Emlyn expanded these three points thus:

> First, Jesus speaks of another God distinct from himself.
> Several times we find him saying, "My God My God" of
> another (Matthew 27.46), "My God My God, why hast
> Thou forsaken me?" (John 20.17). Surely, he intended not
> saying "My Self My Self why hast thou forsaken me?"
> This God was distinct from himself, as he declares in other
> places in John 8.42, where it is to be noted that he does
> not distinguish himself from Him as the Father, but as
> God, and therefore, in all just construction, he cannot be
> supposed to be the selfsame God, from whom he distin-
> guished himself...
>
> Secondly, Jesus owns, not only another than himself
> to be God, but also that he is above or over himself, which
> is plainly intimated also by his Apostles. He himself loudly
> proclaims his subjection to the Father in many instances.
> In general, he declares his Father to be greater than him-
> self. He says he came not to do anything on his own, but
> only in his Father's name and authority. He sought not
> his own, but God's Glory; nor made his own will, but
> God's his rule. In such a posture of subjection he came

down from heaven into this earth. Again he owns his dependence upon God, even for those things, which it is pretended belong to him, as God, viz., the power of working miracles, of raising the dead, of executing universal judgement: all of which he says, "of my own self I can do nothing."

Thirdly, Jesus disclaims those infinite perfections (underived power, absolute goodness, unlimited knowledge), which belong only to the Supreme God of Gods. And it is most certain that, if he lacks one or any of these perfections that are essential to the Deity he is not God in the same sense. If we find him disclaiming the one, he cannot challenge the other, for to deny himself to have all Divine Perfections, or to deny himself to be the Infinite God is the same thing."

Emlyn then went on to give some instances for the proof of this last point:

One great and peculiar Perfection of the Deity, is absolute and underived Omnipotence. He who cannot work all miracles, and do whatever he wills by himself can never be the Supreme Being if he cannot do it without the help of another. He appears to be an imperfect defective being, comparatively, since he needs help, and asks for additional strength from another than himself.

Now it is most evident, that Jesus, (whatever power he had), confesses again and again, that he had not infinite power by himself: "Of myself I can do nothing." (John 5.30) He had been speaking of great miracles, viz.: raising the dead, of executing universal judgement; he makes it quite clear, that men should know that his sufficiency for these things was of God. In the beginning he says, "The son can do nothing but what he sees the Father do." So in the middle he says the same thing. As if he could never too much inculcate this great truth, he adds towards the conclusion, "I can do nothing of myself..." Surely this is not the Voice of God, but of man! The Most High can receive from none. He cannot be made more mighty or wise, because to absolute Perfection, there can be no addition. Since power in God is an essential Perfection, it follows that if it be derived, then so would be the essence or Being itself, which is blasphemy against the most High.

To number him among dependent derivative beings will tantamount to "Un-God" him. The supreme God indeed is only He who is the first Cause and absolute original of all.

Emlyn also examined the statement attributed to Jesus in Mark 13.32. Speaking of the Day of Judgement he says, "Of that day knows no man, no, not the angels of heaven, not the son, but the Father only." Emlyn observed that for anyone who believed in the divinity of Jesus this statement would imply that God had two natures, or two different states of awareness simultaneously. It would put Him in the ridiculous position of knowing and not knowing something at the same time. If Jesus was Divine and God had this knowledge then Jesus would not have made this statement, since by having this nature he too would have possessed that knowledge.

Thomas Emlyn was well aware that he would be misunderstood by a large number of Christians. In defending his belief he made clear his "Confession of Christianity" by saying that he regarded Jesus as his teacher, whom he admired and loved beyond father, mother or friends. He continued, "I know that Jesus loves nothing but Truth, and will never be offended with anyone who stands by his words, viz., that "the Father is greater than I" (John 14.28). In view of this statement, argued Emlyn, it would be dangerous to say, "God is not greater than Jesus." [50]

Thomas Emlyn was a learned man of God who is distinguished by his learning and integrity and for the firmness with which he endured persecution rather than compromise his beliefs. He belongs to the galaxy of saints who defied those who opposed them. They suffered imprisonment, torture and even death, but did not falter before the might of the Church and State which so often combined forces to eliminate them. On the whole, each instance of persecution only added to the popularity of their message which was simply,

There are not Three but One God.

Emlyn was one of the first among the Protestant dissenters who had the courage to publicly pronounce their disbelief in the doctrine of the Trinity. The number of Presbyterian ministers who joined him, and who embraced Arian and other unitarian beliefs at the beginning of the eighteenth century was considerable. Ten years after Emlyn's trial, the muffled unrest, which had been felt in the Church of England as a result of the questioning of Jesus's supposed divinity, exploded with the publication of Samuel Clarke's "Scripture Doctrine of the Trinity" in 1712. In this book, he cited 1,251 passages from the Scriptures to prove that God the Father was supreme, and Christ and the Holy Spirit were subordinate. Clarke later published an edited version of the Book of Common Prayer omitting the Athanasian Creed and other trinitarian features.

Thomas Emlyn died in July 1741.

Theophilus Lindsey (1723-1808)

Theophilus Lindsey was born in 1723. He was the organiser of the first Unitarian congregation in England. Using a re-formed order of service based on Samuel Clarke's revision of sixty years earlier, and robed without the traditional white surplice, Lindsey conducted the first service in an auction room on Essex Street in London. It was April the seven-teenth, 1774. The service was attended by a large congre-gation including Benjamin Franklin and Joseph Priestly. Here is Lindsey's account of the occasion, contained in a letter which he wrote to a friend the next day.

> You will be pleased to hear that everything passed off very well yesterday; a large and much more respectable audience than I could have expected, who behaved with great de-cency and in general appeared, and many of them expressed themselves, to be much satisfied with the whole of the service. Some disturbance was apprehended, and forboded to me by the great names, but not the least movement of the kind. The only fault found with it, was that it was too small. From the impressions that seemed to be made, and the general seriousness and satisfaction, I am persuaded that this attempt will, through the divine blessing, be of singular usefulness. The contrast between ours and the church-service strikes everyone. Forgive me for saying, that I should have blushed to have appeared in a white garment. No one seemed in the least to want it. I am happy not to be hampered with anything — but entirely satisfied with

the whole of the service; a satisfaction never before known —
I must again say it, and bless God for it, that we were en-
abled to being well. And we only desire to go on as through
His blessing we have begun... [51]

The formation of the Essex Street congregation soon inspired other Unitarian "chapels" to be built in Birmingham,
Manchester, and other English cities. Ecclesiastical independence fostered doctrinal freedom, so that in 1790, in an
address to the students of Oxford and Cambridge, Lindsey
asserted the following "facts, clear and plain to every understanding. . .which all men, who believe the scriptures, sooner
or later must bow down to and acknowledge:

> That there is One God, one single person, who is God,
> the sole creator and sovereign Lord of all things;

> That the holy Jesus was a man of the Jewish nation,
> the servant of this God, highly honoured and distin-
> guished by Him;

> That the Spirit, or Holy Spirit, was not a person, or
> intelligent being; but only the extraordinary power or
> gift of God, imparted to Jesus Christ himself, in his
> life-time; and afterwards, to the apostles and many of
> the first Christians, to empower them to preach and
> propogate the gospel with success (Acts 1.2); and

> That this was the doctrine concerning God, and Christ,
> and the Holy Spirit, which was taught by the apostles,
> and preached to Jews and heathens. [52]

With these almost modern convictions, English unitarianism
entered its greatest age.

In his writings, Lindsey made the following points to
establish the fact that Jesus Christ is not God:

> Jesus never styles himself as God; nor does he drop
> the least intimation that he was the person by whom
> all things were made.

> The Scriptures of the Old Testament throughout speak
> of but one Person, one Jehova, as God by Himself,
> Alone and creator of all things. With reference to John
> 5.7, it is therefore not credible that John, a pious He-
> brew, should all at once introduce another creator, a

new God, without any notice. It is not known whence he drew this strange doctrine, or by what authority he delivered it; especially when we consider that by the law of Moses, whose divine authority he acknowledged, it was the crime of idolatry and blasphemy to have, or to worship, any other God but Jehova. His lord and master, Jesus, made mention of no other God but Jehova, and never took upon himself to speak anything of himself; but as the Father, whose messenger he was, gave him commandment what he should say and what he should speak. (John 12.49)

The writers of the Gospel history speak of one divine person, the Father, as the only true God. (John 17.3)

Mark, Matthew and Luke wrote without consulting each other. They have never thrown any hint of Jesus being God. It cannot be believed or imagined that these men, if they had known him to be God and Creator of the World, would have kept silent on this important subject.

John, who begins his gospel by saying that the Word was God and that Jesus was the Word made flesh, does not ascribe this name to him once in the rest of the Gospel.

An examination of Luke's gospel shows that he believed that Jesus had no existence before he was born of his mother, Mary, since,

> In 3.23.38, a lineal descent of Jesus is given.
> In 4.24 and 8.33, Jesus is acknowledged to be a prophet of God.
> In 7.16 and 24.19, Jesus is called a prophet.
> In 3.13, 26 and 4.27, 30, Peter and some of the other apostles call Jesus the servant of God.
> In 17.24, 30, Luke describes him as the "son of man", appointed to an important office under God that made the world.

Lindsey asked those who worshipped Jesus what their reaction would be if Jesus appeared to them and asked the following questions:

> Why did you address your devotions to me? Did I ever direct you to do it, or propose myself as an object of religious worship?
>
> Did I not uniformly and to the last set you an example myself of praying to the Father, to my Father and your Father, to my God and your God? (John 20.17)
>
> When my disciples requested me to teach them to pray (Luke 11.1-2), did I teach them to pray to myself or to any other person but the Father?
>
> Did I ever call myself God, or tell you that I was the maker of the world and to be worshipped?
>
> Solomon, after building the temple said, "Will God indeed dwell on the earth? Behold the heaven and heaven of heavens cannot contain thee; how much less this house which I have built. (I Kings 8.27) [53]

Lindsey's belief in the Divine Unity is evident from these words of his:

> The Infinite Creator should be worshipped in all places for He is everywhere...no place is more sacred than another, but every place sacred for the prayer. The worshipper makes the place. Whenever there is a devout humble mind that looks to God, God is there. A mind free from sin is the true temple of God. [54]

Joseph Priestly (1733-1804)

Joseph Priestly was born in the little hamlet of Fieldhead six miles south-west of Leeds in 1733. He was the eldest child of a domestic cloth maker. His mother died when he was six years old. At home he was given a strict Calvinist upbringing, but at school his teachers were dissenting ministers, that is to say, priests who did not agree with all the doctrines of the Church of England. With a view to becoming a minister, he became well-grounded in Latin, Greek and Hebrew. The Elders of the Quakers refused to admit him, as he did not demonstrate sufficient repentance for Adam's sins. The universities refused to accept anyone who did not subscribe to all the doctrines of the orthodox church. Instead, he was sent to a well-known academy where the teachers and students were divided between the orthodoxy of the established church and the "heresy" of belief in One

God. Here he began to doubt the truth of the fundamental dogmas of the Christian church in earnest, especially that of the Trinity. The more he studied the Bible, the more convinced he was about his own views. The writings of Arius, Servetus, and Sozini left a profound impression on him. Like them, he also came to the conclusion that the scriptures provided meagre support for the doctrines of the Trinity and Atonement. The result was that on completion of his studies he left the Academy as a confirmed Arian.

He was appointed as an assistant to a minister on the salary of thirty pounds per annum. When it was discovered that he was an Arian, he was dismissed. In 1758 he succeeded in securing another appointment as a minister in Nantwich in Cheshire. He served there for three years. His income was small but he supplemented it by giving private tuition. He soon acquired the reputation of being a good teacher. The Arians had established an Academy at Warrington in 1757, and on leaving Nantwich, Priestly became a teacher there. He used to visit London during the vacations, and it was on one of these visits that he met Benjamin Franklin for the first time. In 1767 he came nearer his old home, becoming the minister in Mill Hill in Leeds. He stayed there for six years. In Leeds, Priestly printed a number of tracts and soon became well-known as an outstanding and authorative spokesman of unitarianism. In his spare time, he began to study chemistry with considerable success. He won recognition from the Royal Society, and in 1774 he made his crowning discovery of oxygen which made him famous. In the research which followed, he discovered more new gases than all his predecessors had done before him. However, he was more interested in religion than in physical science and regarded these discoveries as a theologian's pastime. In his personal memoirs, he passes over these achievements in the space of about a page. He once wrote, "I have made discoveries in some branches of Chemistry. I never gave much attention to the common routine of it, and know but little of the common processes." [55]

He next joined the Earl of Shellburne as his librarian and literary companion. He was given a generous salary and a life annuity with the freedom to do what he pleased. He remained at this post for seven years, spending the summers in the Earl's country mansion and the winters in London. He also accompanied the Earl on his journeys to Paris, Holland, Belgium and Germany. The Earl found Priestly's friendship with Benjamin Franklin an embarrassment, since the latter was all in favour of the revolution taking place in France at this time. Priestly officially terminated his friendship with Franklin and shortly afterwards went to stay in Birmingham. His stay in this city lasted for eleven years, and although it ended in a crushing tragedy, it was perhaps the happiest period of his life. His duties as a priest were confined to Sundays and so during the rest of the week he was free to work in his laboratory and to write whatever he wished.

It was in Birmingham that Priestly produced his most important and influential work, *History of the Corruptions of Christianity*, which greatly angered the established church. He not only denied the validity of the doctrine of Trinity, but also affirmed the humanity of Jesus. He said that the narratives of the birth of Jesus were inconsistent with one another. He believed that Jesus was a man, constituted in all respects like other men, subject to the same infirmities, the same ignorance, prejudices and frailties. He was chosen by God to introduce a moral dispensation into the world. He was instructed in the nature of his mission, and invested with miraculous powers. Jesus was sent to reveal the great knowledge of the next life in which men would be rewarded according to their acts in this life and not merely by virtue of their having been baptized. These views were not liked either by the government or by the church.

Priestly not only affirmed the humanity of Jesus, but also denied the immaculate conception. He thus laid the foundation of the new thinking which resulted in unitarianism becoming like a voyage in a boat without a rudder riding on a turbulent sea. A sense of direction is totally missing in the movement known as Unitarian Universalism. This denial of the immaculate conception led to a totally unnecessary and bitter controversy that did more harm than good to those who affirmed the Divine Unity. A similar movement had contributed towards the French Revolution and its Reign of Terror. These events on the other side of the Channel had unnerved many people in England. The orthodox church made it appear that the teachings of Priestly would result in the same kind of tragedy in England. Countless insulting and threatening letters began to arrive at his doorstep, and his effigy was burned in different parts of the country.

On July the 14th 1791, a group of people were celebrating the anniversary of the fall of the Bastille in a Birmingham hotel. A mob, whose leaders were the justices of the town, gathered outside and, thinking Priestly was taking part in the celebrations, smashed the hotel windows. Dr. Priestly was not there. The mob then went to his house which, Priestly writes in his memoirs, was "plundered and burnt without mercy." [56] His library, his laboratory and all his papers and manuscripts were destroyed in the fire. Priestly, who had been forewarned by a friend, barely escaped with his life. The next day, the house of all the important Unitarians were burnt, and in the two days which followed the mob began to burn the houses of those people who were not professed Unitarians, but who had given shelter and protection to the Unitarians who had been made homeless. During this time the people of Birmingham were in a panic. All the shops were closed, and people cried out and wrote on their houses "Church and King" to escape the fury of the mob. It was not until the army was called in that the rioters melted away.

It was now too dangerous for Priestly to remain in Birmingham, and he left for London in disguise. Writing about his experiences in Birmingham, he said, "Instead of flying from lawless violence, I had been flying from public justice. I could not have been pursued with more rancour." [57] In London he was unable to openly walk on the streets lest he be recognised and the house of his host attacked and destroyed. After a while he rented a house. The landlord was afraid that not only this house, but also his own might be destroyed.

In 1794, Priestly sailed for America with Benjamin Franklin. There they opened some of the first Unitarian churches in and around Philadelphia. In the years that followed, the situation in England became more relaxed. In 1802, Priestly's old congregation opened a chapel, and Bilsham, a leading Unitarian, was invited to preach the opening sermon. Priestly, however, was content to remain in America where he died in 1804.

Joseph Priestly's main contribution to the unitarians in England was a comprehensive argument, both historical and philosophical, in support of the Unity of God. It was drawn from the Scriptures and the writings of the old Christian fathers, interpreted by reason, and rigorously applied to the religious and political problems of his day. "Absurdity supported by power," he wrote, "will never be able to stand its ground against the efforts of reason." [58] Of all his religious works, the most influential was his "History of the Corruptions of Christianity", written in two volumes, in which he sought to show that true Christianity, embodied in the beliefs of the early Church, was unitarian; and that all departures from that faith were corruptions. The book infuriated the orthodox and delighted the liberals in both England and America. It was publicly burned in Holland. Here follows Priestly's own summary:

> To consider the system of Christianity, one would think it very liable to corruption, or abuse. The great outline of it is that the universal parent of mankind commissioned Jesus Christ to invite men to practice virtue, by the assurance of his mercy to the penitent, and of his purpose to raise to immortal life and happiness all the virtuous and good. Here is nothing that any person could imagine would lead to much subtle speculation, at least such as could excite animosity. The doctrine itself is so plain, that one would think the learned and the unlearned were upon a level with respect to it. And a person unacquainted with the state of things, at the time of its promulgation would look in vain for any probable source of the monstrous corruptions and abuses which crept into the system afterwards. Jesus, however, and his apostles, foretold that there would be a great departure from the truth, and that something would arise in the Church altogether unlike the doctrine which they taught, and even subversive of it.
>
> In reality, however, the causes of the succeeding corruptions did then exist, and accordingly, without anything more than their natural operation, all the abuses rose to their full height; and what is more wonderful still, by the operation of natural causes also, we see the abuses gradually corrected, and Christianity recovering its primitive beauty

and glory.

The causes of the corruptions were almost wholly contained in the established opinions of the heathen world, and especially the philosophical part of it, so that when those heathens embraced Christianity, they mixed their former tenets and prejudices with it. Also, both Jews and heathens were so much scandalized at the idea of being disciples of a man who had been crucified as a common malefactor, that Christians in general were sufficiently disposed to adopt any opinion that would most effectually wipe away this reproach.

The opinion that the mental faculties of man belonging to a substance distinct from his body or brain, and of this invisible spiritual part, or soul, being capable of subsisting before and after its union with the body, which had taken the deepest root in all schools of philosophy, was wonderfully calculated to answer this purpose. For by this means Christians were enabled to give to the soul of Christ what rank they pleased in the heavenly region before he was born. On this principle went the Gnostics, deriving their doctrine from the received oriental philosophy. Afterwards, the philosophising Christians went upon another principle, personifying the wisdom, or logos of God the Father, equal to God the Father Himself...

The abuses of the positive institutions of Christianity, monstrous as they were, naturally arose from the opinion of the purifying and sanctifying virtues of rites and ceremonies, which was the very basis of all the worships of the heathens! And they were also similar to the abuses of the Jewish religion. We likewise see the rudiments of all the monkish austerities in the opinions and practices of the heathens, who thought to purify and exalt the soul by mascerating and mortifying the body.

As to the abuses of the government of the Church, they are as easily accounted for as abuses in civil government; worldly-minded men being always ready to lay hold of every opportunity of increasing their power; and in the dark ages too many circumstances concurred to give the Christian clergy peculiar advantages over the laity in this respect.

Upon the whole, I flatter myself that, to an attentive reader of this work, it will appear, that the Corruption of Christianity, in every article of faith or practice, was the natural consequence of the circumstances in which it was promulgated; and also that its recovery from these corruptions is the natural consequence of different circumstances.

To bring the whole (false Christian position) into a short compass,

1) The General Council gave the Son the same nature with the Father.

2) Admitted the Holy Spirit into the Trinity.

3) Consigned to Christ a human soul in conjunction with the Logos.

4) Settled the hypothetical union of the divine and human nature of Christ, and

5) Affirmed, that in consequence of this union, the two natures constituted only one person.

It requires a pretty good memory to retain these distinctions, it being a business of words only, and ideas are not concerned in it. [59]

Priestly also wrote another book called "The History of Jesus Christ", some of which is reprinted here:

When we inquire into the doctrine of any book, or set of books, concerning any subject, and particular passages are alleged in favour of different opinions, we should chiefly consider what is the general tenor of the whole work with respect to it, or what impression the first careful perusal of it would make upon an impartial reader...

If we consult Moses' account of the creation, we shall find that he makes no mention of more than one God, who made the heavens and the earth, who supplied the earth with plants and animals, and who also formed man. The plural number, indeed, is made use of when God is represented as saying, Genesis 1.26, "Let us make man"; but that this is mere phraesology is evident from its being said immediately after, in the singular number, Genesis 5.27, "God created man in His own image", so that the creator was still One Being. Also, in the account of the building of the Tower of Babel, we read, Genesis 11.7, that "God said let us go down and there confound their language"; but we find, in the very next verse, that it was one being only who actually effected this.

In all the intercourse of God with Adam, Noah, and the other patriarchs, no mention is made of more than one being who addressed them under that character. The name by which he is distinguished is sometimes "Jehova", and at other times, "the God of Abraham", etc., but no doubt can be entertained that this was the same being who is first mentioned under the general title of God, and to whom the making of the heavens and the earth is ascribed.

Frequent mention is made in the scriptures of "angels", who sometimes speak in the name of God, but then they are always represented as the creatures and the servants of God...On no account, however, can these angels be considered as "Gods", rivals of the supreme being, or of the same rank with Him.

The most express declarations concerning the unity of God, and of the importance of the belief of it, are frequent in the Old Testament. The first commandment is, Exodus 20.3, "Thou shalt have no other gods before Me." This is repeated in the most emphatical manner, Deutronomy 5.4, "Hear, O Israel, the Lord thy God is one Lord." I have no occasion to repeat what occurs on this subject in the later prophets. It appears, indeed, to have been the great object of the religion of the Jews, and of their being distinguished from other nations by the superior presence and superintendence of God, to preserve among them the knowledge of the divine unity, while the rest of the world were falling into idolatry. And by means of this nation, and the discipline which it underwent, that great doctrine was effectually preserved among men, and continues to be so to this day.

Had there been any distinction of persons in the divine nature, such as the doctrine of the Trinity supposes, it is at least so like an infringement of the fundamental doctrine of the Jewish religion, that it certainly required to be explained, and the obvious inference from it to be guarded against. Had the eternal Father had a Son, and also a Spirit, each of them equal in power and glory to Himself, though there should have been a sense in which each of them was truly God, and yet there was, properly speaking, only One God; at least the more obvious inference would have been, that if each of the three persons was properly God, they would all together make three Gods. Since, therefore, nothing of this kind is said in the Old Testament, as the objection is never made, nor answered, it is evident that the idea had not then occurred. No expression, or appearance, had at that time even suggested the difficulty.

If we guide ourselves by the sense in which the Jews understood their own sacred books, we cannot but conclude that they contained no such doctrine as that of the Christian Trinity. For it does not appear that any Jew, of ancient or modern times, ever deduced such a doctrine from them. The Jews always interpreted their scriptures as teaching that God is simply One, without distinction of persons, and that the same being who made the world, did also speak to the patriarchs and the prophets without the intervention of any other beings besides angels.

Christians have imagined that the Messiah was to be the second person in the divine trinity; but the Jews themselves, great as were their expectations from the Messiah, never supposed any such thing. And if we consider the prophecies concerning this great personage, we shall be satisfied that they could not possibly have led them to expect any other than a man in that character. The Messiah is supposed to be announced to our first parents under the title of "the seed of the woman", Genesis 3.15...

God promised to Abraham, Genesis 12.3, that "in his seed all the families of the earth should be blessed." This, if it relate to the Messiah at all, can give us no other idea than that one of his seed or posterity, should be the means of conferring great blessings on mankind. What else, also, could be suggested by the description which Moses is supposed to give of the Messiah, when he said, Deutronomy 18.18, "I will raise them up a prophet, from among their brethren, like unto thee, and will put my words in his mouth, and he shall speak unto them all that I shall command him."? Here is nothing like a second person in the trinity, a person equal to the Father, but a mere prophet, delivering in the name of God, whatever he is ordered to do...

In the New Testament we find the same doctrine concerning God that we do in the Old. To the scribe who inquired which was the first and the greatest commandment, our Saviour answered, Mark 12.29, "The first of all the commandments is, Hear O Israel, the Lord our God is one Lord," etc., and the scribe answered to him, "Well, Master, thou hast said the truth; for there is one God, and there is none other but He," etc.

Christ himself always prayed to this one God, as his God and Father. He always spoke of himself as receiving his doctrine and his power from Him, and again and again disclaimed having any power of his own, John 5.19, "Then answered Jesus and said unto them, 'Verily, verily, I say unto you, the Son can do nothing of himself.'" Chaldeans 14.10, "The words which I speak unto you, I speak not of myself, but the Father that dwelleth in me, he doth the works," Chaldeans 20.17, "Go to my brethren, and say unto them, I ascend unto my Father, and your Father, and unto my God and your God." It cannot, surely, be God who uses such language as this.

The apostles to the latest period of their writings, speak the same language; representing the Father as the only true God, and Christ as a man, the servant of God, who raised him from the dead, and gave him all the power of which he is possessed, as a reward of his obedience, Acts 2.22, Peter says, "Ye men of Israel, hear these words, Jesus of Nazareth, a man approved of God among you, by miracles, and wonders, and signs, which God did by him, etc., whom God has raised up." Paul also says, I Timothy 2.5, "There is one God, and one mediator between God and men, the man Christ Jesus.". . .

It will be seen in the course of this history that the common people, for whose use the books of the New Testament were written, saw nothing in them of the doctrines of the pre-existence or divinity of Christ, which many persons of this day are so confident that they see in them...Why was not the doctrine of the trinity taught as explicitly, and in as definite a manner in the New Testament at least, as the doctrine of the Divine Unity is taught in both the Old and New Testament, if it be a truth? And why is the doctrine of the unity always delivered in so unguarded a manner, and without any exception made in favour of a trinity, to prevent any mistake with respect to it, as is always now done in our orthodox catechisms, creeds, and discourses on the subject?. . .Divines are content to build the strange and inexplicable doctrine of the trinity upon mere inferences from casual expressions, and cannot pretend to one clear, express, and unequivocal textual source.

There are many, very many, passages of scripture, which inculcate the doctrine of the divine unity in the clearest and strongest manner. Let one such passage be produced in favour of the trinity. And why should we believe things so mysterious without the clearest and most express evidence.

There is also another consideration which should be recommended to those who maintain that Christ is either God, or the maker of the world under God. It is this: The manner in which our Lord speaks of himself, and of the power by which he worked miracles, is inconsistent, according to the common construction of language, with the idea of his being possessed of any proper power of his own, more than other men have.

If Christ was the maker of the world...he could not ...have said that of himself he could do nothing, that the words which he spoke were not his own, and that the Father within him did the works. For if any ordinary man, doing what other men usually do, should apply this language to himself, and say that it was not he that spoke or acted, but God who spoke and acted by him, and that otherwise he was not capable of so speaking or acting at all, we should not hesitate to say that his language was either false or blasphemous...

It would also be an abuse of language...if Christ could be supposed to say that his Father was greater than he, and yet secretly mean his human nature only, while his divine nature was at the same time fully equal to that of the Father. There is nothing that can be called an account of the divine, or even the super-angelic nature of Christ in the gospels of Matthew, Mark, or Luke; and allowing that there may be some colour for it in the introduction to the gospel of John, it is remarkable that there are many passages in his gospel which are decisively in favour of his simple humanity.

Now these evangelists could not imagine that either the Jews or the Gentiles, for whose use their gospels were written, would not stand in need of information on a subject of so much importance, which was so very remote from the apprehensions of them both, and which would at the same time have so effectually covered the reproach of the cross, which was continually abject to the Christians of that age. If the doctrines of the divinity, or pre-

176

existence of Christ are true, they are no doubt in the highest degree important and interesting. Since, therefore, these evangelists give no certain and distinct account of them, and say nothing at all of their importance, it may be safely inferred that they were unknown to them.

It must also be asked how the apostles could continue to call Christ a man, as they always do, both in the book of Acts, and in their epistles, after they had discovered him to be either God, or a super-angelic being, the maker of the world under God. After this, it must have been highly degrading, unnatural, and improper, notwithstanding his appearance in human form...Let us put ourselves in the place of the apostles and first disciples of Christ. They certainly saw and conversed with him at first on the supposition that he was a man like themselves. Of this there can be no doubt. Their surprise, therefore, upon being informed that he was not a man, but really God, or even the maker of the world under God, would be of the same nature as ours on discovering that a man of our acquaintance was supposed to be in reality God, or the maker of the world. Let us consider then, how we should feel, how we should behave towards such a person, and how we should speak of him afterwards. No one, I am confident, would ever call any person a man, after he was convinced he was either God, or an angel. He would always speak of him in a manner suitable to his proper rank.

Suppose that any two men of our acquaintance, should appear, on examination to be the angels Michael and Gabriel, would we call them men after that? Certainly not. We would naturally say to our friends, "those two persons whom we took to be men, are not men, but angels in disguise." This language would be natural. Had Christ, therefore, been anything more than man before he came into the world, and especially had he been either God, or the maker of the world, he never could have been considered as being a man, while he was in it; for he could not divest himself of his superior and proper nature. However disguised, he would always in fact have been whatever he had been before, and would have been so styled by all who truly knew him.

Least of all would Christ have been considered as a man in reasoning, and argumentation, though his external appearance should have so far put men off their guard, as to have led them to give him that appellation...

It must strike every person who gives the least attention to the phraesology of the New Testament, that the terms "Christ" and "God", are perpetually used in contradistinction to each other, as much as "God" and "man"; and if we consider the natural use of words, we become satisfied that this would not have been the case, if the former could have been predicated of the latter, that is, if Christ had been God.

We say "the prince and the king", because the prince is not a king. If he had been, we should have had recourse to some other distinction, as that of "greater and less", "senior and junior", "father and son", etc. When therefore the apostle Paul said, that the Church at Corinth was Christ's, and that Christ was God's, and that manner of distinguishing them is recurrent in the New Testament, it is evident that he could have no idea of Christ being God, in any meaningful sense of the word.

In like manner, Clemens Romanus, calling Christ the "sceptre of the Majesty of God", sufficiently proves that in his idea the sceptre was one thing, and the God whose sceptre it was, another. This, I say, must have been the case when this language was first adopted.

Having shown that the general tenor of the scriptures, and several considerations that obviously may be deduced from them are highly unfavourable to the doctrine of the trinity, or to those of the divinity or pre-existence of Christ, there arises another consideration, which has been little attended to, but which seems very strongly to go against either of these doctrines having been known in the time of the apostles, and therefore against their being the doctrine of the scriptures. That Jesus was even the Messiah, was divulged with the greatest caution, both to the apostles and to the body of the Jews. For a long time our Lord said nothing explicit on this subject, but left his disciples, as well as the Jews at large, to judge him from what they saw. In this manner only he replied to the messengers that John the Baptist sent to him.

If the high-priest expressed his horror, by rending his clothes, on Jesus avowing himself to be the Messiah, what would he have done if he had heard or suspected, that he had made any higher pretensions? And if he had made them, they must have transpired. When the people in general saw his miraculous works, they only wondered that God should have given such power to a man. Matthew

9.8, "When the multitude saw it, they marvelled, and glorified God, who had given such power unto men." At the time that Herod heard of him, it was conjectured by some that he was Elias, by others, a prophet, and by some that he was John risen from the dead; but none of them imagined that he was either the most high God himself, or the maker of the world under God. It was not so much as suggested by any person that Jesus performed his mighty works by any power of his own. If the doctrine of the divinity of Christ had been actually preached by the apostles, and the Jewish converts in general had adopted it, it could not but have been well known to the unbelieving Jews. And would they, who were at that time, and have been ever since, so exceedingly zealous with respect to the doctrine of the divine unity, not have taken the alarm, and have urged this objection to Christianity, as teaching the belief of more Gods than one in the apostolic age? And yet no trace of anything of this nature can be perceived in the whole history of the book of Acts, or anywhere else in the New Testament. To answer the charge of holding two or three Gods, is a very considerable article in the writings of several of the ancient Christian Fathers. Why then do we find nothing of this kind in the age of the apostles? The only answer is, that then there was no occasion for it, the doctrine of the divinity of Christ not then having been put forward.

What was the accusation against Stephen (Acts 6.13) but his speaking blasphemous things against the temple and the law? If we accompany the apostle Paul in all his travels, and attend to his discourses with the Jews in their synagogues, and their perpetual and inveterate persecution of him, we shall find no trace of their so much as suspecting that he preached a new divinity, as the godhead of Christ must have appeared, and always has appeared to them.

Is it possible to give due attention to these considerations, and not be aware that the apostles had never been instructed in any such doctrines as those of the divinity or pre-existence of Christ? If they had, as the doctrines were quite new, and must have appeared extraordinary, we should certainly have been able to trace the time when they were communicated to them. They would naturally have expressed some surprise, if they had intimated no doubt about the truth of the information. If they received them with unshaken faith themselves, they would have taught them to others, who would not have received them so readily. They would have had the doubts of some to encounter, and the objections of others to answer. And yet, in all their history, and copious writings, we perceive no trace of their own surprise, or doubts or of the surprise, doubts, or objections of others.

It must be acknowledged that the proper object of prayer is God the Father, who is called the first person in the trinity. Indeed, we cannot find in the scriptures either any precept that will authorise us to address ourselves to any other person, or any proper example of it. The sort of thing that can be alleged to this purpose, like Stephen's short address to Christ after he had seen him in vision, is very inconsiderable. Jesus himself always prayed to his Father, and with as much humility and resignation as the most dependent being in the universe could possibly do; always addressing him as his Father, or the author of his being; and he directs his disciples to pray to the same being, the One, he says, we ought to serve.

Accordingly, the practice of praying to the Father only was long universal in the Christian church. The short addresses to Christ, as those in the Litany, "Lord have mercy upon us, Christ have mercy upon us," being comparatively of late date. In the Clementine liturgy, the oldest that is extant, contained in the Apostolical Constitutions, which were probably composed about the fourth century, there is no trace of any such thing. Oregen, in a large treatise on the subject of prayer, urges very forcibly the propriety of praying to the Father only, and not to Christ; and as he gives no hint that the public forms of prayer had anything reprehensible in them in that respect, we are naturally led to conclude that, in his time, such petitions to Christ were unknown in the public assemblies of Christians.

Let us now attend to some particulars in the history of the apostles. When Herod had put to death James, the brother of John, and imprisoned Peter, we read, Acts 12.5, that "prayer was made without ceasing of the church unto God," not to Christ, "for him." When Paul and Silas were in prison at Philippi, we read, Acts 16.25, that they "sung praises to God," not to Christ. And when Paul was warned of what would befall him if he went to Jerusalem, Acts 21.14, he said, "the will of the Lord be done." This, it must be supposed, was meant of God the Father, because Christ himself used the same language in this sense, when praying to the Father, he said, "Not my will, but Thine be done..."

It has been shown that there is no such doctrine as that of the Trinity in the scriptures. The doctrine itself, as has been clearly demonstrated, has proved impossible for reasonable men to accept or even hold in their minds, as it implies contradictions which render it meaningless.

The Athanasian doctrine of the trinity asserts in effect that nothing is wanting in either the Father, the Son, or the Spirit, to let any one of them truly and properly be God, each of them being equal in eternity, and all divine perfections; and yet these three are not three Gods, but only one God. They are therefore both one and many in the same respect — in each being perfect God. This is certainly as much a contradiction, as to say that Peter, James, and John, having each of them everything that is requisite to constitute a complete man, are yet all together not three men, but only one man. For the ideas annexed to the words "God", or "man", cannot make any difference in the nature of the two propositions. After the Council of Nice, there are instances of the doctrine of the trinity being explained in this very manner. The Fathers of that age being particularly intent on preserving the full equality of the three persons, entirely lost sight of their proper unity. Thus no matter how this doctrine is explained, one of these always has to be sacrificed to the other. As people are apt to confuse themselves with the use of the words "person" and "being", these should be defined.

The term "being" may be predicated of every thing, and therefore of each of the three persons in the trinity. For to say that Christ, for instance, is God, but that there is no being, no substance, to which His attributes may be referred, would be manifestly absurd; and therefore when it is said that each of these persons is by himself God, the meaning must be that the Father, separately considered, has a being; that the Son, separately considered, has a being, and likewise that the Holy Spirit, separately considered, has a being. Here then are no less than three beings, as well as three persons, and what can these three beings be but three Gods, without supposing that there are "three co-ordinate persons, or three Fathers, three Sons, or three Holy Ghosts?"

If this mysterious power of generation be peculiar to the Father, why does it not still operate? Is He not an unchangeable being, the same now that He was from the beginning, His perfections the same, and His power of contemplating them the same? Why then are not more sons produced? Has He become incapable of this generation, as the orthodox Fathers used to ask, or does it depend upon His will and pleasure whether He will exert this power of generation? If so, is not the Son as much a creature, depending on the will of the Creator, as anything else produced by Him, though in another manner; and this whether he be of the same substance with Him, or not?

It must also be asked in what manner the third person of the trinity was produced. Was it by the joint exertion of the two first, in the contemplation of their respective perfections? If so, why does not the same operation in them produce a fourth and so on.

Admitting, however, this strange account of the generation of the trinity, that the personal existence of the Son necessarily flows from the intellect of the Father exerted on itself; it certainly implies a virtual priority, or superiority in the Father with respect to the Son; and no being can be properly God, who has any superior. In short, this scheme effectually overturns the doctrine of the proper equality, as well as the unity of the three persons in the trinity.

The great objection to the doctrine of the trinity is that it is an infringement of the doctrine of the unity of God, as the sole object of worship, which it was the primary design of Divine Revelation to establish. Any modification of this doctrine, therefore, or any other system whatever, ought to be regarded with suspicion, in proportion as it makes a multiplicity of objects of worship, for that is to introduce idolatry. [60]

The Unitarian movement in England had a profound effect in America. It started as an off-shoot of Calvinism, but by the seventeenth century, the different foundations gradually changed into religious covenants and there was not so much emphasis placed on dogma. Thus the way was opened for gradual theological change. Charles Chauncy, (1705-1757), of Boston, gave a definite direction to the establishment of belief in the Divine Unity. Under James Freeman, (1759-1835), the congregation of King's chapel purged their Anglican Liturgy of all references to the doctrine of Trinity. This took place in 1785. Thus, the first Unitarian Church came into existence in the New World. The doctrines of Priestly were openly printed and freely distributed. They were received by the majority of the people. The result was that unitarianism was accepted by all the ministers in Boston except one.

William Ellery Channing (1780-1842)

William Channing was born in 1780. At the age of twenty-three he came to Boston and began his ministry which was to have a great influence on unitarian thought. Channing never accepted the doctrine of Trinity, but it was then not considered safe to denounce it openly. Together with other Unitarian ministers, he was accused of secretly spreading his views against the doctrine of Trinity. Channing replied that their views on Trinity were not concealed, but that they preached as if this doctrine had never been known. Channing said they had adopted this approach so as not to divide the Christians against each other. Thus, at this stage, the unitarian movement had not come out into the open.

In 1819, Channing gave a discourse at the ordination of the Reverend Jared Sparks. In his inimitable way, he outlined the salient features of the unitarian belief. He said that the New Testament was based on the Old Testament. The teaching dispensed to the Christians was a continuation of the Jewish one. It was the completion of a vast scheme of Providence which required a vast perspective to be understood.

Keeping this in mind, he said, he affirmed the belief that God never contradicts in one part of the Scripture what He teaches in the other, and "never contradicts in revelation, what He teaches in His works and providence. And we therefore distrust every interpretation, which, after deliberate attention, seems repugnant to any established truth." Channing was insistent that man should make use of his reason: "God has given us a rational nature, and will call us to account for it. We may let it sleep, but we do so at our peril. Revelation is addressed to us as rational beings. We may wish, in our sloth, that God had given us a system demanding no labour of comparing, limiting, and inferring. But such a system would be at variance with the whole character of our present existence; and it is the part of wisdom to take revelation as it is given to us, and to interpret it by the help of the faculties, which it everywhere supposes, and on which it is founded." He went on to say that "if God be infinitely wise He cannot sport with the understanding of His creatures. A wise teacher discovers his wisdom in adapting himself to the capacities of his pupils, not in perplexing them with what is unintelligible, not in distressing with apparent contradictions. . .It is not the mark of wisdom to use an unintelligible phraesology to communicate what is above our capacity, to confuse and unsettle the intellect by appearance of contradictions. . .A revelation is a gift of light. It cannot thicken our darkness and multiply our perplexities."

Following these principles, Channing continued,

> ...in the first place, we believe in the doctrine of God's Unity, or that there is One God and One only. To this truth we give infinite importance and we feel ourselves bound to take heed lest any man spoil us of it by vain philosophy. The proposition that there is One God seems to us exceedingly plain. We understand by it that there is One Being. One Mind, One Person, One Intelligent Agent and One only to whom underived and infinite perfection and dominion belongs. We conceive that these words could have conveyed no other meaning to the simple and uncultivated people who were set apart to be the depositaries of this great truth and who were utterly incapable of understanding those hair-breadth distinctions between being and person which the sagacity of later ages has discovered. We find no intimation that God's unity was a quite different thing from the one-ness of other intelligent beings.
>
> We object to the doctrine of the Trinity, that whilst acknowledging in words, it subverts in effect, the unity of God. According to this doctrine, there are three infinite and equal persons, possessing supreme divinity, called the Father, Son and Holy Ghost. Each of these persons, as described by theologians, has his own particular consciousness, will and perceptions. They love each other, converse with each other, and delight in each other's society. They perform different parts in man's redemption, each having his appropriate office, and neither doing the work of the other. The Son is mediator and not the Father. The Father

sends the Son, and is not himself sent; nor is he conscious, like the Son, of taking flesh. Here, then, we have three intelligent agents, possessed of different consciousness, different wills, and different perceptions, performing different acts, and sustaining different relations; and if these things do not imply and constitute three minds or beings, we are utterly at a loss to know how three minds or beings are to be formed. It is a difference of properties, and acts, and consciousness, which leads us to the belief of different intelligent beings, and if this mark fails us, our whole knowledge falls; we have no proof, that all the agents and persons in the universe are not one and the same mind. When we attempt to conceive of three Gods, we can do nothing more than represent to ourselves three agents, distinguished from each other by similar marks and peculiarities to those which separate the persons of the Trinity; and when common Christians hear these persons spoken of as conversing with each other, loving each other, and performing different acts, how can they help regarding them as different beings, different minds?

We do, then with all earnestness, though without reproaching our brethren, protest against the irrational and unscriptural doctrine of the Trinity. "To us," as to the Apostle and the primitive Christians, "there is one God, even the Father." With Jesus, we worship the Father, as the only living and true God. We are astonished, that any man can read the New Testament, and avoid the conviction, that the Father alone is God. We hear our Saviour continually distinguished from Jesus by this title. "God sent His Son." "God annointed Jesus." Now, how singular and inexplicable is this phraesology, which fills the New Testament, if this title belong equally to Jesus, and if a principal object of this book is to reveal him as God, as partaking equally with the Father in supreme divinity! We challenge our opponents to adduce one passage in the New Testament, where the word God means three persons, where it is not limited to one person, and where, unless turned from its usual sense by the connection, it does not mean the Father. Can stronger proof be given, that the doctrine of three persons in the Godhead is not a fundamental doctrine of Christianity?

This doctrine, were it true, must, from its difficulty, singularity, and importance, have been laid down with great clearness, guarded with great care, and stated with all possible precision. But where does this statement appear? From the many passages which treat of God, we ask for one, one only, in which we are told, that He is a three-fold being, or, that He is three persons, or that He is Father, Son, and Holy Ghost. On the contrary, in the New Testament, where, at least, we might expect many express assertions of this nature, God is declared to be one, without the least attempt to prevent the acceptation of the words in their common sense; and He is always spoken of and addressed in the singular number, that is, in language which was universally understood to intend a single person, and to which no other idea could have been attached, without an express admonition. So entirely do the Scriptures abstain from stating the Trinity, that when our opponents would insert it into their creeds and doxologies, they are compelled to leave the Bible, and to invent forms of words altogether unsanctioned by Scriptural phraseology. That a doctrine so strange, so liable to misapprehension, so fundamental as this is said to be, and requiring such careful exposition, should be left so undefined and unprotected, to be made out by inference, and to be hunted through distant and detached parts of Scripture, this is a difficulty, which, we think, no ingenuity can explain.

We have another difficulty. Christianity, it must be remembered, was planted and grew up amidst sharp-sighted enemies, who overlooked no objectionable part of the system, and who must have fastened with great earnestness on a doctrine involving such apparent contradictions as the Trinity. We cannot conceive an opinion, against which the Jews, who prided themselves on an adherence to God's unity, would have raised an equal clamour. Now, how happens it, that in the apostolic writings, which relate so much to objections against Christianity, and to the controversies which grew out of this religion, not one word is said, implying that objections were brought against the Gospel from the doctrine of the Trinity, not one word is uttered in its defence and explanation, not a word to rescue it from reproach and mistake? This argument has almost the force of demonstration. We are persuaded, that had three divine persons been announced by the first preachers of Christianity, all equal, and all infinite, one of whom was the very Jesus who had lately died on a cross, this peculiarity of Christianity would have almost absorbed every other, and the great labour of the Apostles would have been to repel the continual assaults, which it would have awakened. But the fact is, that not a whisper of objection to Christianity, on that account, reaches our ears from the apostolic age. In the Epistles we see not a trace of controversy called forth by the Trinity.

We have further objections to this doctrine, drawn from its practical influence. We regard it as unfavourable to devotion, by dividing and distracting the mind in its communion with God. It is a great excellence of the doctrine of God's Unity, that it offers to us One object of supreme homage, adoration, and love, One Infinite Father, One Being of beings, One Original and Fountain, to Whom we may refer all good, in Whom all our powers and affections may be concentrated, and Whose lovely and venerable nature may pervade all our thoughts. True piety, when directed to an undivided Deity, has a chasteness, a singleness, most favourable to religious awe and love. Now the Trinity sets before us three distinct objects of supreme adoration; three infinite persons, having equal claims on our hearts; three divine agents, performing different offices, and to be acknowledged and worshipped in different relations. And is it possible, we ask, that the weak and limited mind of man can attach itself to these with the same power and joy, as to One Infinite Father, the only First Cause, in Whom all the blessings of nature and redemption meet as their centre and source? Must not devotion be distracted by the equal and rival claims of three equal persons, and must not the worship of the conscientious, consistent Christian be disturbed by an apprehension, lest he withhold from one or another of these, his due proportion of homage?

We also think, that the doctrine of the Trinity injures devotion, not only by joining to the Father other objects of worship, but by taking from the Father the supreme affection, which is His due, and transferring it to the Son. This is a most important view. That Jesus Christ, if exalted into the infinite Divinity, should be more interesting than the Father, is precisely what might be expected from history, and from the principles of human nature. Men want an object of worship like themselves, and the great secret of idolatry lies in this propensity. A God, clothed in our form, and feeling our wants and sorrows, speaks to our weak nature more strongly than a Father in heaven, a pure spirit, invisible and unapproachable, save by the re-reflecting and purified mind. We think too, that the peculiar offices ascribed to Jesus by the popular theology, make him the most attractive person in the Godhead. The Father is the depository of the justice, the vindicator of the rights, the avenger of the laws of the Divinity. On the other hand, the Son, the brightness of the divine mercy, stands between the incensed Deity and guilty humanity, exposes his meek head to the storms, and his compassionate breast to the sword of the divine justice, bears our whole load of punishment, and purchases with his blood every blessing which descends from heaven. Need we state the effect of these representations, especially on common minds, for whom Christianity was chiefly designed, and whom it seeks to bring to the Father as the loveliest being?

Having thus given our views of the unity of God, I proceed in the second place to observe, that we believe in the unity of Jesus Christ. We believe that Jesus is one mind, one soul, one being, as truly as we are, and equally distinct from the one God. We complain of the doctrine of the Trinity, that not satisfied with making God three beings, it makes Jesus Christ two beings, and thus introduces infinite confusion into our conceptions of his character. This corruption of Christianity, alike repugnant to common sense and to the general strain of Scripture, is a remarkable proof of the power of a false philosophy in disfiguring the simple truth of Jesus.

According to this doctrine, Jesus Christ, instead of being one mind, one conscious intelligent principle, whom we can understand, consists of two souls, two minds; the one divine, the other omniscient. Now we maintain, that this is to make Christ two beings. To denominate him one person, one being and yet to suppose him made up of two minds, infinitely different from each other, is to abuse and confound language, and to throw darkness over all our conceptions of intelligent natures. According to the common doctrine, each of these two minds in Christ has its own consciousness, its own will, its own perceptions. They have in fact no common properties. The divine mind feels none of the wants and sorrows of the human, and the human is infinitely removed from the perfection and happiness of the divine. Can you conceive of two beings in the universe more distinct? We have always thought that one person was constituted and distinguished by one consciousness. The doctrine, that one and the same person, should have two consciousnesses, two wills, two souls, infinitely different from each other, this we think an enormous tax on human credulity.

We say, that if a doctrine so strange, so difficult, so remote from all the previous conceptions of men, be indeed a part and an essential part of revelation, it must be taught with great distinctions, and we ask our brethren to point to some plain, direct passage, where Christ is said to be composed of two minds infinitely different, yet constituting one person. We find none. Other Christians, indeed, tell us, that this doctrine is necessary to the harmony of the Scriptures, that some texts ascribe to Jesus Christ human, and others, divine properties, and that to reconcile these, we must suppose two minds, to which these properties may be referred. In other words, for the purpose of reconciling certain difficult passages. . .we must invent an hypothesis vastly more difficult, and involving gross absurdity. We are to find our way out of a labyrinth, by a clue which conducts us into mazes more inextricable.

Surely, if Jesus Christ felt that he consisted of two minds, and that this was a leading feature of his religion, his phraseology respecting himself would have been coloured by this peculiarity. The universal language of men is framed upon the idea, that one person is one person, is one mind, and one soul; and when the multitude heard this language from the lips of Jesus, they must have taken it in its usual sense, and must have referred to a single soul all of which he spoke, unless expressly instructed to interpret it differently. But where do we find this instruction? Where do you meet, in the New Testament, the phraseology which abounds in Trinitarian books, and which necessarily grows from the doctrine of two natures in Jesus? Where does this divine teacher say, "This I speak as God, and this as man; this is true only of my human mind, this only of my divine"? Where do we find in the Epistles a trace of this strange phraseology? Nowhere. It was not needed in that day. It was demanded by the errors of a later age.

We believe then, that Christ is one mind, one being, and, I add, a being distinct from the one God. . .We wish, that those from whom we differ, would weigh one striking fact. Jesus, in his preaching, continually spoke of God. The word was always in his mouth. We ask, does he, by this word, ever mean himself? We say, never. On the contrary, he most plainly distinguishes between God and himself, and so do his disciples. How this is to be reconciled with the idea, that the manifestation of Christ, as God, was a primary object of Christianity, our adversaries must determine.

If we examine the passages in which Jesus is distinguished from God, we shall see, that they not only speak of him as another being, but seem to labour to express his inferiority. He is continually spoken of as the Son of God, sent of God, receiving all his powers from God, working miracles because God was with him, judging justly because God taught him, having claims on our belief, because he was annointed and sealed by God, and was able of himself to do nothing. The New Testament is filled with this language. Now, we ask, what impression this language was fitted and intended to make? Could any, who heard it, have imagined that Jesus was the very God to whom he was so industriously declared to be inferior; the very Being by whom he was sent, and from whom he professed to have received his message and power.

Trinitarians profess to derive some important advantages from their mode of viewing Christ. It furnishes them, they tell us, with an infinite atonement, for it shows them an infinite being suffering for their sins. The confidence with which this fallacy is repeated astonishes us. When pressed with the question, whether they really believe, that the infinite and unchangeable God suffered and died on the cross, they acknowledge that this is not true, but that Christ's human mind alone sustained the pains of death. How have we, then, an infinite sufferer? This language seems to us an imposition on common minds, and very derogatory to God's justice, as if this attribute could be satisfied by a sophism and a fiction... [61]

Thus, although Channing believed that Jesus was crucified and was resurrected, he was still able to illustrate the absurdity of the doctrine of atonement, despite his ignorance of the fact that the events this doctrine is based on never took place. Channing refuted the doctrine of atonement on the following grounds:

There is no passage in the Bible in which we are told that the son of man is infinite and needs an infinite atonement. This doctrine teaches us that man, although created by God a frail, erring and imperfect being, is regarded by the Creator as an infinite offender. Channing said that the unitarians believed that God can forgive sin without this rigid expedient. This doctrine which talks of God becoming a victim and a sacrifice for his own rebellious subjects is as irrational as it is unscriptural. Atonement should be made to and not by God. If infinite atonement was necessary, which only God can make so, then God must become a sufferer and must take upon Himself our pain and woe a thought which the mind cannot conceive. To escape this difficulty, we are told that Christ suffered as man and not as God. But if man only suffered for a short and limited period, then what was the necessity for infinite atonement? If we have God in heaven with infinite goodness and power, we need no other infinite person to save us. This doctrine dishonours God when it says that without the help of a second and a third deity, He could not save man. If an infinite satisfaction to justice was indispensable to man's salvation, this should have been expressed clearly and definitely in at least one passage of the Bible. This doctrine is like a judge punishing himself for the crime committed by a transgressor appearing in his court.

The Bible says, "Everyone must appear before the judgement seat of Christ to receive according to things done in the body according to that he hath done whether it be good or bad." (II Corinthians 5.10) And again, "Everyone of us must give account of himself to God." (Romans 14.10) If by the crucifixion of Jesus, God's justice is satisfied for sins past, present and to come, then God has lost all power to enjoin godliness and a virtuous life, and also all perogative in punishing disobedience. If God punishes a sinner on the Day of Judgement, then it clearly means that either God commits a breach of faith or else the doctrine of atonement is not true.

Up until 1819, the congregations of the Unitarians were held either in private houses or in the hall of the Medical College in Barclay Street, in Boston. In 1820, the construction of a building for unitarian worship was started. It was completed in 1821. Despite this proof of their becoming more established, the unitarians were still called "a crew of heretics, infidels, or atheists." [62] However, this year saw a reversal of the policy of cautious preaching by the Unitarians. Channing, who had so far received the narrow and bitter attacks from the pulpits of the orthodox church without retaliating, felt that the time had come for him to strike back with all the force at his command and speak out boldly in support of his faith, and against the prejudices of orthodoxy. In his book, "A History of Unitarianism", E. M. Wilber writes of Channing that, "His theme was that the Scriptures, when reasonably interpreted, teach the doctrine held by the Unitarians. It took up the main doctrines on which the Unitarians depart from the orthodox and held them up one by one for searching examination. . .it made an eloquent and lofty appeal against a scheme so full of unreason, inhumanity and gloom as Calvinism. . .and impeached the orthodoxy of the day before the bar of the popular reason and conscience." [63]

The cause of Unitarianism in America was further helped by a convention held at Massachusetts in 1823, when the orthodox church made an unsuccessful attempt to impose a doctrinal test on ministers who wished to preach to Unitarian congregations. This failure, however, succeeded in bringing the unitarian movement out into the open, and served to unite its different members in the defence of a common cause.

In 1827, a second church was opened with a famous sermon by Channing. To him, writes E. M. Wilber, should go the credit of being primarily responsible for the result that "even if not explicitly acknowledged, the doctrine of Trinity, even if still formally confessed, had ceased to be the centre of orthodox faith, and was no longer given its old emphasis; and that the outstanding doctrines of Calvinism had received new interpretations which the fathers would have rejected with horror." [64] These developments did not take place without resistance. In 1833, the Unitarians were attacked as "cold-blooded infidels" and abuses were hurled that were "unparallelled even in the days of theological intolerance and bigotry." [65]It is recorded that as late as 1924, thirty or forty Unitarians met in Boston and formed an Anonymous Association. This indicates that although there was no likelihood of their sharing the same fate as earlier Unitarians, there was still an element of danger for a Christian who affirmed the Divine Unity.

Channing remained a firm Unitarian to the end of his days. To him, Jesus was not only human, but also an inspired prophet of God. In contrast with the Calvin doctrines of human depravity, the wrath of God, and the atoning sacrifice of Christ, Channing proclaimed "one sublime idea" which he defined as "the greatness of the soul, its union with God by spiritual likeness, its receptivity of His spirit, its self-forming power, its destination to the ineffable and its immortality." [66] This was a refreshing change from the cold logic and over emphasis on the phenomenal world of Priestly. It breathed life into the Unitarian movement, not only in America, but also in England. Priestly was after all a physical scientist. His reasoning was sound, but his outlook was materialistic. Channing elevated it to sublime spiritual heights. His words made a deep impression on both sides of the Atlantic when he said, "man's rational nature was from God." [67] He protested against every form of sectarian narrowness. Denominational aggression was foreign to his nature and this spirit was infused in the leaders of the movement which culminated in the founding of the Divinity School of Harvard University in 1861.

Part of its constitution reads, "It being understood that every encouragement be given to the serious, impartial and unbiased investigation of Christian truth and that no assent to the peculiarities of any denomination be required of either the students or professors or instructors." [68]In 1825, the American Association was formed, the same year as was done in England. Ralph Waldo Emerson, (1803-1882), resigned the pulpit in Boston and the breach between the old and the new thinking was complete. The religion of Jesus was proclaimed to be the love of God and service of man and this was an "absolute religion."

Unitarianism within Christianity has continued up to the

present day. Many of the Christian sects, although they have little access to the existential reality of Jesus — of how he behaved towards people and conducted his transactions with them, of how he did everything and lived his life — do believe in One God and seek to live according to the Bible's precepts, despite the contradictions within it. However, the confusion caused by the doctrines of atonement and redemption and Trinity, together with the absence of any real guidance as to how to live the way Jesus lived, have caused the now almost complete rejection of Christianity. Today the churches lie empty.

Chapter 8

CHRISTIANITY TODAY

In order to ascertain the nature of Christianity today, it is necessary to bear in mind the distinction between knowledge which is arrived at by observation and deduction, and knowledge which is revealed to man through no power of his own. Deductive knowledge is always changing in the light of fresh observations and new experience. It therefore lacks certainty. Revealed knowledge is from God. In every revealed message, there is a metaphysical aspect and a physical. The metaphysical teaches the nature of the Divine Unity. The physical provides a code of behaviour. Revealed knowledge has always been brought by a messenger who embodied it. The way he lives is the message. To behave as the messenger did is to have knowledge of the message, and in this knowledge is certainty. Christianity today is said to be based on revealed knowledge, but none of the Bible contains the message of Jesus intact, and exactly as it was revealed to him. There is hardly any record of his code of behaviour. The books in the New Testament do not even contain eye-witness accounts of his sayings and actions. They were written by people who derived their knowledge second-hand. These records are not comprehensive. Everything which Jesus said and did which has not been recorded has been lost forever.

Those who seek to verify what is in the New Testament claim that even if by no means comprehensive, it is at least accurate. However, it is significant that all the oldest surviving manuscripts of the New Testament, from which all the present translations of the Bible derive, were written after the Council of Nicea. The Codex Sinaiticus and the Codex Vaticanus date from the late fourth century, and the Codex Alexandrius from the fifth century. As a result of the Council of Nicea, nearly three hundred other accounts of the life of Jesus, many of them eye-witness accounts, were systematically destroyed. The events of the Council of Nicea indicate that the Pauline Church had every reason to change the four gospels which survived. Clearly, the manuscripts of the New Testament which were written after the Council of Nicea are different from the manuscripts which existed before the Council. It is significant that publication of some of the Dead Sea Scrolls, when they do not verify the post-Nicene manuscripts, have been withheld.

The unreliability of the gospels appears to be admitted by the Church itself: The metaphysics of Christianity today is not even based on what is in the gospels. The established church is founded on the doctrine of original sin, of atonement and redemption, of the divinity of Jesus, of the divinity of the Holy Ghost and of Trinity. None of these doctrines are to be found within the gospels. They were not taught by Jesus. They were the fruits of Paul's innovations and the influence of Greek culture and philosophy. Paul never experienced the company nor the direct transmission of knowledge from Jesus. Before his "conversion", he vigourously persecuted the followers of Jesus, and after it he was largely responsible for abandoning the code of behaviour of Jesus when he took "Christianity" to the non-Jews of Greece and beyond. The figure of "Christ" whom he claimed taught him his new doctrine is an imagination. His teaching is based on an event which never took place, the supposed death and resurrection of Jesus.

Despite their doubtful origins, these doctrines form an integral part of the conditioning of anyone who is given a "Christian education". Although many have rejected some or all of them, the magic they exercise is such that those who give them credibility are lead by their logic to believe in the notorious principle: Outside the Church, no salvation." The Church's metaphysical construct is this: The doctrine of atonement and redemption says that Christ who was of God took on human form and became Jesus, who then died for mankind to atone for all its sins. The Church guarantees forgiveness of sins and salvation on the Day of Judgement, for any man who believes in "Christ" and who follows the guidance of the church. Further, it is believed that this contract is available to all people until the end of the world. The natural consequences of this belief are these:

Firstly, it implies that a man is not responsible for his actions and that he will not be held to account for them after his death; for whatever he does he yet believes he will be redeemed by "Christ's sacrifice". However, this does not mean a life of joy on earth. His belief in the doctrine of original sin, which states that because of the fall of Adam, all men are born sinful, means that while he is alive it follows that his condition is one of unworthiness and incompleteness. This tragic view of life is reflected in the following statement of J. G. Vos, a Christian, in which he compares Islam and Christianity:

> There is nothing in Islam to lead a man to say, "Oh wretched man that I am, who shall deliver me from the body of this death?" or "I know that in me; that is, in my flesh, dwelleth no good thing." A religion with reasonable attainable objectives...does not give the sinner the anguish of a guilty conscience nor the frustration of trying without success to attain in practical living the requirements of an absolute moral standard. In brief, Islam makes a man feel good, while Christianity necessarily first, and often thereafter, makes a man feel bad. The religion of the broken heart is Christianity, not Islam. [1]

Secondly, belief in the doctrine of atonement and redemption leads to confusion when a Christian attempts to reconcile the other teachings God has revealed to man with his own belief. It implies that "Christ's sacrifice" and "message" are unique and final, and therefore he cannot accept the teachings of other prophets. At the same time, he cannot deny the truth he finds in them. Thus, a Christian rejects Judaism, yet accepts the Old Testament, which is derived from the teachings which Moses brought to the Jews. He puts himself in the impossible position of having to accept two contradictory beliefs simultaneously, as this passage shows:

> There are elements of relative good in the non-Christian faiths. While the call for separation from false religions is certainly Biblical, and the demonic character of pagan religions is taught in Scripture...still it is also true that

> elements of limited relative good exist in these religions. While it is true that they are demonic in character, it is also true (and Scriptural) that they are products of man's distorted interpretation of God's revelation in nature. Even though they may be works of the devil, still they are not simply works of the devil, but partly products of God's common grace and partly products of sinful man's abuse of God's revelation in nature. [2]

It is significant that Vos does not mention all the distortions the Bible has undergone.

Attempts to avoid the dilemma of simultaneous acceptance and rejection of non-Christian faiths has been made by arguing that some Christians "discern in them the influence of the 'cosmic Christ' who, as the eternal Logos or revealer of the Godhead, is the 'light that enlightens every man.' This view...was summed up by William Temple when he wrote: "By the word of God — that is to say, Jesus Christ — Isaiah and Plato, Zoroaster, Buddha, and Confucius uttered and wrote such truths as they declared. There is only one Divine Light, and every man in his own measure is enlightened by it." [3] The reasoning in this passage relies on the assumption that the "one Divine Light" and "Christ" are the same. Since "Christ" is an imagination, the doctrine fails, and the dilemma remains. It can only be avoided by resorting to George Orwell's 'doublethink'. He defined it thus:

> Doublethink means the power of holding two contradictory beliefs simultaneously, and accepting both of them. The party intellectual knows that he is playing tricks with reality, but by the exercise of doublethink he also satisfies himself that reality is not violated. [4]

Doublethink lies at the root of a Christian's basic assumption that Christ is God. It is around this assumption that the controversy of the two natures of Jesus has raged. One moment he is human. The next moment he is divine. First he is Jesus, then he is Christ. It is only by the exercise of doublethink that a man can hold these two contradictory beliefs simultaneously. It is only by the exercise of doublethink that belief in the doctrine of Trinity can be maintained.

Article VII of the Thirty-nine Articles of the Church of

England begins: "The Old Testament is not contrary to the New..." As Milton has so clearly shown, the Old Testament is full of passages affirming the One-ness of God. There is not one passage which describes the Divine Reality in the terms of the doctrine of Trinity. The act of affirming what is in the Old Testament, and the gospels for that matter, and at the same time affirming belief in the doctrine of Trinity, is perhaps the greatest illustration of the exercise of doublethink within Christianity today. Thus the logic of the established Church's metaphysic, based on doctrines which were not taught by Jesus, obscures not only the nature of Jesus, but also the Divine Unity. The metaphysic of Christianity today is totally opposed to the metaphysic which Jesus brought. The physical aspect of what Jesus brought, his code of behaviour, is today irrecoverably lost. To live as Jesus lived is to understand his message, yet there is virtually no existing record of how Jesus behaved. And what little knowledge exists is often ignored. The most fundamental act of Jesus was that of worship of the Creator, the whole purpose for which man was created. Yet it is evident that no Christian today makes the same acts of worship which Jesus made. Jesus usually prayed in the synagogue. He prayed at appointed times each day, in the morning, at mid-day, and in the evening. The exact form of his prayer is no longer extant, but it is known that it was based on the prayer which Moses was given. Jesus said that he had come to uphold the law and not to destroy it one jot or one tithe. Jesus was educated in the synagogue in Jerusalem from the age of twelve. He preached in the synagogue. He used to keep the synagogue clean. No Christian today can be found performing these actions. How many Christians have even been circumcised in the manner that Jesus was? The services now held in today's churches were developed long after Jesus had disappeared. Many of them come directly from the pagan Graeco-Roman mythological rites. The prayers they use are not the prayers which Jesus made. The hymns they sing are not the praises which Jesus sung. Due to the innovations of Paul and his followers, there is no revealed teaching left as to what to eat and what not to eat. Anyone given a "Christian education" today eats what he feels like. Yet Jesus and his true followers only ate kosher meat and were forbidden to eat pig's flesh. The last meal Jesus is known to have eaten before his disappearance was the Passover meal. No Christian today celebrates this longstanding Jewish tradition to which Jesus so meticulously held. It is no longer known in what manner Jesus ate and drank, who he would eat with and who he would not eat with, where he would eat and where he would not eat, when he would eat and when he would not eat. Jesus fasted, but again it is not known how, where and when he fasted. His science of fasting has been lost. There is no record of the food he liked especially, and the food of which he was not particularly fond. Jesus did not marry while he was on earth, but he did not forbid it. There is no passage in the gospels which states that a follower of Jesus must take a vow of celibacy. Nor is there any authority for the establishment of single-sex communities such as monasteries or convents, although these could owe their origin to communities such as the Essenes. The early followers of Jesus who were married must have followed the code of behaviour in marriage which Moses brought. Their example is no longer emulated today.

The breakdown of the family structure in the West demonstrates the lack of an effective guide to behaviour within a Christian marriage, of how a man should behave towards a woman, and a woman towards a man. Extracting a moral principle from the gospels and trying to live by it is not the same as acting in a certain manner because it is known that Jesus acted that way in that situation. One course of action is the fruit of deductive knowledge, the other course of action is by revealed knowledge.

There is no record of how Jesus walked, how he sat, how he stood, how he kept himself clean, how he went to sleep, how he woke up, how he greeted people, how he was with old people, how he was with young people, how he was with old women, how he was with young women, how he was with strangers, how he was with guests, how he was with his enemies, how he conducted his transactions in the market place, how he travelled, what he was allowed to do and what he was not allowed to do.

The records of Jesus' message as revealed to him by God are incomplete and inaccurate. The doctrines on which Christianity today is based are not to be found within these records. The record of how Jesus acted is almost non-existent, and what little is known is virtually ignored. Yet the institution of the Church, in whatever form, has always claimed to be the interpreter and guardian of Jesus' message. The Church was not instituted by Jesus. He did not establish a hierarchy of priests to act as mediators between God and man. Yet the established Pauline church, from very early on, always taught Christians to believe that their salvation was assured if they acted and believed as the Church told them. From where did the Church derive its authority?

This claim for authority, in its most extreme form, is to be found in the Roman Catholic Church's doctrine of papal infallibility. Cardinal Heenan has summed it up in these words:

> This secret of this wonderful unity of our Church is Christ's promise that the Church will never fail to teach the truth. Once we know what the Church teaches we accept it. For we know it must be true...All Catholic priests teach the same doctrine because they all obey the Vicar of Christ. The word "vicar" means "one who takes the place of another." The Pope is the Vicar of Christ because he takes the place of Christ as Head of the Church on earth. The Church remains one because all her members believe the same Faith. They believe it because the Church cannot teach what is false. This is what we mean when we say that the Church is infallible. Christ promised to guide his Church. One of the ways Christ chose to guide the Church was by leaving his Vicar on earth to speak for him. That is why we say the Pope is infallible. He is the Head of the infallible Church. God could not allow him to lead it into error." [5]

It is significant that Cardinal Heenan talks only of "Christ", and not of Jesus. He does not refer to the gospels to support his claims.

This dogma has often proved awkward. For if all the popes were infallible, why was Pope Honorius anathematised? Does the recent papal encyclical which states that the Jews were not responsible for the supposed crucifixion of Jesus mean that all the preceding popes were not infallible after all?

Many Roman Catholics today have rejected the validity of "Christ's promise that the Church will never fail to teach the truth" which is not to be found in any of the gospels: The great gap between church teaching and practice troubles Cincinnati's Archbishop Joseph L. Bernadin...Said Bernadin in an interview in U.S. Catholic: "So many consider themselves good Catholics, even though their beliefs and practices seem to conflict with the official teaching in the Church. This is almost a new concept of what it means to be a Catholic today...Once it became legitimate (in 1966) to eat meat on Friday one could doubt the authority of the Pope, practice birth control, leave the priesthood and get married or indeed do anything else one wanted to." Greely writes, "The practice of abstaining from meat on Friday, meant to emulate Jesus's fasting and to commemorate the day he was crucified, eventually became a church commandment and for centuries served as a kind of Roman Catholic badge."

"Vatican II, (the Second Vatican Council of 1962), amazed me," wrote author, Doris Grumbach, in the Critic, "because it raised the possibility of more answers than one, of gray areas, of a private world of conscience and behaviour. But like all places in human experience of rigour and rule, once the window was opened, everything came under question. No constants remained, no absolutes, and the church became for me a debatable question. I still cling to the Gospels, to Christ and some of his followers as central to my life, but the institution no longer seems important to me. I no longer live in it." [6]

The investment of authority in the church, if not its complete infallibility, still remains. It has taken root even within the churches which rejected the authority of the Pope over them. However, the validity of this authority is today being doubted and rejected on a scale that has never been known before. In the words of George Harrison:

> When you're young you get taken to church by your parents and you get pushed into religion at school. They're trying to put something into your mind. Obviously because nobody goes to church and nobody believes in God. Why?

Because they haven't interpreted the Bible as it was intended. I didn't really believe in God as I'd been taught it.
It was just like something out of a science fiction novel.
You're taught just to have faith, you don't have to worry
about it, just believe what we're telling you. [7]

Between the two poles of complete acceptance and complete rejection of the established Church's reliability as the
guardians of the message of Jesus, there lies every shade of
opinions as to what it is to be a Christian. Wilfred Cantwell
Smith writes:

There is so much diversity and clash, so much chaos, in
the Christian Church today that the old ideal of a unified
or systematic Christian truth has gone. For this, the ecu-
menical movement is too late. What has happened is that
the Christian world has moved into that situation of open
variety, of optional alternatives. It would seem no longer
possible for anyone to be told or even to imagine that he
can be told, what it means or should mean, formally and
generically, to be a Christian. He must decide for himself -
and only for himself. [8]

This conclusion implies that there are as many versions of
Christianity today as there are Christians, and that the role
of the church, as an institution which is the guardian of
Jesus's message, has largely ceased to exist: A graduate
student at U.C.L.A. asks: "What is the point of a church
if it's always up to my own conscience?" [9] However, the
church remains an integral part of Western culture today,
and the relationship between the two is an interesting one.

Vast amounts of literature have been written in the West
during the last few centuries, in the attempt to understand
the nature of existence. They provide a catalogue of all the
possible avenues of thought a man's mind will pursue when
he does not have the certainty of revealed knowledge to
live and understand his life by. Some writers such as Pascal
have realised that the mind is a limited tool, and that the
heart is the centre of their being, and the container of real
knowledge:

The heart has its reasons which are unknown to reason...
It is the heart which is aware of God and not reason.
This is what faith is: God perceived intuitively by the

heart, not by reason. [10]

In the attempt to gain access to the heart many have rejected Christianity and experimented with other means:

> Mystical experience is said to lead to real knowledge of "the truth" about the universe. This truth is inexpressible in words, but it can be felt. The medium can be music, drugs, meditation... [11]

These alternative approaches to understanding Reality have been adapted by people in the West on a vast scale, often only as a means of self-gratification.

The Church has greatly accommodated itself to these new trends in the culture of the West. In their attempt to keep the churches full, some priests have introduced pop-groups and discotheques into their routine to attract young people. Concerts, exhibitions and jumble-sales cater for the more conservative tastes. Charitable concerns help establish a sense of purpose for those who indulge in them. These attempts to "modernise" the church and keep it "up to date" are in keeping with the Pauline church's longstanding tradition of compromise by all means. If it cannot pass on the message of Jesus, it must at least provide a "useful social function."

This process of compromise, especially during the last decade, has resulted both in the continued absorption of the Church into the culture, and of the re-absorption of the culture into this changing structure of the Church. It is a two-way process which has endlessly been alternating since Paul and his followers set it in motion. Many people have "returned to Christianity" as a result of their experience with music, drugs and meditation. They tend either to completely reject these experiences, and adopt a puritannical form of Christianity, or else to incorporate their new way of life into their own updated version of Christianity. Both these trends cover up the prophethood of Jesus. He is either exalted as God or regarded as a charismatic cult figure who meant well, but was misunderstood.

The identification of the Church with the culture of the West is clearly apparent by observing how people live today. With the exception of those who have withdrawn into monasteries and convents to remember God, the life-style of those who call themselves Christians closely resembles the life-styles of those who claim to be agnostics, humanists or atheists. Their beliefs may be different, but their general behaviour is the same.

The laws which exist in the "Christian" countries of the West, the laws governing birth and death, the formation and dissolution of marriage, the rights over property within and outside marriage or in the event of divorce or death, adoption and guardianship, commerce and industry, are not to be found in the gospels. They are not laws which have been revealed to man by God. They are the fruits of deductive knowledge. They are either inherited from the Roman system of law, or are based on the common practice of people over a long period of time, or are statutes erected and ammended in accordance with the democratic method, which is the bequest of the ancient Greeks. No one in today's courts of law can refer to the gospels as a binding authority in his dealings with another man, and have it accepted.

The Christianity of today is inseparable from the culture of the West. The Christian Church and the State are one. And the individuals who work within these institutions do not live as Jesus lived. The total sickness of Christianity today is due to the inescapable fact that the Christians of today lack a science of social behaviour and that lack has left them impoverished in this life and unprepared for what happens after death. As Wilfred Cantwell Smith writes:

> To say that Christianity is true is to say nothing significant; the only question that concerns either God or me, or my neighbour is whether my Christianity is true, and whether yours is. And to that question, a truly cosmic one, in my case the only valid answer is a sorrowful "not very..." [12]

It is scarcely surprising in the light of all this that as the churches of the world are emptying — the mosques of Islam are filling up.

Chapter 9

JESUS IN QUR'AN

The Qur'an, the last of the Divine Books, revealed by the Creator to the last of the Messengers, is a source of knowledge about Jesus which is not generally known to most students of Christianity. The Qur'an not only leads us towards a better understanding of who he was, but also, through that understanding, it increases our respect and love for him. The last Revelation, coming as it does some six hundred years after Jesus's birth, tells what is important for us to know about his life and teachings, and places his role as Prophet in the vast perspective that the Unitarians realised lay behind prophecy itself. Qur'an gives that perspective which no other source can provide.

The Qur'an does not cover the life of Jesus in any great detail as regards specific events. The miracles and powers which he was given are referred to, but mostly in general terms. Similarly, the Book he was given by Allah, the Ingeel, is mentioned several times, but its exact contents are not indicated. However, the Qur'an is very specific as to his purpose, how he appeared on earth, who he was, and, equally important, who he was not, and how his mission ended.

Before looking at his life, it would be helpful to examine what his function on earth was, and how he fits into the pattern of what came before him and what was to come after him: it is stated again and again that Jesus was one of the long line of prophets who had been sent to the peoples of this earth; that he was a Messenger whose guidance and teachings were a reaffirmation and extension of the guidance which the prophets before him had brought, and were a preparation for the guidance which the prophet coming after him would bring.

The first mention of Jesus is made very early on in the Qur'an:

> And truly We gave to Moses the Books and
> We caused a train of messengers to follow after him,
> and We gave to Jesus, son of Mary, clear proofs
> and We supported him with the Pure Spirit.* (2.87)

The following passage reminds us of the line of messengers, of which Jesus was a part. After mentioning Abraham, it continues:

> And We bestowed on him Isaac and Jacob; each of them
> We guided; and Noah did We guide in an earlier time,
> and of his seed David and Solomon and Job and Joseph
> and Moses and Aaron. Thus do We reward the good.
> And Zachariah and John and Jesus and Elias.
> Each one was of the righteous. And Ishmael and Elisha
> and Jonah and Lot. Each one of them did We prefer
> above the (other) creatures. (6.84-86)

And this list of messengers is by no means complete, for there are,

> ...messengers We have mentioned to you before and
> messengers We have not mentioned to you... (4.164)

In fact, Sayidina Muhammad, peace of Allah be upon him, said that Jesus was one of one hundred and twenty-four thousand prophets, between whom there is no cause for conflict or argument. Allah tells His Messenger in one passage of Qur'an:

> Say: We believe in Allah and what is revealed to us
> and what was revealed to Abraham and Ishmael and
> Isaac and Jacob and the tribes, and what was entrusted
> to Moses and Jesus and the prophets from their Lord.
> We make no distinction between any of them,
> and to Him we have surrendered. (3.84)

*The Pure Spirit refers to the Angel Gabriel.

All the prophets are well aware that they have been sent by Allah for the same purpose and with the same message:

> And when We exacted a covenant from the Prophets,
> And from you (O Muhammad) and from Noah
> and Abraham and Moses and Jesus, son of Mary.
> We took from them a solemn covenant;
> that He may ask the loyal of their loyalty.
> And He has prepared a painful doom
> for the unfaithful. (33.7-8)

> O you Messengers! Eat of the good things,
> and do right. See! I am Aware of what you do.
> And see! This your life-transaction is one
> life-transaction and I am your Lord,
> so keep your duty to Me. (23.51-52)

> He has ordained for you that life-transaction
> which He commended to Noah, and that which
> We inspire in you (Muhammad), and that which
> We commended to Abraham and Moses and Jesus,
> saying: Establish the life-transaction
> and do not be divided in it. (42.13)

Thus, the picture which unfolds is not that of some remarkable man who appeared on earth as an isolated event in an otherwise chaotic world, but of a messenger who, like all the other messengers, was sent for his time and his age, a part of the ordered unfolding of the universe:

> And We caused Jesus, son of Mary, to follow
> in their footsteps, confirming what was before him,
> and We bestowed on him the Gospel
> wherein is guidance and a light, confirming
> that which was before it in the Torah —
> a guidance and an admonition to those
> who are careful. (5.46)

And furthermore, a time which, as Jesus was well aware, had limits; a time which was bounded by the time before his, and by the time after his:

> ... Jesus, son of Mary, said: O Children of Israel!
> See! I am the messenger of Allah to you, confirming
> what was before me in the Torah, and bringing
> good news of a messenger who will come after me,
> whose name is the Praised One (Ahmad) ...(61.6)

Jesus' conception and birth are recorded by the Qur'an in great detail. It would be illuminating to begin with his mother's birth and upbringing, for it helps us to see how she was made ready by Allah to be the mother of Jesus, and that she was chosen by Him.

> Remember when the wife of Imran said: My Lord!
> I have vowed to you what is within my womb
> Accept it from me. See! You, only You,
> are the Hearer, the Knower! And when she was
> delivered, she said: My Lord! See! I am delivered
> of a female — Allah knew best of what she was
> delivered — the male is not as the female;
> and see! I have named her Mary,
> and I crave Your protection for her
> and for her offspring from Satan the outcast.
> And her Lord accepted her with full acceptance
> and accorded her a goodly growth; and made
> Zachariah her guardian. Whenever Zachariah
> went into the sanctuary where she was, he found
> that she had food. He said: O Mary! Where does
> this come from? She answered: It is from Allah.
> Allah gives without stint to whom He will.
> Then Zachariah prayed to his Lord and said: My Lord!
> Bestow on me of Your bounty goodly offspring.
> See! You are the Hearer of Prayer. And the angels
> called to him as he stood praying in the sanctuary;
> Allah gives you good news of (a son whose name is)
> John, who comes to confirm a word from Allah,
> lordly, chaste, a Prophet of the righteous.
> He said: My Lord! How can I have a son when age has
> overtaken me already and my wife is barren? The angel

answered: So (it will be). Allah does what He will.
He said: My Lord! Appoint a token for me.
(The angel) said: The token to you (shall be) that you
shall not speak to mankind three days except by
signs. Remember your Lord much, and praise (Him)
in the early hours of night and morning. (3.35-41)

John was the prophet who directly preceded Jesus. The
miraculous birth of John is mentioned again in the Sura
called "Maryam":

A mention of the mercy of your Lord to His servant
Zachariah. When he cried to his Lord a cry in secret,
saying: My Lord! See! My bones wax feeble and my head
is shining with grey hair, and I have never been unblest
in prayer to You, my Lord. I fear my kinfolk after me,
since my wife is barren. Oh, give me from Your presence
a successor, who shall inherit of me and inherit of the
house of Jacob. And make him, my Lord, acceptable
(to You)! (It was said to him): O Zachariah!
We bring you tidings of a son whose name is John;
We have given the same name to none before (him).
He said: My Lord! How can I have a son when
my wife is barren and I have reached infirm old age?
He said: So (it will be). Your Lord says: It is easy
for Me, even as I created you before, when you
were naught. He said: My Lord! Appoint for me
some token. He said: Your token is that you,
with no bodily defect, shall not speak to mankind
three nights. Then he came out to his people
from the sanctuary, and signified to them;
Glorify your Lord at break of day and fall of night.
(And it was said to his son): O John! Hold fast
the Book. And We gave him wisdom when a child,
and compassion from Our presence and purity;
and he was devout, and dutiful toward his parents.
And he was not arrogant, rebellious. Peace on him
the day he was born, and the day he dies and the day
he shall be raised alive! (19.2-15)

The story of the birth of Jesus is related in two different places in the Qur'an:

And when the angels said: O Mary! See! Allah has
chosen you and made you pure, and has preferred
you above (all) the women of creation. O Mary!
Be obedient to your Lord, prostrate yourself
and bow with those who bow (in worship).
This is of the news of things hidden. We reveal it
to you (Muhammad). You were not present
with them when they threw their pens (to know)
which of them should be the guardian of Mary,
nor were you present with them when they quarrelled
(about it). (And remember) when the angels said:
O Mary! Allah gives you glad tidings of a word from
Him, whose name is the Messiah, Jesus, son of Mary,
illustrious in the world and the Hereafter and one
of those brought near (unto Allah). He will speak
to mankind in his cradle and in his manhood,
and he is of the righteous. She said: My Lord! How
can I have a child when no mortal has touched me?
He said: So (it will be). Allah creates what He will.
If He decrees a thing, He says to it only: Be! and it is.
And He will teach him the Book and the wisdom,
and the Torah and the Gospel. And will make him
a messenger to the Children of Israel, (saying):
I come to you with a sign from your Lord. See!
I fashion for you out of clay the likeness of a
bird, and I breathe into it and it is a bird,
by Allah's leave. I heal him who was born blind,
and the leper, and I raise the dead, by Allah's leave.
And I announce to you what you eat and what
you store up in your houses. Here truly is a portent
for you, if you are to be believers. And (I come)
confirming what was before me of the Torah,
and to make lawful some of what was forbidden
to you. I come to you with a sign from your Lord,
so keep your duty to Allah and obey me.
Allah is my Lord and your Lord, so worship Him.
That is a straight path. But when Jesus became

conscious of their disbelief, he cried: Who will be
my helpers in the cause of Allah? The disciples said:
We will be Allah's helpers. We believe in Allah, and
bear you witness that we have surrendered (to Him).
Our Lord! We believe in what You have revealed
and we follow him whom You have sent. Enroll us
among those who witness (to the Truth). (3.42-53)

The story is also told in the Sura of "Maryam":

And make mention of Mary in the Book,
when she had withdrawn from her people
to a chamber looking East, and had chosen
seclusion from them. Then We sent to her
Our spirit* and it assumed for her the
likeness of a perfect man. She said: I seek
refuge in the Compassionate One from you,
if you are God-fearing. He said: I am only
a messenger of your Lord, that I may
bestow on you a faultless son. She said:
How can I have a son when no mortal has
touched me, neither have I been unchaste?
He said: So (it will be) Your Lord says:
It is easy for Me. And (it will be) that We
may make of him a revelation for mankind
and a mercy from Us, and it is a thing ordained.
And she conceived him, and she withdrew with
him to a far place. And the pangs of childbirth
drove her to the trunk of the palm tree.
She said: Oh, would that I had become a
thing of naught, forgotten! Then (one) cried
to her from below her, saying: Grieve not!
Your Lord has placed a rivulet beneath you.
And shake the trunk of the palm tree toward
you. You will cause ripe dates to fall on you.
So eat and drink and be consoled. And if
you meet any mortal, say: I have vowed a
fast to the Compassionate, and may not speak
this day to any mortal. Then she brought him

*This refers to the Angel Gabriel.

own folk, carrying him. They said: O Mary!
You have come with an amazing thing. Oh
sister of Aaron! Your father was not a wicked
man nor was your mother a harlot. Then she
pointed to him. They said: How can we talk
to one who is in the cradle, a young boy?
He spoke: See! I am the slave of Allah.
He has given me the Book and has appointed
me a Prophet, and has made me blessed
wherever I may be, and has enjoined on me
prayer and almsgiving so long as I remain
alive. And (has made me) dutiful toward her
who bore me, and has not made me arrogant,
unblest. Peace on me the day I was born,
and the day I die, and the day I shall be
raised alive! Such was Jesus, son of Mary:
(this is) a statement of the Truth
concerning which they doubt. It does not
befit (the Majesty of) Allah that He should
take to Himself a son. Glory be to Him!
When He decrees a thing, He saith to it
only: Be! and it is. And see! Allah is my
Lord and your Lord. So serve Him.
That is the right path. (19.16-36)

The place where Jesus was born is mentioned in one other
passage in Qur'an:

And We made the son of Mary and his mother
a portent, and We gave them refuge on a height,
a place of flocks and water-springs. (23.50)

His childhood and early manhood are not mentioned. The
response of the men who became his disciples is also described in the following passage:

O you who believe! Be Allah's helpers, even as Jesus,
son of Mary, said to the disciples: Who are my
helpers for Allah? They said: We are Allah's
helpers. And a party of the Children of Israel
believed, while a party disbelieved...(61.14)

And again in greater detail:

> And when I inspired the disciples, (saying):
> Believe in Me and My messenger, they said: We
> believe. Bear witness that we have surrendered
> (to You). When the disciples said: O Jesus,
> son of Mary! Is your Lord able to send down
> for us a table spread with food from heaven?
> He said: Observe your duty to Allah, if you
> are true believers. (They said:) We wish to eat
> from it, that we may satisfy our hearts and know
> that you have spoken truth to us, and that we
> may be witnesses to this. Jesus, son of Mary,
> said: O Allah, our Lord, send down for us a
> table spread with food from heaven, that it
> may be a feast for us, for the first of us and
> for the last of us, and a sign from You. Give
> us sustenance for You are the Best of Sustainers.
> Allah said: See! I send it down. And whoever
> disbelieves in you afterwards, him I will surely
> punish with a punishment with which I have
> not punished any of (My) creatures. (5.111-115)

When Jesus's teaching began to spread, some accepted the
guidance, and some did not:

> And when the son of Mary is quoted as an example,
> behold! the folk laugh out, and say: Are our gods
> better or is he? They raise not the objection save
> for argument. No! but they are a contentious people.
> He is nothing but a slave on whom We bestowed
> favour, and We made him a pattern for the
> Children of Israel. (43.57-59)

> ...and We caused Jesus, son of Mary, to follow,
> and gave him the Gospel, and placed compassion
> and mercy in the hearts of those who followed him.
> But they invented monasticism — We did not ordain
> it for them — only seeking Allah's pleasure, and
> they did not observe it with correct observance.
> So We gave those of them who believe their reward,
> but many of them are evil-livers. (57.27)

The message he brought was simple:

> When Jesus came with clear proofs (of Allah's
> sovereignty), he said: I have come to you
> with wisdom, and to make plain some of
> that about which you differ. So keep your
> duty to Allah, and obey me. Allah, He is
> my Lord and your Lord. So worship Him.
> This is the right path. (43.63-64)

His miracles are mentioned again:

> When Allah says: O Jesus, son of Mary! Remember
> My favour to you and to your mother; how I
> strengthened you with the holy spirit*, so that
> you speak to mankind in the cradle as in maturity;
> and how I taught you the Scripture and Wisdom
> and the Torah and the Gospel; and how you
> shaped of clay the likeness of a bird by My
> permission, and blew upon it and it was a bird
> by My permission, and you healed him who
> was born blind and the leper by My permission;
> and how I restrained the Children of Israel from
> (harming) you when you came to them with
> clear proofs, and those of them who disbelieved
> exclaimed: This is nothing but mere magic. (5.110)

A misconception which arose from the circumstances of
Jesus' birth is that he was therefore the "son of God":

> They say: Allah has taken a son. Glorified be He!
> He has no needs! His is all that is in the heavens
> and all that is in the earth. You have no warrant
> for this. Do you tell concerning Allah what you
> do not know? (10.68)

*This refers to the Angel Gabriel.

(And remember) when Allah said: O Jesus! See!
I am gathering you and causing you to ascend
to Me, and am cleansing you of those who
disbelieve and am setting those who follow you
above those who disbelieve until the Day of
Resurrection. Then to Me you will (all) return,
and I shall judge between you as to that in which
you used to differ. As for those who disbelieve,
I shall chastise them with a heavy chastisement
in the world and the Hereafter; and they will
have no helpers. And as for those who believe
and do good works, He will pay them their wages
in full. Allah loves not wrong-doers. This (which)
We recite to you is a revelation and a wise reminder.
The likeness of Jesus with Allah is as the likeness
of Adam. He created him of dust, then He said
to him: Be! and he is. (3.55-59)

And they say: Allah has taken to Himself a son.
Be He glorified! No! But whatever is in the
heavens and the earth is His. All are subservient
to Him. The Originator of the heavens and the
earth! When He decrees a thing, He says to it
only: Be! and it is. (2.116-117)

And they say: The Compassionate has taken
to Himself a son. Be He glorified! No, but
(those whom they call sons) are honoured
slaves; they do not speak until He has spoken,
and they act by His command. He knows what
is before them and what is behind them, and
they cannot intercede except for him whom
He accepts, and they quake for awe of Him.
And one of them who should say: Look! I am
a god beside Him, that one We should repay
with hell. Thus We repay wrong-doers. (21.26-30)

And they say: The Compassionate has taken to
Himself a son. Certainly you utter a disastrous
thing, whereby almost the heavens are torn,
and the earth is split open and the mountains
fall in ruins, that you ascribe to the Compassionate
a son! When it is not fitting for (the Majesty of)
the Compassionate that He should choose a son.
There is none in the heavens and the earth but
comes to the Compassionate as a slave. (19.88-93)

The Qur'an denies the divinity of Jesus:

They indeed have disbelieved who say: Allah is
the Messiah, son of Mary. Say: Who then can do
anything against Allah, if He had willed to destroy
the Messiah, son of Mary, and his mother and
everyone on earth? Allah's is the Sovereignty of
the heavens and the earth and all that is between
them. He creates what He will. And Allah is able
to do all things. (5.17)

And when Allah says: O Jesus, son of Mary! Did
you say to mankind: Take me and my mother
for two gods beside Allah? he says: Be glorified!
It was not mine to utter that to which I had no
right. If I used to say it, then You know it.
You know what is in my mind, and I know not
what is in Your mind. You, only You, are the
Knower of Things Hidden. I spoke to them
only what You commanded me, (saying):
Worship Allah, my Lord and your Lord. I was
a witness of them while I lived among them,
and when You took me You were the Watcher
over them. You are Witness over all things. If
You punish them, they are Your slaves, and
if You forgive them (they are Your slaves).
You, only You are the Mighty, the Wise. (5.116-118)

And the Jews say: Ezra is the son of Allah, and the
Christians say: The Messiah is the son of Allah.
That is their saying with their mouths. They imitate
the saying of those who disbelieved of old.
Allah (Himself) fights against them. How perverse
are they! They have taken as lords beside Allah
their rabbis and their monks and the Messiah,
son of Mary, when they were ordered to worship
only One God. There is no god except Him.
Be He glorified from all that they ascribe
as partner (to Him)! If they could they would
put out the Light of Allah with their mouths,
but Allah disdains anything except that
He shall perfect His Light, however much
the disbelievers are against it. (9.30-32)

The Qur'an rejects the concept of Trinity:

O people of the Book! Do not exaggerate in your
religion nor utter anything concerning Allah
except the Truth. The Messiah, Jesus, son of Mary,
was only a messenger of Allah, and His word
which He conveyed to Mary, and a spirit from Him.
So believe in Allah and His messengers, and do not
say "Three" — Stop! (it is) better for you! —
Allah is only One God. It is far removed from
His transcendant majesty that He should have a son.
His is all that is in the heavens and all that is in the
earth. And Allah is enough as Defender. The Messiah
will never scorn to be a slave to Allah nor will the
favoured angels. Whoever scorns His service and
is proud, all such will He assemble to Him; then
as for those who believed and did good works,
to them He will pay their wages in full, adding to
them of His bounty; and as for those who were
scornful and proud, them will He punish with a
painful doom; and they will not find for them,
against Allah, any protecting friend or helper.
(4.171-173)

The Qur'an rejects the crucifixion of Jesus, but affirms the ascension:

> And because of their saying: We killed the Messiah
> Jesus, son of Mary, Allah's messenger — They did not
> kill or crucify him, but it appeared so to them;
> and look! — those who disagree concerning it are
> in doubt about it; they have no knowledge of it
> except pursuit of a conjecture; they did not kill
> him for certain; but Allah took him up to Himself.
> Allah was ever Mighty, Wise. (4.157-158)

Finally,

> They surely disbelieve who say: Lo! Allah is the
> Messiah, son of Mary. The Messiah (himself) said:
> O Children of Israel, worship Allah, my Lord
> and your Lord. Lo! Whoever ascribes partners
> to Allah, for him Allah has forbidden the Garden.
> His abode is the Fire. For evil-doers there will be
> no helpers. They surely disbelieve who say:
> Allah is the third of three; when there is
> no God save the One God. If they desist not
> from saying it, a painful doom will fall on
> those of them who disbelieve. Will they
> not rather turn to Allah and seek forgiveness
> of Him? For Allah is Forgiving, Merciful.
> The Messiah, son of Mary, was no other
> than a messenger, messengers (the like of
> whom) had passed away before him. And
> his mother was a saintly woman. And they
> both used to eat (earthly) food. See how
> We make the revelation clear for them,
> and see how they are turned away! (5.72-75)

> Of these messengers, some of whom We have
> caused to excel others, and of whom there are
> some to whom Allah spoke, while some of them
> He exalted (above others) in degree; and We gave
> Jesus, son of Mary, clear proofs (of Allah's

Sovereignty) and We supported him with the
holy spirit.* And if Allah had so willed it, those
who followed after them would not have fought
one with another after the clear proofs had come
to them. But they differed, some of them believing
and some disbelieving. And if Allah had so willed
it, they would not have fought one with another;
but Allah does what He will. (2.253)

But,

You will find the most vehement of mankind
in hostility to those who believe (to be) the Jews
and the idolaters. And you will find the nearest
of them in affection to those who believe (to be)
those who say: Look! We are Christians. That is
because there are among them priests and monks,
and because they are not proud. (5.82)

*This refers to the Angel Gabriel.

Chapter 10

JESUS IN HADITH AND MUSLIM TRADITIONS

The Hadith are another source of knowledge about which students of Christianity have been kept in the dark. The Hadith consist of records of eyewitness accounts of what the Prophet Muhammad, peace and blessings of Allah be upon him, said and did in his life. A highly sophisticated pseudo-scholarship was set up by the Roman Church and the Christian missionaries in the last century to discredit the Muslim Hadith literature which had already undergone the most scrupulous checking and verification in the history of recorded scholarship. Unlike the gospels of the New Testament, a hadith is not accepted unless the chain of transmission can be traced back through reliable men, to a man who was a companion of the Prophet Muhammad, peace and blessings of Allah be upon him, and who actually witnessed the event or heard the words which the hadith relates. The most reliable sources of hadith were those men who loved and feared Allah most. The most important collections of hadith, made by Imam al-Bukhari and Salih Muslim, were gathered together about a hundred and twenty years after the Prophet Muhammad's death, peace and blessings of Allah be upon him, and cover every aspect of his life and knowledge. The Hadith are an essential part of the teaching of Muhammad, may the peace and blessings of Allah be upon him. It was from these contemporary eyewitness accounts that the collections of Imam al-Bukhari and Salih Muslim were gathered.

As well as the Hadith which refer to Jesus, there are also many Muslim traditions which give accounts of the sayings and deeds of Jesus. These were originally gathered together by the earlier followers of Jesus, especially those who spread to Arabia and North Africa. When the Prophet Muhammad, peace and blessings of Allah be upon him, came, many of

221

the followers of these followers embraced Islam. They retained all the accounts they had about Jesus who had foretold the coming of the Prophet Muhammad, peace and blessings of Allah be upon him. These traditions were passed down from generation to generation by the Muslims, and many of them were finally gathered together in Tha'labi's *Stories of the Prophets* and in Al-Ghazzali's *Revival of the Life- Transaction Sciences.* It is significant to see how these traditions give a clear and unanimous picture of the ascetic Prophet who prepared the way for the final Messenger:

Ka'b al-Akbar said: Jesus, son of Mary, was a ruddy man, inclined to white; he did not have long hair, and he never annointed his head. Jesus used to walk barefoot, and he took no house or adornment, or goods, or clothes, or provision except his day's food. Wherever the sun set, he arranged his feet in prayer till the morning came. He was curing the blind from birth and the leper and raising the dead by Allah's permission and was telling his people what they were eating in their houses and what they were storing up for the morrow, and he was walking on the surface of the water in the sea. His head was dishevelled and his face was small; he was an ascetic in the world, longing for the next world and eager for the worship of Allah. He was a pilgrim in the earth till the Jews sought him and desired to kill him. Then Allah raised him up to heaven; and Allah knows best.

Malik, son of Dinar, said: Jesus, peace be upon him, and the disciples with him passed by the carcass of a dog. A disciple said, "What a stench this dog makes!" Then he, (blessings and peace by upon him), said, "How white are its teeth!"

It is related on the authority of Ma'ruf al Karkhi that Jesus, peace be upon him, said, "Remember cotton when it is put over your eyes."

In a tradition (it is said) that Jesus, son of Mary, peace be upon him, met a man and said to him, "What are you doing?" He replied, "I am devoting myself to God." He said, "Who is giving you what you need?" He said, "My brother." (Jesus) said, "He is more devoted to Allah than you."

Jesus, son of Mary, peace be upon him, said: "The world consists of three days: yesterday which has passed, from which you have nothing in your hand; tommorow of which you do not know whether you will reach it or not; and today in which you are, so avail yourself of it."

The disciples said to Jesus, peace be upon him, "How is it that you can walk on water and we cannot?" Then he said to them, "What do you think of the dinar and the dirham?" (pieces of money). They replied, "They are good." He said, "But they and mud are alike to me."

When Jesus was asked, "How are you this morning?", he would answer, "Unable to forestall what I hope, or to put off what I fear, bound by my works, with all my good in another's hand. There is no poor man poorer than I."

And he said also, "The world is both seeking and sought. He who seeks the next world, this world seeks him until his provision in it is complete; and he who seeks the present world, the next world seeks him until death comes and seizes him by the neck."

If you wish, you may follow him who was the Spirit and the Word, Jesus, son of Mary, peace be upon him, for he used to say, "My seasoning is hunger, my undergarment is fear of Allah, my outer-garment is wool, my fire in winter is the rays of the sun, my lamp is the moon, my riding beast is my feet, and my food and fruit are what the earth brings forth (i.e. without cultivation). At night I have nothing and in the morning I have nothing, yet there is no one on earth richer than I.

Jesus, peace be upon him, said, "He who seeks after the world is like one who drinks sea water; the more he drinks, the more his thirst increases, until it kills him."

It is related that the Messiah, peace be upon him, passed in his wandering a man asleep wrapped up in his cloak; then he wakened him and said, "O sleeper, arise and glorify Allah! Exalted is He!" Then the man said, "What do you want from me? Truly I have abandoned the world to its people." So he said to him, "Sleep then, my friend."

Obaid, son of 'Omar, said, the Messiah, son of Mary, peace be upon him, used to wear hair clothing, and eat wild fruits, and he had no son to die, and no house to be demolished, and he stored up nothing for the morrow. He slept wherever the evening overtook him.

Jesus, the Messiah, peace be upon him, used to take nothing with him but a comb and a jug. Then he saw a man combing his beard with his fingers, so he threw away the comb; and he saw another drinking from a river with the palms of his hands, so he threw away the jug."

Jesus, peace be upon him, said to the disciples, "Take the places of worship as houses and the houses as alighting-places; and eat wild vegetables and drink pure water, and escape safe from the world."

Jesus, son of Mary, peace be upon him, said, "In the last days there will be learned men who teach abstinence in the world but will not be abstinent themselves, who will teach men to take delight in the next world but will not take delight in it themselves, and who will warn men against coming before rulers but will not refrain themselves. They will draw near to the rich and keep far from the poor; they will be pleasant to great men but will shrink from humble men. Those are the brethren of the devils and the enemies of the Merciful."

The following is related on the authority of Janir, on the authority of Laith. A man accompanied Jesus, son of Mary, peace be upon him, and said, "I will be with you and will accompany you." So they set off and came to the bank of a river and sat down to breakfast; and they had three loaves. They ate two loaves, and a third loaf was left over. Then Jesus, peace be upon him, rose up and went to the river and drank, after which he returned, but did not find the loaf; so he said to the man, "Who took the loaf?" He replied, "I do not know." Then he set off with his companion and saw a gazelle with two of her young. The narrator says, he called one of them and it came to him; then he cut its throat and roasted part of it, and he and that man ate. Then he said to the young gazelle, "Rise, by the permission of Allah." When it rose and went away, he said to the man, "I ask you by Him who has shown you this sign, who took the loaf?" He replied, "I do not know." Afterwards they came to a wadi with water in it and Jesus took the man's hand and they walked on the water. Then, when they had crossed, he said to him, "I ask you by Him who has shown you this sign, who took the loaf?" He replied, "I do not know." Then they came to a desert and sat down, and Jesus, peace be upon him, began to collect earth and a heap of sand, after which he said, "Become gold, by the permission of Allah, Exalted be He!" It became gold, and he divided it into three parts and said, "A third is for me, a third for you, and a third for him who took the loaf." Then he said, "I am the one who took the loaf." He said, "It is all yours." Jesus, peace be upon him, then left him and two men came to him in the desert while he had the wealth with him and wished to take it from him and kill him. He said, "It is among us in thirds; so send one of you to the village to buy food for us to eat." The narrator said: They sent one of them, and he who was sent said to himself, "Why should I divide this wealth with these men? I shall put poison in this food and kill them and take the wealth myself." So he did so. And these two men said, "Why should we give this man a third of the wealth? When he returns we shall kill him, and divide the wealth between us." The narrator said: So when he returned they killed him and ate the food and died; and that wealth remained in the desert with those three men lying dead beside it. Then Jesus, peace be upon him, passed them in that condition and said to his companions, "This is the world, so beware of it."

It is related that Jesus, peace be upon him, passed three people whose bodies were wasted and who were pale and said, "What has brought on you that which I see?" They replied, "Fear of the Fire." He said, "It is Allah's duty to render secure him who fears." Afterwards he passed from them and came to another three, and lo! they were in greater emaciation and paleness, so he said, "What has brought on you that which I see?" They replied, "Desire for the Garden." He said, "It is Allah's duty to give you what you hope for." After that he passed from them and came to another three, and lo! they were in still greater emaciation and paleness as though mirrors of light were over their faces, so he said, "What has brought on you that which I see?" They replied, "We love Allah, Great and Glorious is He." He said, "You are those who are nearest to Allah; you are those who are nearest to Allah; you are those who are nearest to Allah."

It is related on the authority of Muhammad, son of Abu Musa, concerning Jesus, son of Mary, peace be on him, that he passed an afflicted man and treated him kindly and said, "Oh Allah, I beseech You to heal him." Then Allah, Exalted is He, revealed to him, "How can I heal him from that which I am healing him?"

It is related that Jesus, peace be upon him, one day passed a hill in which he saw a cell. He drew near it and found in it a devotee whose back was bent, whose body was wasted, and in whom austerity had reached its utmost limits. Jesus saluted him and wondered at his evidences (of devotion) which he saw. So Jesus said to him, "How long have you been in this place?" He replied, "For seventy years I have been asking Him for one thing which He has not granted me yet. Perhaps you, O Spirit of Allah, may intercede for me concerning it; then possibly it may be granted." Jesus said, "What is your requirement?" He replied, "I asked Him to let me taste the amount of an atom of His pure love." Jesus said to him, "I shall pray to Allah for you about that." So he prayed for him that night, and Allah, Exalted is He, revealed to him, "I have accepted your intercession and granted your request." Jesus, peace be upon him, returned to him to the place after some days to see what the condition of the devotee was, and saw the cell had fallen down and a great fissure had appeared in the ground below it. Jesus, peace be upon him, went down into that fissure and went some leagues in it and saw the devotee in a cave under that hill standing with his eyes staring and his mouth open. Then Jesus, peace be upon him, saluted him, but he did not give him an answer. While Jesus was wondering at his condition someone shouted to him, "O Jesus, he has asked Us for something like an atom of Our pure love, and We knew that he was not able for that, so We gave him a seventieth part of an atom, and he is bewildered in it thus; so what would it have been like if We had given him more than that?"

Abd'Allah bin Umar reported Allah's messenger, peace and blessings of Allah be upon him, as saying, "Last night I found myself in a vision at the Ka'ba and saw a ruddy man like the most good-looking of that type that you can see with the most beautiful lock of hair you can see. He had combed it out, and it was dripping with water. He was leaning on the shoulders of two men and going round the House. When I asked who he was, I was told that he was the Messiah, son of Mary..." (From Bukhari and Muslim)

Abu Huraira reported Allah's Messenger, peace and blessings of Allah be upon him, as saying, "By Him in whose hand my soul is, the son of Mary will soon descend among you as a just judge. He will break crosses, kill swine and abolish the jizya (a tax payable by a community which accepts the protection of a Muslim ruler but whose members do not embrace Islam), and wealth will pour forth to such an extent that no one will accept it, and one sajda, (the position in a Muslim's prayer where the forehead is placed on the ground), will be better than the world and what it contains." Abu Huraira used to say: Recite if you wish, *"Not one of the people of the Book will fail to believe in him before his death..."* — *Qur'an 4.159* (From Bukhari and Muslim)

Abd'Allah bin Amr reported Sayyidina Muhammad, peace and blessings of Allah be upon him, as saying, "Jesus, son of Mary, will descend to the earth, will marry, have children, and remain forty-five years, after which he will die and be buried along with me in my grave. Then Jesus, son of Mary, and I shall arise from one grave between Abu Bakr and 'Umar.'' (Ibn al-Jauzi transmitted it in the *Kitab al-Wafa'*).

Abu Huraira reported Allah's Messenger, peace and blessings of Allah be upon him, as saying, "I am the nearest of kin to Jesus, son of Mary, in this world and the next. The prophets are brothers, sons of one father by co-wives. Their mothers are different, but their religion is one. There has been no prophet between us." (From Bukhari and Muslim)

In this famous statement, the last of the Prophets and Messengers, our Master Muhammad, peace and blessings of Allah be upon him, summed up the whole matter:

The prophets are brothers: they are all the same; there is no distinction between them.

Sons of one father: they all declare one doctrine — *La ilaha il'Allah. There is no god but Allah, the One.* Nothing can be associated with Him in His Divinity.

Their mothers are different: each Prophet has been sent to a particular people at a particular time. The Prophet of the time has had revealed to him a *Sunna*, or life-form, a practice, a social pattern by which his community should live. When a new Prophet came to a people, he brought a new form of this Sunna to accord with the new age. This is the *Shari'a* or Road of the Prophets. Thus, with the coming of Sayyidina Muhammad, peace and blessings of Allah be upon him, the Divine Transaction is complete. Messengership is sealed in the last revealed Book, the *Glorious Qur'an.*

Prophethood is sealed with the Shari'a and the Sunna of the compassionate Prophet, Muhammad, peace and blessings of Allah be upon him.

The science of worship, itself the means of approach to Allah, is sealed in the Book and the Sunna of the first of the sons of Adam, peace be upon him. The Way of Jesus, Prophet of Islam, is over. The Way of Muhammad, Prophet of Islam, has begun.

This ayat of the Qur'an disclosed the tremendous matter to be complete:

> This day have I perfected your life-transaction for you, and completed My favour to you, and have chosen for you as life-transaction, AL-ISLAM.

CHAPTER NOTES

Chapter One

1) *The Apostolic Fathers,* E.J. Goodspeed.

2) *Articles of the Apostolic Creed,* Theodore Zahn, pp. 33-37.

3) *Tetradymus,* John Toland.

4) *Outline of the History of Dogma,* Adolf Harnack.

5) *What Is Christianity?,* Adolf Harnack, p. 20.

6) *The Jesus Report,* J. Lehman (quoting from *Krewz Verlag,* Stuttgart, 2nd ed., 1960, p. 112).

7) *Articles of the Apostolic Creed,* Theodore Zahn.

8) *Erasmi Epistolai,* 1334 ed., P.S. Allen, V, pp. 173-92.

Chapter Two

1) *The Jesus Report,* J. Lehman, pp. 14-15.

2) *The Wilderness Revolt,* Bishop Pike, p. 101.

3) *The Dead Sea Scrolls,* Edmund Wilson.

4) *The Death of Jesus,* Joel Carmichael, p. 141.

5) *The Dead Sea Scrolls,* Edmund Wilson, p. 94.

6) *The Death of Jesus,* Joel Carmichael, p. 139.

7) *The Jesus Scroll,* D. Joyce, p. 126.

8) *The Nazarenes,* John Toland, p. 18.

9) *The Life of Jesus,* Carveri.

Chapter Three

1) *The Nazarenes*, John Toland, pp. 6-8.
2) *Spicilegium i* (ex Cod. Barocc. 39), Grabe.
3) *The Nazarenes*, John Toland, pp. 15-16.
4) *The Apostolic Fathers*, E. J. Goodspeed, p. 266.

Chapter Four

The Apostolic Fathers, Edgar J. Goodspeed.

Chapter Five

1) *The Kingdom of God and Primitive Christian Belief*, Albert Schweitzer, p. 149.
2) *Lebuch II*, Heinrich Holzmann, pp. 256, 376.
3) *The Jesus Report*, Johannes Lehman, p. 123.
4) *The Beginning of the Christian Church*, Hanz Lietzman, p. 104.
5) *Paul and His Interpreters*, Albert Schweitzer, p. 198.
6) *The Nazarenes*, John Toland, p. 6 (preface).
7) *A History of Christianity in the Apostolic Age*, A.C. MacGiffert, pp. 216, 231, 424-5.
8) Quoted in *The Jesus Report*, Johannes Lehman, p. 126.
9) Quoted in *The Jesus Report*, Johannes Lehman, p. 127.
10) Quoted in *The Jesus Report*, Johannes Lehman, p. 128.
11) *The Nazarenes*, John Toland, pp. 73-76.

Chapter Six

1) *Constantine the Great*, J.B. Firth, pp. 190-191.
2) *A History of the Eastern Church*, A.R. Stanley, p. 94.

3)   *A History of Christianity in the Apostolic Age,* A.C.
     MacGiffert, p. 172.

4)   *The Donatist Church,* W.H.C. Frend, p. 153.

5)   *The Donatist Church,* W.H.C. Frend, p. 164.

6)   *The Donatist Church,* W.H.C. Frend.

7)   *The Donatist Church,* W.H.C. Frend.

8)   *The Donatist Church,* W.H.C. Frend.

9)   *Constantine the Great,* J.B. Firth.

10) *Constantine the Great,* J.B. Firth.

11) *The Donatist Church,* W.H.C. Frend, p. 164.

12) *The Donatist Church,* W.H.C. Frend, p. 326.

13) *John 14.28,* The Bible.

14) *Constantine the Great,* J.B. Firth.

15) *Constantine the Great,* J.B. Firth.

16) *Constantine the Great,* J.B. Firth.

17) *Constantine the Great,* J.B. Firth.

18) *Constantine the Great,* J.B. Firth.

19) *The Council of Nicea,* J. Kaye, pp. 23-25.

20) *Constantine the Great,* J.B. Firth, p. 60.

21) *Arius,* Prof. Gwatkin.

22) *Arius,* Prof. Gwatkin.

23) *Arius,* Prof. Gwatkin.

24) *Tetradymus,* J. Toland.

25) *Tetradymus,* J. Toland.

26) *Tetradymus,* J. Toland.

27) *Tetradymus,* J. Toland.

28) *Tetradymus,* J. Toland.

29) *A History of Christianity in the Apostolic Age,* A.C.
     MacGiffert.

30) *The Condemnation of Pope Honorius,* John Chapman.

31) *The Condemnation of Pope Honorius,* John Chapman.

32) *The Condemnation of Pope Honorius*, John Chapman.

Chapter Seven

1) *The Hunted Heretic*, R.H. Bainton.

2) *A History of Unitarianism*, E.M. Wilbur.

3) *Challenge of a Liberal Faith*, G.N. Marshall.

4) *Anti-trinitarian Biographies*, A. Wallace.

5) *Rise of the Dutch Republic*, Motley.

6) *The Epic of Unitarianism*, D.B. Parke, pp. 5-6.

7) *Treatises Concerning the Mohametons*, A. Reland, pp. 215-223.

8) *Francis David*, W.C. Gannett.

9) *Francis David*, W.C. Gannett.

10) *A History of Unitarianism*, E.M. Wilbur.

11) *Francis David*, W.C. Gannett.

12) *Francis David*, W.C. Gannett.

13) *Francis David*, W.C. Gannett.

14) *A History of Unitarianism*, E.M. Wilbur, p. 78.

15) *Treatises Concerning the Mohametons*, A. Reland, p. 190.

16) *Francis David*, W.C. Gannett.

17) *Anti-trinitarian Biographies*, A. Wallace.

18) *A History of the Reformation in Poland*, Lubinietski.

19) *Anti-trinitarian Biographies*, A. Wallace.

20) *Anti-trinitarian Biographies*, A. Wallace.

21) *Anti-trinitarian Biographies*, A. Wallace, Introduction, p. 79.

22) *Anti-trinitarian Biographies*, A. Wallace, p. 44.

23) *Anti-trinitarian Biographies*, A. Wallace, p. 45.

24) *Historical and Critical Reflections Upon Mohametonism and Socianism*, A. Reland.

25) *The Nazarenes*, John Toland.

26) *Anti-trinitarian Biographies. III*, A. Wallace.

27) *Anti-trinitarian Biographies, III*, A. Wallace.

28) *Anti-trinitarian Biographies, III*, A. Wallace.

29) *The Religion of the Protestants*, W. Chillingworth.

30) *The Religion of the Protestants*, W. Chillingworth.

31) *Anti-trinitarian Biographies. III*, A. Wallace.

32) *True Opinion Concerning the Holy Trinity*, J. Biddle.

33) *Anti-trinitarian Biographies. III*, A. Wallace.

34) *The Epic of Unitarianism*, D.B. Parke, pp. 31-32.

35) *Anti-trinitarian Biographies. III*, A. Wallace.

36) *Anti-trinitarian Biographies. III*, A. Wallace.

37) *Anti-trinitarian Biographies. III*, A. Wallace.

38) *The Christian Doctrine*, J. Milton.

39) *The Christian Doctrine*, J. Milton.

40) *Anti-trinitarian Biographies. III*, A. Wallace.

41) *The Christian Doctrine*, J. Milton.

42) *The Christian Doctrine*, J. Milton.

43) *Anti-trinitarian Biographies. III*, A. Wallace, p. 428.

44) *Anti-trinitarian Biographies. III*, A. Wallace, p. 438.

45) *Anti-trinitarian Biographies. III*, A. Wallace.

46) *Anti-trinitarian Biographies. III*, A. Wallace.

47) *Anti-trinitarian Biographies. III*, A. Wallace, p. 517.

48) *Anti-trinitarian Biographies. III*, A. Wallace.

49) *Anti-trinitarian Biographies. III*, A. Wallace.

50) *Anti-trinitarian Biographies. III*, A. Wallace.

51) *The Epic of Unitarianism*, D.B. Parke, p. 46.

52) *The Epic of Unitarianism*, D.B. Parke, p. 47.

53) *A List of False Reading of the Scripture*, T. Lindsey.

54) *Two Dissertations*, T. Lindsey.

55) *Memoirs of Dr. Priestly*, J. Priestly.

56) *Memoirs of Dr. Priestly*, J. Priestly, p. 76.

57) *Memoirs of Dr. Priestly*, J. Priestly, p. 89.

58) *The Epic of Unitarianism*, D.B. Parke, p. 48.

59) *A History of the Corruptions of Christianity*, J. Priestly.

60) *The History of Jesus Christ*, J. Priestly.

61) *Anti-trinitarian Biographies*, A. Wallace.

62) *Anti-trinitarian Biographies*, A. Wallace.

63) *A History of Unitarianism*, E.M. Wilbur, p. 424.

64) *A History of Unitarianism*, E.M. Wilbur.

65) *Anti-trinitarian Biographies*, A. Wallace.

66) *The Epic of Unitarianism*, D.B. Parke.

67) *Challenge of a Liberal Faith*, G.N. Marshall.

68) *A History of Unitarianism*, E.M. Wilbur.

Chapter Eight

1) *A Christian Introduction to Religions of the World*, J.G. Vos, pp. 66-67.

2) *A Christian Introduction to Religions of the World*, J.G. Vos, p. 27.

3) *The World's Religions*, N. Anderson, p. 232.

4) *"1984"*, G. Orwell, p. 220.

5) *Christianity on Trial, I*, Colin Chapman, pp. 32-33.

6) *Time Magazine*, May 24th, 1976, pp. 42-43.

7) *Christianity on Trial, I*, Colin Chapman, p. 37.

8) *Christianity on Trial, I*, Colin Chapman, pp. 51-52.

9) *Time Magazine*, May 24th, 1976, p. 46.

10) *Christianity on Trial, I*, Colin Chapman, p. 63.

11) *Christianity on Trial, I*, Colin Chapman, p. 74.

12) *Christianity on Trial, I*, Colin Chapman, p. 61.

BIBLIOGRAPHY

The Qur'an

The Hadith of al-Bukhari and Muslim

The Bible

'Abd al-Qadir as-Sufi, *The Way of Muhammad,* Diwan Press, 1975.

Alton, *Religious Opinions of Milton, Locke, and Newton,* 1833.

Allegro, *The Dead Sea Scrolls.*

Anderson, Norman, *The World's Religions,* 1975.

Apuleius, Lucius, *Metamorphosis - The Golden Ass,* (translated by T. Taylor), 1822.

Backwell, R.H., *The Christianity of Jesus,* 1972.

Bainton, R.H., *Hunted Heretic,* 1953.

Beattie, *The New Theology and the Old,* 1910.

Becker, *The Dead Sea Scrolls.*

Begin, Menachem, *The Revolt. The Story of the Irgun.* (translated by Samuel Karr).

Belloc, J.H.D., *An Open Letter on the Decay of Faith,* 1906.

Biddle, John, *The Opinion Concerning the Holy Trinity (XII Arguments),* 1653.

Bigg, *The Origin of Christianity,* 1909.

Blackney, E.H., *The Problems of Higher Criticism,* 1905.

Brown, David, *The Structure of the Apocalypse,* 1891.

Brown, W.E., *The Revision of the Prayer Book - A Criticism,* 1909.

Bruce, Frederick, *Jesus and Christian Origins Outside the New Testament,* 1974.

Bruce, F.F., *The New Testament Documents,* 1943.

Bruce, F.F., *The Books and the Parchments,* 1950.

Burnet, Gilbert, *An Abridgement of the History of the Reformation.*

Bury, Arthur, *The Naked Gospel,* 1699.

Carmichael, Joel, *The Death of Jesus,* 1962.

Carnegie, W.H., *Why and What I Believe in Christianity,* 1910.

Cary, *Parsons and Pagans - An Indictment of Christianity,* 1906.

Celsus, *Arguments of Celsus* (translated by Lardner), 1830.

Chadwick, H., *Alexandrian Christianity,* 1954.

Chadwick, H., *The Early Church,* 1967.

Channing, W.E., *The Character and Writing of Milton,* 1826.

Channing, W.E., *The Superior Tendency of Unitarianism,* 1831

Channing, W.E., *The Works of Channing,* 1840-1844.

Chapman, Colin, *Christianity on Trial,* 1974.

Chapman, John, *The Condemnation of Pope Honorius,* 1907.

Charles, R.H., *The Book of Jublilees,* 1917.

Charles, R.H., *The Apocrypha and Pseudo-Epiapapha of the Old Testament.*

Chesterton, G.K., *Orthodoxy,* 1909.

Chillingworth, W., *The Religion of the Protestants.*

Clarke, Samuel, *The Bible,* 1867.

Clodd, Edward, *Gibbon and Christianity,* 1916.

Cooke, Rev., *Reply to Montgomery,* 1883. ·

Cooke, Rev., *True to Himself,* 1883.

Corelli, Marie, *Barnabas - A Novel,* 1893.

Council of Nicea and St. Athanasius, 1898.

Cox, Edwin, *The Elusive Jesus.*

Craver, Marcello, *The Life of Jesus,* 1967.

Cross, Frank Moore, *The Ancient Library of Qumran and Modern Biblical Studies.*

Culligan, *The Arian Movement,* 1913.

Cummins, G.D., *The Childhood of Jesus,* 1972.

Cunningham, Francis, *A Dissertation on the Books of Origen Against Celsus,* 1812.

Curll, Edward, *Historical Account of the Life of John Toland,* 1728.

Davies, W.D., *Paul and Rabbinic Judaism.*

Dinwiddie, *The Times Before the Reformation,* 1883.

Disciple, *Gospel of the Holy Twelve.*

DuPont-Sommer, *The Jewish Sect of Qumran and the Essenes,* (translated by R.D. Barnett).

Emlyn, T., *An Humble Enquiry into Scripture,* 1756.

Everett, C.C., *Theism and the Christian Faith.*

Eusebius, *Church History - Life of Constantine the Great,* (translated by MacGiffert), 1890.

Eusebius, *The Ecclesiastic History,* 1847.

Eusebius, *A Select Library of Nicene and post-Nicene Fathers of the Christian Church,* (translated by A.C. MacGiffert, Ph.D.), 1890.

Firth, J.B., *Constantine the Great,* 1890.

Frazer, W., *The Golden Bough.*

Frend, W.H.C., *The Early Church.*

Frend, W.H.C., *Persecution in the Early Church.*

Frend, W.H.C., *An Address to the Inhabitants of Cambridge,* 1788.

Frend, W.H.C., *The Rise of the Monophysite Movement.*

Frend, W.H.C., *Coulthurst's Blunders Exposed,* 1788-89.

Frend, W.H.C., *The Donatist Church.*

Froude, *The Life and Letters of Erasmus,* 1916.

Gannett, D., *Francis David, Founder of Unitarianism,* 1914.

Gibbon, E., *Christianity,* 1930.

Gibbon, Edward, *Decline and Fall of the Roman Empire,* 1909-1914.

Gibson, J.M., *Inspiration and Authority of the Holy Scriptures.*

Glover, T.R., *Jesus of History,* 1919.

Goodspeed, E.J., *The Letter of Barnabas,* 1950.

Goodspeed, E.J., *The Apostolic Fathers,* 1950.

Gordon, Alexander, *Heresy.*

Grant & Fridman, *The Secret Sayings of Jesus,* 1960.

Green, *Sir Isaac Newton's Views,* 1871.

Guthrie, D., *A Shorter Life of Christ,* 1970.

Gwatkin, *Arius.*

Hall, L., *The Continuity of Revelation,* 1908.

Harnack, Adolf, *Christianity and History,* (translated by Saunders), 1900.

Harnack, Adolf, *Outlines of the History of Dogma,* 1900.

Harnack, Adolf, *What is Christianity?* 1901.

Harris, J.R., *Celsus and Aristedes,* 1921.

Hay, J.S., *Heliogabalus,* 1911.

Haygood, A.G., *The Monk and the Prince,* 1895.

Hayne, S., *The General View of the Holy Scripture,* 1607.

Haines, *Religious Persecution.*

Harwood, P., *Priestly and Unitarianism,* 1842.

Hastings, *Dictionary of Christ and the Gospel.*

Heinimann, *John Toland,* 1944.

Hermes, *Hermes - A Disciple of Jesus,* 1888.

Hort, F.J.A., *Six Lectures on the Ante-Nicene Fathers,* 1895.

Hone, W., *The Apocryphal New Testament,* 1820.

Huddleston, *Toland's History of the Druids,* 1814.

Hunt, *Jesus Christ,* 1904.

Hynes, S., *The Manifesto,* 1697.

Jan, *John Hus - His Life,* 1915.

Josephus, *The Works of Flavius Josephus,* (translated by William Whitson), 1840.

Joyce, D., *The Jesus Scroll,* 1973.

Kamer, H.A.F., *The Spanish Inquisition,* 1965.

Kaye, J., *The Council of Nicea,* 1853.

Kaye, J., *The Ecclesiastic History of the 2nd & 3rd Centuries,* 1893.

Kaye, J., *The Sermons,* 1850.

Kaspary, J., *The Life of the Real Jesus,* 1904.

Kaspary, J., *The Origin, Growth, and Decline of Christianity,* 1904-10.

Kelly, J.N.D., *Early Christian Creeds,* 1949.

Kirkgaldy, *The New Theology and the Old,* 1910.

Knight, *The Life of Faustus Socianus,* (translated by Biddle), 1653.

Knox, W.L., *The Sources of the Synoptic Gospels,* 1953.

Konstantinides, *Saint Barnabas,* 1971.

Lardner, N., *A History of Heretics,* 1780.

Lardner, N., *Two Schemes of Trinity*, 1829.

Latourette, K.C., *A History of the Expansion of Christianity*, 1953.

Leany, A.R.C., *The Dead Sea Scrolls*.

Leany, A.R.C., *The Rule of Qumran*.

Lehman, Johannes, *The Jesus Report*, 1972.

Lietzman, Hanz, *The Beginning of the Christian Church*, 1949.

Lietzman, Hanz, *A History of the Early Church*, 1961.

Lindsey, T., *Two Dissertations*, 1779.

Lindsey, T., *An Historical View of the State of Unitarian Doctrine*, 1783.

Lindsey, T., *A List of False Readings of the Scripture*, 1790.

Lubinietski, *A History of the Reformation in Poland*.

Major, John, *"Sentences"*.

Marshall, G.N., *Challenge of a Liberal Faith*, 1966.

Marshall, G.N., *Understanding of Albert Schweitzer*, 1966.

Madden, *Life and Martyrdom of Savonarola*, 1854.

Masters, John, *Baptismal Vows, or the Feast of St. Barnabas*, 1866.

Mellone, S.H., *Unitarianism and the New Theology*, 1908.

Miller, F., *The History of the Jewish People in the Age of Jesus Christ*.

Milton, J., *Treatise of Civil Power*.

Milton, J., *The Christian Doctrine*, 1825.

Motley, *Rise of the Dutch Republic*.

Mowry, Lucetta, *The Dead Sea Scrolls and the Early Church*.

Murray, G.G.A., *Five Stages of Greek Religion*.

MacGiffert, *The Apostles' Creed*, 1902.

MacGiffert, *The God of the Early Christians*, 1924.

MacGiffert, *A History of Christianity in the Apostolic Age*, 1897.

MacLachlan, *The Religious Opinions of Milton, Locke, and Newton*, 1941.

Newman, A., *Jesus* (with a preface by Dr. Schmeidal), 1907.

Newman, J.H., *Arianism of the Fourth Century*, 1833.

Newton, *Sir Isaac Newton Daniel*, 1922.

Oxyrhynchus, *New Sayings of Jesus and Fragments of a Lost Gospel*, (translated by B.P. Grenfell & A.S. Hunt), 1897.

Patrick, John, *The Apology of Oregin in Reply to Celsus*, 1892.

Parke, D.B., *The Epic of Unitarianism*, 1957.

Pike, E.R., *Spiritual Basis of Nonconformity*, 1897.

Pike, J.A., *If This Be Heresy*, 1967.

Pike, J.A., *Time for Christian Candour*, 1965.

Pike, J.A., *The Wilderness Revolt*, 1972.

Priestly, Joseph, *A General History of the Christian Church*, 1802.

Priestly, Joseph, *A History of the Corruption of Christianity*, 1871.

Priestly, Joseph, *History of Jesus Christ*, 1786.

Priestly, Joseph, *Memoirs of Dr. Priestly*, 1904.

Priestly, Joseph, *Socrates and Jesus*, 1803.

Priestly, Joseph, *Three Tracts*, 1791.

Priestly, Joseph, *Dr. Priestly's Catechism*, 1796.

Priestly, Joseph, *A New Song*, 1876.

Puccinelli, P., *Vita de S. Barnaba Apostolo*.

Quick, Murid, *The Story of Barnabas*.

Reland, Adrian, *Historical and Critical Reflections upon Mohametanism and Socianism*, 1712.

Rice, D.T., *Byzantine Art*, 1954.

Robinson, J.A., *Barnabas, Hermas and the Didache*, 1920.

Robinson, J.A.T., *Honest to God*, 1964.

Robinson, J.M., *The New Quest of the Historical Jesus*, 1959.

Robinson, J.M., *Problem of History in Mark*, 1957.

Robertson, J.M., *The Historical Jesus*, 1916.

Robson, Rev. James, *Christ in Islam*, 1929.

Ruinus, *Commentary on the Apostles' Creed*, 1955.

Ryley, G.B., *Barnabas, or the Great Renunciation*, 1893.

Sandmel, S., *We Jews and Jesus*, 1973.

Santucci, L., *Wrestling with Jesus*, 1972.

Sanday, *Outlines of the Life of Christ*.

Savonarola, *Verity of Christian Faith*, 1651.

Schmiedel, P.W., *Jesus in Modern Criticism*, 1907.

Schokel, L.A., *Understanding Bibical Research*, 1968.

Schweitzer, Albert, *Christianity and the Religions of the World*, 1923.

Schweitzer, Albert, *The Mysticism of Paul the Apostle*, 1953.

Schweitzer, Albert, *The Kingdom of God and Primitive Christianity*, 1968.

Schweitzer, Albert, *The Philosophy of Civilization*, 1946.

Schweitzer, Albert, *A Psychiatric Study of Jesus*, 1958.

Schweitzer, Albert, *The Story of Albert Schweitzer.*

Spark, *Unitarian Miscellany.*

Spark, *Christian Reformer.*

Stanley, A.P., *The Eastern Church*, 1869.

Stanley, A.P., *The Athanasian Creed*, 1871.

Stanley, A.P., *Lectures on the History of the Eastern Church*, 1883.

Stevenson, J., *Creeds, Councils, and Controversies.*

Stevenson, J., *Studies in Eusebius*, 1929.

Stevenson, J., *The New Eusebius.*

Taylor, John, *The Scriptural Doctrine of Original Sin.*

Taylor, John, *A History of the Octagon Church.*

Thomas-A-Kempis, *Imitation of Christ*, (translated by John Wesley), 1903.

Thompson, E.A., *Goths in Spain*, 1969.

Toland, John, *Hypathia*, 1753.

Toland, John, *Nazarenes*, 1718.

Toland, John, *Theological and Philosophical Works*, 1732.

Toland, John, *Tetradymus.*

Towgood, *Serious and Free Thoughts on the Present State of the Church.*

Vermas, G., *Jesus, the Jew*, 1973.

Vos, J.G., *A Christian Introduction to Religions of the World*, 1965.

Wallace, *Antitrinitarian Biographies*, 1850.

Warchaurr, J., *Jesus or Christ?*, 1909.

Warfield, B.B., *Jesus or Christ?*, 1909.

Wilbur, E.M., *A History of Unitarianism in Transylvania, England, and America.*

Williamson, G.A., *The History of the Church*, 1965.

Williamson, G.A., *The Jewish War*, 1959.

Wilson, E.M., *The Dead Sea Scrolls*, 1969.

Wisaart, H.S., *Socialism and Christ, the Great Enemy of the Human Race*, 1905.

Whittaker, T., *The Origins of Christianity*, 1933.

Workman, H.B., *Persecution in the Early Church*, 1960.

Zahn, T., *The Articles of the Apostles' Creed*, 1899.

Zahn, T., *Introduction to the New Testament*, 1909.

Zahn, T., *Peter, Saint and Apostle*, 1889.

Periodicals

Christian Examiner, Jan. 1924-Dec. 1925.

Edinburgh Review, Vol. XII, 1825.

Hibbert Journal Supplement, *Jesus or Christ*, Vol. VII, 1909.

Harvard Theological Review, *Theism and the Christian Faith*, 1909.

Review Biblique, 1950.

Neale, Samuel, *A select series of biographical narratives, etc.*, Vol. VIII, 1845.

Time Magazine, May 24, 1976.